L.A.'s LAST STREET COP

Surviving Hollywood Freaks, the Aryan Brotherhood, and the L.A.P.D.'s Homicidal Vendetta Against Me

AL MORENO

HIGHPOINT
LIT

L.A.'s Last Street Cop
Surviving Hollywood Freaks, the Aryan Brotherhood,
and the L.A.P.D.'s Homicidal Vendetta Against Me

This edition published by Highpoint LIT, an imprint of Highpoint Executive Publishing, New York, New York. Michael Roney, President and Publisher, Maya Ziobro, Development Editor. For information, write to info@highpointpubs.com.

First Edition

ISBN: 978-1-7344497-0-9

Library of Congress Cataloging-in-Publication Data

Moreno, Al
L.A.'s Last Street Cop

Summary: *"This gripping memoir vividly recounts the career of a gifted and fearless Los Angeles police officer in the late 1970s and early 1980s as he battled gangs and dealt with multiple homicidal situations on gritty city streets. It culminates in his vocal stand against corruption within the L.A.P.D., and the political retribution that ensued, including a dirty internal investigation and the murderous vendetta of a violent member of the Aryan Brotherhood."*—Provided by publisher.

ISBN: 978-1-7344497-0-9 (hardcover)
1. Memoir

Library of Congress Control Number: 9781734449709

Cover and interior design by Sarah M. Clarehart

10 9 8 7 6 5 4 3 2 1

Dedication

THIS BOOK IS DEDICATED to the 23,000 (and counting) police officers killed in the line of duty since 1791 throughout our country, in all jurisdictions. And to their mothers, fathers, children, brothers, sisters, and friends.

Please visit the Officer Down Memorial Page at www.odmp.org.

Semper Fi, my brothers and sisters.

Al Moreno

Acknowledgments

*"Render unto Caesar the things that are Caesar's
and unto God the things that are God's."*

Highpoint LIT stands alone in the cut, color, clarity, and carat of manuscript development.

Dear Lord, thank you for my indomitable faith and your celestial forgiveness. For truly, without your love, I would have perished into darkness.

Contents

But the Consul's brow was sad,
And the Consul's speech was low,
And darkly looked he at the wall,
And darkly at the foe.
"Their van will be upon us
Before the bridge goes down;
And if they once may win the bridge,
What hope to save the town?"

Then out spake brave Horatius,
The Captain of the Gate:
"To every man upon this earth
Death cometh soon or late.
And how can man die better
Than facing fearful odds,
For the ashes of his fathers,
And the temples of his gods,

"And for the tender mother
Who dandled him to rest,
And for the wife who nurses
His baby at her breast,
And for the holy maidens
Who feed the eternal flame,
To save them from false Sextus
That wrought the deed of shame?"

—Thomas Macaulay, "Lays of Ancient Rome"

Prologue

February 1982

I WAS JUST LYING THERE on the couch in the living room when a group of monstrous, heavily tattooed white men walked in armed with knives and sawed-off shotguns. What was really strange was they all looked at me as they slowly filed by but made no attempt to take the two-inch .38 backup I carried on the job or my .44 Magnum Smith and Wesson. The firearms were lying within my reach next to me on the floor. But I was frozen in place—no matter how hard I tried, I couldn't move.

Then came the horrid screams and cries for mercy as the Aryan Brotherhood gang members systematically slaughtered my little brothers, my sisters, and my mom.

It was the most vivid and horrifying dream I ever had.

For years, I had this recurring nightmare and similar ones as well. I went into a paranoia of sorts but fortunately recognized I was teetering on losing my mind. So I immersed myself in my faith and started working out twice a day instead of falling into the axiomatic trap of alcohol and drugs to sedate my overwhelming psychological pain and fear.

I went nowhere for months, not even my usual Saturday night date with Maria Elena, the beautiful Mexican foreign-exchange student I met when I was working Hollywood Division a few years back. One Saturday as I sat in Mom's car—parked in front of the house listening to the radio and armed with Rosco and Gun-zalez (my two-inch .38 and .44 Mag)—I called her and told her what was going on. That angel drove over and joined me in the car, bringing a picnic of wonderful homemade sandwiches, chips, a pint of tequila, and a six-pack of the "Champagne of Beers," my favorite, Miller High Life.

I looked into Maria Elena's magnetic brown eyes and told her everything—my whistleblowing, the terrifying fight with the Aryan Brotherhood and the death threats, and the vendetta the department unleashed against me. Her full lips parted and she gasped, "Al, your L.A.P.D. sounds as corrupt as our Mexican police." Then she tried to change the subject. It wasn't because she didn't care; she just wanted to take me away from my living nightmare, a nightmare that was the consequence of fulfilling my childhood dream of wanting to became a twenty-first-century Praetorian Guard.

1

The Praetorians' Vision

OCTOBER 10, 1975—Our Los Angeles Police Academy class, "8-75," was at the halfway point to our scheduled graduation day—and we didn't know shit about almost anything.

At this point, eight cadets had dropped out, six men and the only two females in the class. We were now down to fifty-six. Everyone was chomping at the bit because for the next four weekends, we were each going to work as a third man in an A-car (two-man patrol car) in one of the department's eighteen geographical divisions.

It was an intimidating experience. I was assigned to work my Friday and Saturday p.m. watches at Wilshire Division. I got to Wilshire Station early to familiarize myself with the station. I walked into the watch commander's (W/C) office and introduced myself to Sergeant II Frank Windsor.

Windsor was old school with thirty-plus years on the job. Six foot four, lean and handsome, he looked immaculate in his navy-blue uniform sporting his Sergeant II chevron on the upper sleeves. The lower part of his uniform sleeve was covered from the cuff to the elbow with diagonal hash marks denoting four years of service per hash mark. He had a full head of pure white hair, a heavily wrinkled face with piercing blue eyes, and a soft but deep voice. He would have made a much richer character than Theodore Roberts who played Moses in the 1923 Cecil B. DeMille film, *The Ten Commandments*.

I expected him to give me the standard rookie treatment we were all accustomed to at the Academy. As I started to introduce myself, he raised his arm in a "just a moment" gesture while he spoke to two other officers about some police business.

A few moments later, he wheeled around and asked, "Military?"

"Yes sir, Marine Corps."

He extended his long arm for a handshake and said, *"Semper Fi."* No doubt, I was shaking the hand of a World War II Marine Corp veteran. He looked at my name tag. "Officer Moreno, who were you with?"

"India Company 3/7, sir, First Marine Division."

"I was with the First Marine Division on the Canal [Guadalcanal]." Shit, this old Corps Marine was in the first offensive of the hellish Pacific Island fighting. At this point, several other officers queued behind him waiting to talk to him before roll call. So, it was a short but memorable conversation with this old Praetorian Guard. "Marine, have a seat in the roll-call room."

I had a flashback of my Dutch beauty, Danique—she always called me "Marine." It seemed like just yesterday when we were spending endless summer days spearfishing in her Palos Verdes coves. My God, I miss her. But I made my choice and fulfilled my childhood dream. I was well on my way to becoming a twenty-first-century Praetorian.

—

When I walked into the roll-call room, it was still empty. So I looked around for something to read and noted a stack of sheets on the desk up front. The sheets were known as *Daily Crime and Arrest Summaries* (DCAS). The officers called them D.O. sheets. They categorically listed the previous days' crimes in the division, including the officers' names who made the arrests.

The crime categories on the D.O. sheets included both crimes against person and property. *Crimes against person* include murder, attempted murder, felony, and misdemeanor assault, rape, and kidnapping. *Crimes against property* are robbery, burglary, grand theft auto (GTA), fraud, forgery, arson, and the like. In some cases, a detailed description of the suspect(s), their vehicle(s), and weapons used were listed as well. The D.O. included the crime report (D.R.) number; the type of arrest; the suspect's name and booking number; the date, time, and location of the crime; and a line describing the suspect's modus operandi.

The countless numbers of stolen vehicles were listed in a separate sheet called the "hot-sheet," which also listed the license plates.

By now the p.m. watch officers were filing into the roll-call room, and I instinctively knew there was a pecking order in the seating arrangement. The boots were in the first row, followed by the senior officers, with the old-timers in the very back of the room.

It was 1500 hours, the start of the p.m. shift. Sergeant Windsor walked in followed by two p.m. field supervisors, Sergeants Darr and Kunz. Damn! All the officers and sergeants looked really big and squared away.

There was a height requirement back then of five feet nine. I don't know why, but just then I thought about another background hiring requirement called *moral turpitude,* a legal concept in the United States and some other countries that refers to "conduct that is considered contrary to community standards of justice, honesty, and good moral character." This term appears in US immigration law beginning in the nineteenth century.

Moral turpitude was strictly enforced back in the day. For example, if your background investigator found that a police candidate was living with his girlfriend out of wedlock, he was perceived as lacking in moral character and was disqualified from becoming a Los Angeles police officer.

The roll-call room fell completely silent when Sergeant Windsor started handing out the daily patrol assignments. "Brophy, Wilder, and Moreno, 7-A-77." "7" denoted the division; "A" signified a two-man patrol unit; and "77" designated which reporting district (R/D) or quadrant of the division the unit was to patrol.

While Windsor went on, all the officers were dutifully making entries into their field notebooks. The cover of the notebook displayed the Admonition of Rights, or Miranda Rights—a 1966 landmark decision by the United States Supreme Court in *Miranda v. Arizona.* The Supreme Court held in a 5–4 majority that both inculpatory and exculpatory statements made in response to interrogation by a defendant in police custody will be admissible at trial *only* if the prosecution can show that the defendant was informed of the right to consult with an attorney before and during questioning and of the right against self-incrimination before police questioning, and that the defendant not only understood these rights but voluntarily waived them.

Roll call is supposed to be forty-five minutes long, but it never went longer than fifteen to twenty minutes before we were all hustled the hell out to relieve the previous watch. When I walked out into the hallway, I was approached by my partners, Officers Brendan Brophy and Jack Wilder, both in their midtwenties, just under six feet in height. They were fit, motivated street cops, each with a bit over five years on the job. I could sense that these two had worked together for some time, and they were indeed an impressive pair. Brophy did most of the talking and asked me how old I was and if I had been in the military. I gave them the same short introduction I gave Sergeant Windsor. "We're not going to give you any shit," Brophy said. "Just do exactly as we say and we'll be good. And don't call me fucking sir!"

I followed them to the kit room where the officers collected their print kit (fingerprint box) and the Ithaca model 37 pump-action .12-gage shotgun and ammunition. The shotgun rounds were monster slayers.

We walked out to the parking lot to our black-and-white. To a rookie like me, the inside of the police vehicle looked like the late-1960s *Starship Enterprise* because of all of the equipment. Before we left the station, Wilder lifted the removable backseat to check for any discarded contraband left by an arrested suspect while being transported in the backseat to the station from the previous watch, then we gassed up.

Brophy picked up the radio mic and cleared us for service. "7-A-77, p.m. watch clear."

Communications replied, "7-A-77 p.m. watch clear, good evening."

I was toast. I didn't understand a damn thing coming out of the radio. The radio transmissions were going ballistic with calls for service from the "Glass House," our name for Parker Center, L.A.P.D.'s headquarters downtown. Each RTO (radio telephone operator) was hemorrhaging out radio calls for service to two additional divisions on the same frequency. That meant that an A-car officer needed to distinguish his calls from the other two divisions' radio calls for service. And you damn sure didn't want to ask the RTO to repeat any information. That would tie up the radio for all three divisions. Brophy somehow managed to write down three radio calls like a court stenographer, then looked down and locked the shotgun rack running along the floorboard of the front seat.

In between handling our radio calls, we were dashing back and forth to "Officer Needs a Backup," "Officer Needs Assistance," and the mother of all radio calls, "Officer Needs Help." It was to be a night of service and mayhem in the City of the Seraphs.

Our first call was at 1645 ½ Gramercy Street, a dilapidated four-plex quadrant of the division with the heaviest calls for service and crime. Wilder parked our black-and-white a residence down from the call. I followed my two partners as we approached the fourplex. We could hear violent screams coming out of the unit.

"Motherfucker, I'm going to kill you!"

"Fuck you, you're not my father!"

This cadence of mixed vulgarities got louder and louder as we approached. Both officers stood on each side of the front door and tapped it with their batons.

An obese woman about five feet tall answered the door. "Edna, what is it this time?" Brophy asked. Evidently, my partners had been here several times before to deal with this mind-bending dysfunctional horror.

As we entered, I thought to myself, hell, this little apartment is half the size of my little home on Lou Dillon, in the gang-infested Florencia-13 part of South Central Los Angeles. There were seven little souls in the squalid apartment ranging in age from one to Edna's eldest daughter, Katrina, fifteen.

Edna's latest live-in boyfriend was Thomas. He was twenty-three years old with a three-page rap sheet, mostly for violations of the 11350 Health & Safety Code, which was being under the influence of an opiate (heroin). The rest of his arrests were for petty theft and residential burglaries. Brophy and Wilder had arrested him numerous times before.

While my partners were trying to sort out the problem and keep the peace, everything was still in a state of vulgar ear-piercing shouts from Edna, Thomas, and Katrina.

All of a sudden, Brophy screamed at the top of his lungs, "Shut the fuck up!" He was speaking their language, and it finally silenced the lot of them, including the crying babies.

Wilder hustled Thomas outside. Brophy told me to take Katrina to the kitchen. I walked her into the tiny kitchen and she was all smiles. She was a darling little girl. While standing there, I looked at all the little ones in the tiny living room. They were sickly, skinny, all dressed in rags, and barefoot. The kitchen floor and walls were filthy, and the stench of the apartment was sickening. My Lord, I was raised in the barrio and knew poverty, but this was a whole different and unspeakable nightmare. Edna was only thirty-five but looked fifty-five. Five of the seven children were from different fathers.

Once Brophy secured a little order, he asked Edna what the problem was. When Edna started talking, Katrina jumped in screaming, "That motherfucker (Thomas) is always trying to fuck me! And that bitch (her mother) ain't doing a fucking thing about it!"

Brophy gave Katrina the thousand-yard stare, and she chilled for a minute. I thought to myself, what on earth are Brophy and Wilder going to do to resolve this plethora of madness?

Just then, Katrina ran the few feet to the living room and kicked Edna in the ass, then went at her with lefts and rights. Brophy took Katrina by the arm, wheeled her around, and cuffed her. That was my first arrest as a Los Angeles police officer, and I hated it. I would shortly come to learn that these types of radio calls are the norm, not the exception, in South and Central Bureau.

Katrina was placed in the right-rear seat of our patrol car with me to her left. Brophy grabbed the mic: "7-A-77, cancel our two other calls and show us 'time and mileage' to Wilshire Station from 1645 Gramercy." When we arrived, Brophy radioed "7-A-77 arriving at Wilshire Station, your time and our mileage." This communication protocol protects the transporting officers from unfounded accusations of sexual assault. The officers recorded the location and time from the arrest locations to the station.

Once in the station, the arresting officers inform one of the supervisors, normally the watch commander (W/C), of the arrest and receive booking approval. Then it was filling out one report after another for hours. Katrina was placed in a small interview room as opposed to the station's holding cell. Once the reports were completed, she would be off to either Eastlake in Los Angeles or Los Padrinos Juvenile Hall in Downey where minors are detained. Katrina was detained at Los Padrinos.

The arrest took us almost five hours before we were cleared for service once again. When we got back to the Wilshire area, Brophy requested Code-7 (a forty-five-minute meal break). Brophy and Wilder were surprised when communications OK'd the request. Normally, the RTO denies the request and assigns the officer three more radio calls.

We stopped at this greasy spoon on Western Boulevard just south of the Santa Monica Freeway. It was Wilder's favorite burger joint. It was indeed a hole-in-the-wall with only outdoor seating, but the burgers and fries were delicious.

I asked endless questions about the arrest. There was a shitload of violations. Wilder listed everything from child abuse, possible sex abuse, physical abuse, emotional abuse, and general neglect of the children.

Edna has overdosed half a dozen times from prescription pills and street drugs. If we arrested her again, she would spend a few days in County (the general hospital), then be sent back home to her kids. Thomas is a known hype (heroin addict) and burglar who just completed his parole. He wasn't under the influence of heroin when we were there, and he had just cleaned up all his warrants.

Twice within the last two years, Brophy and Wilder took the whole household into the system. They arrested Edna's previous boyfriend, Big Eddie, another hype. That time, they arrested Edna for a slew of child endangerment violations, and the seven children were entered into the worthless California Child Protection Services. Everyone would be back home in that shithole house within a couple months.

"Al, always remember this: This world out here is a shithole with no long-term fixes," Brophy philosophized. "We go to the same homes throughout the division, time after time, for some type of 415 (disturbing the peace) calls, and it's the same drill every time. Remember this: Your main responsibility is to *keep the fucking peace* for that instant in real time and prevent the situation from escalating into another senseless killing or something like that. We just keep the peace, then move on to the next Edna insane asylum."

Our forty-five-minute break was over, and it was back to work. "7-A-77, clear." There was a short lull over the net—all radio transmissions from the entire city went silent. A Code-3 call was about to be assigned to a unit in one of the eighteen geographic divisions. A Code-3 call is always proceeded by three beeps on the net. "Wilshire units and 7-A-77, a 211 (robbery) in progress at 4222 Pico Boulevard; your call is Code-3."

We were only a couple miles from the call. Brophy activated the red lights and siren, Wilder put the pedal to the metal northbound on Western, then blew the red light on Pico turning westbound. (Vehicle seatbelts weren't used back then, and officers did not wear body armor.) Wilder was driving at least sixty miles per hour on that busy boulevard, weaving in and out of traffic that didn't pull over half the time. Brophy reached down and unlocked the Ithaca shotgun, then chambered a round of "get-some." The mere sound of that action can cause a suspect to have an unscheduled bowel movement.

Brophy screamed out the hundred-block numbers while Wilder continued driving like a possessed man. Brophy knew the call was a Kentucky Fried Chicken joint from previous robbery calls there. As we got within a block, Brophy screamed, "Slow down, you're going to pass it, slow down!"

Wilder locked up the brakes, and the car slid from side to side before coming to rest up against a high curb.

The fast-food restaurant was located on the northwest corner of Pico and Crenshaw Boulevard. Our car was in a tactically inferior location, stopped diagonally up against the curb, just in front of a large metal door on the south side of the building. If the suspects happened to exit through that heavy door just then, there was only the width of the sidewalk between us and being shot.

The main entrance to the restaurant was on the Crenshaw side, with a large parking lot in front. The customer entrance was the same as all other Kentucky Fried Chicken restaurants, with a heavy glass front door flanked by huge windows on either side for all to see inside from the street. Sergeant Edwin Darr was already standing in front of the metal door just in front of us armed with a shotgun and barking out to us, "It's a good call; there's two armed suspects inside with hostages."

Brophy had the shotgun and Wilder was armed with his .38 caliber revolver, both behind the left-front part of our patrol unit. I was behind the right-rear door closest to the metal door on the street side on Pico.

Sergeant Darr ran to a position of advantage behind his vehicle south of our car. Brophy shuffled to his right and reached into the patrol car for the radio to put out an "Officer Needs Help." I was amazed at how calm his voice was. It was as if he were at home with his wife and two young children having dessert after a Sunday night dinner. This was the consummate street cop. They don't get any better.

If the robbery came down to a firefight, all of us in the department had little to no confidence in our standard-issue Smith and Wesson piss-ant .38 six-shot revolvers. They had absolutely no knockdown power. The .38 fired a 158-grain soft-nosed lead slug at an ineffective muzzle velocity of 767 feet per second with little to no stopping power. The weapon earned the nickname "Widow Maker" because of its repeated failure to knock down suspects, putting both the officers' lives and the public in great jeopardy.

After Brophy put out the help call, he switched the radio to the P.A. system and ordered the suspects inside to release the hostages and come out unarmed. The suspects refused to comply, thereby escalating the armed incident into a S.W.A.T. call-out. Brophy radioed the communications center downtown about the armed and barricaded situation with numerous hostages. At this point, our responsibility was to put everything on ice until S.W.A.T. arrived.

By this time, it seemed that half of the department's patrol units had responded to our help call, and more were rolling in at breakneck speed with their sirens blaring and red lights flashing. Then I heard a familiar sound overhead. It was Air-6, one of our helicopters. The rotor noise was deafening and made it difficult for us to communicate with each other.

There must have been fifty guns by now covering the front entrance on Crenshaw and the employee entrance on Pico. L.A.'s Praetorians do this on a daily basis, and it is stunning to see how calm they are.

A few moments later, the metal door directly in front of us opened slightly inward. It was one of the two armed suspects having a look-see outside. Then the door abruptly slammed shut. I took a quick look to my left and saw Brophy and Wilder zeroed in on the door. Just then, a pair of plainclothes officers working a juvenile unit (J-unit) parked next to Sergeant Darr's car. These two were full-on, old-school gunfighters. One was of Sioux descent and fondly called Chief; the other was Asian.

Again, the door slightly opened, and this time I could see one of the teenage female hostages. She was being used as a shield in front of the armed suspect. The suspect had his left arm wrapped around her throat and a six-inch .357 Magnum up against her right temple. She couldn't have been more than sixteen years old, dressed in her red-and-white-striped uniform. Her sweet face was frozen in sheer horror.

The suspect was a black male, about six feet in height, in his midthirties, with a resolute look in his bloodshot eyes. His hair was styled like Don King's, straight up like a porcupine. I couldn't get over how evil his eyes looked.

Then all at once, he stepped out and started screaming, "Give me the fucking keys (to our patrol car), or I'll blow her fucking brains out!"

I had the perfect shot—about four inches of the left side of his face was exposed between him and the hostage. He was no more than four and a half feet away from me behind the right rear door of our car. I was 100 percent confident I could make the shot. I wasn't going to give him the opportunity to murder that innocent little girl. His .357 was in the cocked position, and I knew it would only take the slightest jerk form either the suspect or the hostage to cause the trigger to slam into the chambered cartridge.

Without thinking, my Marine Corps firearms training went into overdrive. There was zero margin for error. I centered my weapon's rear sight aperture with the front sight blade at the suspect's left eye, an instant kill shot. I started slowly pulling the trigger back for the shot, incorporating the B.R.A.S.S. system: breathe, relax, aim, slack, squeeze...

But a nanosecond before the hammer slammed into the chambered round, an explosion went off to my left. It was Chief! He took a "Hail Mary" shot and miraculously made it, striking the suspect through the mouth. I lost my stationary target and released the trigger from completing my shot. The suspect's face violently spasmed sideways from the impact of the slug precisely when the round slammed into his face. The hostage tore away from his death grip and rolled down and away from the "Contagious Fire" (all officers firing at once). Unbelievably, the suspect didn't go down immediately and raised his weapon to get a kill shot before he went to hell.

Simultaneously, Brophy, Wilder, Chief, and his partner, including a reserve officer, opened up at the same time. It was one of the most extraordinary things I've ever seen in a firefight. Brophy hit the suspect center mass with all four Ithaca shotgun rounds, at the same time the suspect was being hit with bullets from the other officers' revolvers. I checked my fire the whole time.

That malevolent soul never got a round off. The whole street was covered in a fog of gray smoke from the gunfire, but it wasn't over. We all maintained our positions for about two long minutes more until the other perpetrator inside the building released the remaining four hostages. They came out through the metal door hysterically crying. Brophy, Wilder, a couple other officers, and I ran from around our cover and hustled all four remaining hostages out of harm's way.

Just then, the remaining suspect walked out with his hands up. Chief and a few other officers quickly slammed him to the ground and cuffed him.

S.W.A.T. arrived moments later and gave their blue-suiter (street cops) brothers a thumbs-up. Brophy, Wilder, several other officers, and I walked up to the deceased suspect and were surprised when this big slick-sleeve (an officer with no chevrons on his sleeves) walked between us and handcuffed the obviously dead man. We all looked at him with a "What the fuck? He's dead." It was Big John Petrovitch, an ass-kicking street cop from Wilshire patrol.

"The department manual says that all suspects 'shall' be hand-cuffed including suspects who have been shot in an Officer Involved Shooting (O.I.S.). Big John was studying the department manual in preparation for an upcoming promotion to Police Officer III (P-III). He was simply following department procedures to the letter.

I thought to myself, oh well, what the hell. Years later, I would be partnered-up with Big John. He ended up becoming one of the department's premier Robbery/Homicide Detectives.

The gray fog from all the shooting was finally clearing up when a rescue ambulance (R.A.) arrived and pink-tagged (confirmed the death of) the suspect's body, although it would be eight to twelve hours before the coroner would transport the body to the morgue because of the extensive shooting investigation by Robbery Homicide Division (R.H.D.) out of Glass House. The body was evidence and could not be moved until Scientific Investigation Division (S.I.D.), working in conjunction with R.H.D., completed their laborious task of collecting the crime scene evidence, including taking hundreds of photographs of the crime scene, taking endless measurements, and analyzing the trajectory, angle, and path of every bullet fired.

Within a short time, Brophy, Wilder, Chief, his partner, the reserve officer, and I were separated and individually transported to the station for at least eight hours of interrogation ending with the "walk-through." In a walk-through, each officer gets back into soft clothes (civilian clothes) and is transported back to the shooting scene to reenact every single second of every individual action taken from the time the call was received until the conclusion of the shooting.

When I got to the station, one of the Wilshire captains asked me how many rounds I fired. I told him I had "checked my fire" (did not fire my weapon). He walked over to a handful of other plainclothes detectives and department brass. They deliberated for a couple of minutes. The captain walked back to me and said. "We don't need to include you in the O.I.S. investigation if you didn't fire your weapon." He told me, "Go home and have a beer. Good job, Officer."

What in the hell was that all about? It was our radio call—Brophy, Wilder, and me. I was closest to the suspect when he was killed, but they felt I didn't need to be part of the investigation? Well shit, I was still in the Academy, and my probationary period was months away, so I kept my mouth shut.

⁓

On my way home, I thought about stopping at Mom's to have a talk and blow off some steam or maybe paying a visit to my friend, Spanky, to have a few beers. He was a member of the hierarchy in the ruthless Florencia-13 gang in our community. For some reason, he was endeared to and protected our family from the savage multitude of gangsters in the neighborhood and was personally responsible for saving my life from a planned gang hit.

But when I got to Mom's, it was well after 2 a.m., and Spanky and his homies across the street must have called it an early night because his porch was deserted.

It isn't that I hadn't seen violent death before. By this point, I'd seen more death than most men though not as much as some. Still, I needed to decompress. I needed a soulful conversation with a friend. And it wasn't that I felt any guilt or remorse for the death of that piece of shit. The dead man had a hole in his heart, and the only way he could fill it was by destroying innocence in his path—men, woman, children, it made no difference—so fuck him!

I wanted to drive directly to Cabrillo Beach in San Pedro where Danique and I used to spend those sweet summer days and nights drinking Dutch spirits and eating homemade sandwiches on that wonderful Dutch rye bread. But I was only about five minutes away from the A & N liquor store just around the corner on Alameda and Nadeau, so I decided to stop there first.

When I arrived at the liquor store, it was closed. Fortunately, I saw that Mike, the owner's son and a longtime family friend, was still inside moving merchandise around. When he saw me, he smiled and unlocked the glass door. "Corky, how are you doing? Your brother Arty told me you're a cop now with the L.A.P.D."

I wasn't about to tell him what I had just been through. I just wanted a few beers. I gave him a cursory progress report on how I was doing in the Academy and got a six-pack of Rainier Ale, the "green death." Nostalgia washed over me as I looked at those green-and-gold sixteen-ounce cans. I immediately thought of my two Cathedral High School friends, Tyron Seals and Lourie McCray. My lovable, cheeky soul brothers who introduced me to the world of alcohol for the first time in the tenth grade.

I thanked Mike and continued on my way to the beach. As I was driving across the Vincent Thomas Bridge, I had another sweet thought of my best Huntington Park High School friend and Marine Corps warrior brother, Rick Beach, who once persuaded me to follow him in hanging off the suspension cables from the top of the bridge. Shit, those were insane but priceless times. Pure magic, care-free days! Rick had titanium balls then but was married now with a couple kids and in the department. The days of *A Summer Place* were indeed gone forever.

I arrived at Cabrillo Beach and pulled into the parking lot; there wasn't a soul around. The October weather was nothing like I remember back in 1969 when I was dating Danique, just back from Vietnam. It was colder than hell, but there was still something magical about this little beach. I stayed in the car with the motor running to keep the heater on while I listened to the radio and drank my Rainer. A 1965 recording by Marvin Gaye played on the radio— "Pretty Little Baby"—it was Danique's favorite song. She loved the haunting lyrics "...*Darlin', you give me joy, am I your toy?...*" and so did I.

———

When the warm sun started to rise, I walked out to the sand and sat with a single remaining can of Cathedral High School brew. Funny, I wasn't cold, tired, sleepy, or hungry. I was just thinking about Danique, and that gave me all the comfort and warmth I needed.

I don't regret my decision in choosing a life as an L.A. Praetorian, but I would forever live with a hole in my heart for choosing the department over Danique. I chose working the murderous streets of L.A. instead of a life on a hilltop in Palos Verdes with a couple of kids and her lovely parents, Jos and Huberta.

When I popped my last beer open. I heard something shuffling from behind. It was a couple of Harbor Division morning-watch blue-suiters. These coppers were as old as the sand I was sitting on and still working patrol, a real rarity for their time on the job.

The older, shorter one had a voice that sounded like he was chewing on gravel as he talked. "What in the hell are you doing out here? It's colder than a well-digger's ass," he mumbled.

I stood up and ID'd myself. I knew this could mean trouble for me because I was drinking and still in the Academy. But I sensed a welcome brotherhood from these two old salts. "I'm just having a couple of beers, officers. I was in an Officer Involved Shooting last night, in Wilshire Division."

These two were old-school P-IIIs (two-stripers) with beaucoup time on the job. The next step up would be a management position, but they didn't want any part of that bullshit. They loved being around their street-cop brothers too much. God only knows what these two honorable souls had seen and experienced. They both lit up big-ass cigars and smiled. "Shit, we heard about it. You blew those two assholes up!"

I told them that it was only one of the two armed-robbery suspects who was killed, the other surrendered. This type of news travels like wildfire in the department. The old cops introduced themselves. Mel had twenty-three years in and looked like he was right out of central casting—tall, thin, and distinguished looking, with slightly receding, perfectly combed gray hair. His uniform was spotless and pressed and his black shoes were heavily polished.

His partner, Harry, was a bit the opposite. He had served twenty-five years and was just five foot nine with a beer belly that would put Saint Nick's to shame and a nose that resembled W.C. Fields's—pitted and bright red, taking up a third of his deeply wrinkled face. However, his uniform and shoes were as spotless as Mel's.

"Let's get in the damn car; it's freezing out here!" Harry shouted. "Got any booze left?"

"Sorry, Harry, this is my last can." I told them all about the shooting and could see they were all in on the street justice of it all. Neither of them, like 90 percent of all officers on the job, had ever dropped the hammer on an asshole.

Harry asked me if I wanted to join them for a beer when they got off. They wanted to treat me for excising that worthless cancer from society. I didn't tell them that out of the six officers in the shooting, I was the only one to check my fire. I thought that may have dulled their opinions of me for some reason or another. I thanked them but declined and drove to my apartment in Downey. It was Saturday morning, and I didn't have to return to work until Monday morning.

When I got home to my little apartment, it felt warm, quiet, and secure. I didn't even undress; I just collapsed on the bed and immediately fell into a deep sleep. When I woke up, it was almost five in the afternoon, and I needed to hit the books.

———

I spent the weekend memorizing the plethora of class subjects and riveted into a monk-like existence. Monday morning came, and I was off to start my eleventh week of twenty in the Academy. Our class designation was "8-75" (August 1975) and we were still losing cadets.

The camaraderie was much like that in the Marine Corps, and many of the guys were combat veterans from the various services. I gravitated toward personalities like Mark Fuhrman—a low-key, well-liked former Marine who did a tour of duty in Vietnam as an 0331 machine gunner. Years later, he and I would be two of the original forty-four officers and detectives picked from the entire department to work the first-ever gang suppression unit in the department—Community Resources against Street Hoodlums, or CRASH. After a few years in CRASH, Mark transferred to the West Los Angeles Division and eventually become one of their top robbery/homicide detectives. Mark gained international exposure when he and his partner were assigned to the O.J. Simpson double-murder case.

Despite the workload, I especially loved our law classes in the Academy. They reminded me of the days when I cut virtually all of my classes my senior year at Huntington Park High School to spend endless hours watching court proceedings at the local criminal courthouse.

California has twenty-nine governing state codes of which law enforcement principally addresses six: The Penal Code (enacted on February 14, 1882); the Vehicle Code; the Evidence Code; the Health and Safety Code; the Welfare and Institutions Code; and the Business and Profession Code.

In addition, there was the ever-morphing "case law" coming down from the state and federal courts, which affected law enforcement arrests, search and seizures, and just about every other aspect of criminal law. These were groundbreaking cases like:

Miranda v. Arizona (1966), where police must advise criminal suspects of their rights under the Constitution to remain silent and the right to consult with a lawyer and to have one appointed to you if one is indigent;

Escobedo v. Illinois (1964), where criminal suspects have a right to counsel during police interrogations under the Sixth Amendment;

Terry v. Ohio (1968), where police may stop a person if they have a reasonable suspicion that the person has committed or is about to commit a crime and frisk the suspect for weapons if they have a reasonable suspicion that the suspect is armed and dangerous;

Schmerber v. California (1966), the application of the Fourth Amendment's protection against warrantless searches and the Fifth Amendment privilege against self-incrimination; and,

Katz v. United States (1967), the Fourth Amendment's ban on unreasonable searches and seizures that applies to all places where an individual has a "reasonable expectation of privacy."

These five cases are but a mere pebbles in the sand of what your everyday street cop has to know when dealing with suspects in the field. And if you get it wrong, you could arrest a suspect with a car trunk full of dead bodies and the perpetrator could ultimately walk scot-free.

In addition to the endless law class modules, we were constantly on the firing range practicing with our piece-of-shit .38 caliber six-shot revolvers on the twenty-five yard line. I enjoyed the shotgun range more than practicing with the revolver. Throughout our weapons training, I always felt we lacked guidance on specific shooting scenarios about when to drop the hammer and use lethal force and when not to.

After firing our .38s on the range, we formed small groups to practice speed loading our weapons with a metal speedy loader that held six cartridges in a single file. There was a flange at the end of the speedy loader to grasp while you held your weapon in the other hand with the cylinder in the open position. Then you fed cartridges into the cylinder, one round at a time. I never won a single speed-loading contest in those groups.

The trick was to precisely feed the head of the bullet into the individual cylinder slot or else the round would spill off. Bear in mind, this was intended to be accomplished in the middle of a firefight while suspects were often armed with superior weapons.

The city fathers forced my brothers and sisters to go into harm's way with that worthless weapon (the aforementioned "Widow Maker"). In May of 1986, the Los Angeles Police Commission authorized the use of the fifteen-shot 9 mm semiautomatic Beretta Model 92-FS. However, the initial ammunition authorized was an inferior round-nosed brass bullet. As the years went on, the department authorized more effective ammunition.

In retrospect, I reckon this was considered the best possible training at the time. We were instructed that the use of deadly force was only authorized in the protection of human life or in a situation where a citizen or the officer would sustain great bodily harm if we didn't shoot. There is a universe of variables of when to use deadly force and when not too. These life-altering decisions must be done in a nanosecond!

Today, the larger law enforcement agencies have state-of-the-art, life-sized screen simulators that provide realistic field situations of *when and when not to* shoot. For example, when faced with a possible Officer Involved Shooting (O.I.S.), you must instantly analyze your surroundings, including populated sidewalks, vehicle traffic, businesses, and homes. When a suspect is holding a hostage, is it really a hostage? Or, is it his or her partner mimicking a hostage? If you fire, would the bullet pass through the suspect and hit an innocent onlooker? If you miss, will the bullet strike an innocent bystander a couple blocks away? Is the suspect using a toy gun that resembles a real firearm? Is the suspect attempting "suicide by cop"? Is the suspect mentally impaired? Is he or she on drugs? Is he or she a violent felon fleeing form a serious crime?

The variables could fill the Library of Congress, and the officer needs to make that life-or-death decision instantly or risk being killed or severely injured for life. And to hell with you if you get it wrong. You, your family, your job, your future, and your mental health are fucked for life!

The weeks in the Academy were flying by, and I had successfully passed the three remaining English modules, but not before failing two of the three twice. And I still had to retake the spelling test I failed twice before; three strikes and you're out!

The daily physical fitness (P.T.) and officer defense classes were taking their toll. The Geek Squad's ranks were increasing exponentially from so many injuries, and surprisingly, we lost a couple more cadets. Our self-defense classes included baton training with our twenty-six-inch "hickory stick," also called a "straight stick" or "Billy club." This weapon was primarily used for self-defense in parrying a suspect's fist and leg strikes against an officer. It also served as a valuable tool in protection against violent crowd assaults, and, on occasion, it was used against a violent suspect in a fight before having to ultimately use a firearm. Defense kicks and hand and arm restraint techniques, pat-down searches, and handcuffing were also a major part of our self-defense classes.

Watching our classmate Ray Sua practicing the martial arts leg kicks was always a sight to behold. You could hear the impact of his leg and hand strikes against the foam pads throughout the entire Academy grounds. No one fancied being his partner in practice and on the receiving end of those blows.

We learned the proper position for an officer to stand in when interviewing a suspect in the field—take an oblique stance with your holstered gun opposite to the suspect's reach. You were to assume the same stance while writing a traffic ticket or completing a field interview (F.I.) card. And you should never get so involved in writing that short missive that you fail to continually glance up at the suspect who could take you out with a sucker punch or blow your brains out with a gun.

I learned that lesson the hard way when I was practicing a simulated field interview and started writing an F.I. on my classmate Jim Moran, who was playing the suspect. I got so involved in doing a good job completing multiple little box entries when Jim hit me with a "come to Jesus" thunderous shoulder smash and then wheeled me around into a bar arm choke hold. You could hear the shoulder smash a block away. It caught the attention of the cadets practicing the same module and the P.T. staff as well. The instructors gave Jim a faint look of approval that brought home the seriousness of the exercise. I felt like a jerk, but thank you, Jim. I never duplicated that mistake out in the field regardless of who I was conducting police business with—male, female, granny, or juvenile.

We went over various scenarios on suspect vehicle stops, ranging from the generic traffic violation stops to pulling over a carload of armed felons. When you approach a traffic violator, you should never let complacency get the better of you. It will kill you just as fast as getting hit with one of Ray's kicks. Always run the suspect's vehicle for wants and warrants (W&Ws) before you stop a vehicle for any reason. Then wait for Communications to come back with the information, and don't light them up (use your red lights) until you find a tactically suitable location to make the stop. If Communications comes back with hot information, request a rolling backup before making the stop.

Once the suspect's vehicle comes to a stop, offset your vehicle a few feet left to act as a protective barrier to the traffic from behind. Both you and your partner must exit your vehicle immediately without forgetting to retrieve your baton from its sheath on the door panel and to secure it in your Sam Brown utility ring. When you approach the suspect's door, assume the oblique profile to decrease your target profile while your partner does the same from the opposite side of the suspect's vehicle. Look into the suspect's vehicle for any suspicious movements or actions before you reach the driver's window. And stay in verbal contact with your partner at all times—don't assume he sees what you see!

When you respond to any radio call, always park your sled a safe distance away from the Person Requesting's (P.R.'s) residence or business. When approaching the door, stand to the side of the doorway before knocking. Look and listen first, then strike the side of the door with the far end of your baton. This prudent and tried technique will ensure that you and your partner don't take a shotgun blast through the door.

These timeless officer safety drills are not meant to graduate a class of paranoid, gun-toting, trigger-happy, robo-cops on the street. They are meant to develop an alert, well-trained Praetorian who will maintain a civil and safe society protected from those who will harm you and your family. The training will enhance your chances of getting home to your family that night.

All the reality training is worthless without real-life examples of what our brother officers have experienced in the field. The Academy staff used the following true stories to show what we might experience a short time after graduation.

On August 5, 1968, L.A.P.D. Officers Rudy Limas and Norman Roberge were on routine patrol in the West Adams area of Los Angeles when they saw a black 1955 Ford with four male black suspects. The car was continually driving up and down a private driveway. Finding this suspicious, the officers followed the Ford. Limas called in for a wants and warrants check before stopping the vehicle. Before Communications returned the vehicle status, the Ford stopped in a gas station. Roberge exited his vehicle and walked toward the driver and asked him for his license and registration.

The driver informed the officer that he did not have a license. Officer Roberge ordered the four suspects to exit the vehicle and place their hands on top of their patrol car for the officers' safety. Suddenly, one of the suspects reached into his waistband and produced a gun. The suspect screamed, "Okay, motherfucker!" then shot Limas in the abdomen and thigh. Officer Roberge cleared leather while he rushed toward his downed partner and took two bullets to both legs. In the following firefight, Limas fatally shot two suspects, and Roberge emptied his revolver at a third suspect while the fourth suspect fled. All four suspects were later identified as members of the Black Panthers.

This incalculably heroic story serves as a standard for all in law enforcement to emulate, and for many years served as a valuable training film for police academies throughout the United States. Both Officers Limas and Roberge survived their wounds and returned to work.

On June 21, 1973, L.A.P.D. Officer Charles Caraccilo, working out of Van Nuys Division as a motorcycle officer, made a routine traffic stop with the intent to cite the violator for a traffic infraction. Unbeknown to Officer Caraccilo, the motorist, Michael Hunter, age twenty-one, was an escapee from the California Youth Authority driving an unreported stolen vehicle.

As Officer Caraccilo approached Hunter's vehicle, Hunter exited and fired six rounds at the officer who, fortunately, was wearing body armor. Unfortunately, one of the bullets entered an unprotected side of the vest, striking the officer in the heart. It was a mortal wound, but Caraccilo still managed to get off six rounds at the suspect. Hunter was captured and sentenced to twenty years for second-degree murder.

Caraccilo was eulogized as one of the finest and most decent men who ever wore L.A.'s blues. To this day, family, friends, and strangers visit the "Officer Down Memorial Page" website (https://www.odmp.org) and leave heart-wrenching missives:

> *Almost 39 years since Chuck has been gone. I rode motors with him on a Valley task force of about 21 or so motor officers. Most of us were on duty the night he was killed. He was one of the nicest guys you would ever want to know, and I have never forgotten him.*
>
> *Rest in Peace, Chuck.*
>
> *Ed, May 10, 2012*
>
> *I was 10 years old when we lost Uncle Chuck, and I still think of him and how much he taught me about being honest and sincere. He was always smiling, and I am sure it was because of his wonderful wife and children. To me he was a true living hero. He rode his police motorcycle like a knight riding a stallion. He always seemed to have a little smile going and had such a comical good attitude while home from work. He requested me to address him as "Uncle Chuck." My Father was his close family friend as well as the godfather of his son Ricky. My father, Frank, helped Chuck's kids cope with the tragedy of losing their father and months later, they're (sic) mother as well.*
>
> *I cried for days and at 10 years of age, I learned the true meaning of heartache and deep loss. We lived in the same neighborhood, and I would hang out in his garage while he was working on the boat or just drinking a cold one. He was patient enough to have a 10-year-old as a friend. Chuck will never be forgotten by the many friends and fellow officers whom he rode with.*
>
> *With the respect and honor he taught me, I have to say I am a*

better man for having him in my childhood life. Thank you all for such kind words and for sharing a moment to reflect.

Paul, son of close family friend Frank De Prizio, December 31, 2006

Officer Gary Murakami was the first Asian Los Angeles police officer to be killed in the line of duty. His tragic death was a real wake-up call for all the "fucking new guys" (FNGs) who choose the life of today's modern-day Praetorian.

After graduating in the upper 10 percent of his Academy class in 1968, he was assigned to University Division in South Central Los Angeles (today's Southwest Division). On the second day of working uniform patrol day watch with his training officer, William Brote, they got a radio call: "311 man (naked individual) at 3236 W. 60th Street."

They handled the radio call by the numbers, parked their sled a safe distance from the location, and looked and listened for anything that just wasn't right. Then they walked across the street to the two-story shithole apartment building. As they walked across the unkempt lawn and approached the first floor, Officer Brote yelled out to his partner, "Look out!" Just then, the new officer took a shotgun blast to the face and fell to the ground, bleeding to death. Officer Brote managed to run back to his car without getting hit and broadcast, a "Shots Fired, Officer Down" call. Officer Murakami's brothers from all over the city rolled Code-3 to his aid.

One of the first units to arrive were Officers Frank Pettinato and his partner, Richard Harsma. They both walked into the first-floor apartment building hallway looking for the armed suspect, at which time the suspect flung his apartment door open, striking both officers with a volley of shotgun blasts. After being hit, both officers returned fire with their pathetic .38s. The suspect managed to close the door and walk to the apartment window facing the street and continued firing at the officers. The whole time, Officer Murakami was lying on the lawn just feet from the suspect's window, crying out for help, but the officers were unable to render aid because of the suspect's withering fire.

This is when Officer Murakami's L.A.P.D. brothers continued to show their steel. While the suspect was firing through the window, Officers Timothy Walgren and Dale Stevens drove their patrol car onto the front lawn in front of the apartment between the downed officer and the suspect. At this time, Officer Gerald Woempner made his way to the window, reached up and tore out the screen and drapes, giving the officers a better view inside the apartment.

Officer Woempner also provided covering fire for Walgren and Stevens as they dragged Murakami into the backseat of their patrol car and rushed him to the hospital. Officer Murakami died of his injuries while in surgery. He was survived by his mother and father, Mary and Georgy, his sister Dian, and his pregnant wife, Jill.

Arguably, the most chilling example of the risk to an officer's safety while making a generic vehicle stop occurred on April 6, 1970, in an unincorporated part of Los Angeles County. The O.I.S. was coined the "Newhall Massacre." This lesson serves as a "death notice" to all in law enforcement of what you may encounter on a typical day serving your community anywhere in the United States.

California Highway Patrol Officers James Pence and Roger Gore were on routine patrol when they received an information broadcast about two male suspects brandishing a firearm. The broadcast included the suspect's vehicle make, model, and plate. Shortly after the broadcast, they spotted the vehicle and called for a rolling backup unit. Before their backup arrived, the two suspects stopped in a parking lot.

Both Officers Pence and Gore were immediately gunned down by suspects Jack Twinning and Bobby Davis, both career criminals. Moments later, California Patrol Officers Walt Frago and George Alleyn were also murdered as they arrived to help their fallen brothers.

This bloodbath all happened within four minutes. Twinning and Davis split up after the murders. Nine hours later, the fallen officer's brothers ascertained that Twinning had broken into a home and taken a hostage. However, the hostage managed to escape, allowing the officers to fire tear gas into the residence before storming in. The suspect killed himself with the shotgun he took from Officer Frago.

Suspect Bobby Davis was captured and tried for the murders of Officers Pence, Gore, Frago, and Alleyn. He was found guilty and sentenced to die in the California gas chamber. In 1972, the California Supreme Court declared the death penalty to be cruel and unusual punishment, and in 1973, the court modified Davis's death sentence to life in prison.

Officers Pence, Gore, Frago, and Alleyn were all married and left a total of seven children ranging in age from nine months to four years, in addition to their wives, mothers, fathers, brothers, sisters, extended family, and friends.

After the Newhall Massacre, the California Highway Patrol radically changed their entire training manual for officers' safety, including issuing better weapons and firearms training. Today, their new training and procedures mirror that of big-city law enforcement departments. The California Highway Patrol learned a brutal lesson that balmy day in April 1970: They're not "just traffic cops"!

So, take heed my brothers and sisters—once you strap on your blues, Sam Brown, weapon and shield, although you may have the best of intentions for our capricious society, you may meet an ugly death just like so many of your law enforcement family. Death is always just a heartbeat away when you're on the street protecting folks you've never met. And in today's America, more than ever before, there are endless forces out there that wish you ill.

———

At times in my Academy training, I would pause and take a stealthy look at my brothers while they were going through some of the more difficult training modules. All of them more than once looked like the grim reaper was at their doorstep. But they never once faltered in their commitment in serving you.

"Protect and Serve" is the L.A.P.D.'s motto. I know it sounds corny, but the truth is, those first responders are the best souls of mankind. When I reflect on the character of my Academy brothers, the British essayist Thomas Macaulay's "Lays of Ancient Rome" comes to mind. Here, he eloquently describes the heroism of Horatius Cocles, Captain of the Gate:

> *But the Consul's brow was sad,*
> *And the Consul's speech was low,*
> *And darkly looked he at the wall,*
> *And darkly at the foe.*

"Their van will be upon us
Before the bridge goes down;
And if they once may win the bridge,
What hope to save the town?"

Then out spake brave Horatius,
The Captain of the Gate:
"To every man upon this earth
Death cometh soon or late.
And how can man die better
Than facing fearful odds,
For the ashes of his fathers,
And the temples of his gods,

"And for the tender mother
Who dandled him to rest,
And for the wife who nurses
His baby at her breast,
And for the holy maidens
Who feed the eternal flame,
To save them from false Sextus
That wrought the deed of shame?"

Sleep well, America, in your warm homes with your little ones. Enjoy your outings to the parks, beaches, and entertainment venues. Enjoy your trips to the mountains, your shopping centers, movie houses, and restaurants. Like brave Horatius, our modern-day Praetorians "have your six."

—

It was time for some pure, unadulterated, kick-ass fun—a full week of driving school in San Pedro. This was our opportunity to get behind the wheel of our badass black-and-white and put the pedal to the metal. On that Monday, we all met for roll call in an outdoor classroom and were greeted by a team of driving instructors in light-blue overalls. We were given a cursory overview of the weeklong course, then given an off-the-couch go on the track in a black-and-white.

The racetrack included a long straightaway leading into the chicanes, then more sweeping turns leading back to the straightaway. At the completion of the weeklong course, we got a final go on the racetrack and marveled at the difference in our better times.

Driving school included the "skidpan," which educated the driver about the force of vehicle weight transference and dynamics when turning and braking. The skidpan is a large, circular course that required the driver to maneuver and control the vehicle without losing control and spinning out from either under- or oversteering or from a wrong combination of acceleration and braking. For the life of me, I couldn't nail it, and all the guys ragged me about it.

The braking and acceleration module was put to the test in the next exercise. This course required the driver to approach a series of three lanes from a single lane while driving at a high speed. Then at the last minute, the passenger instructor shouted out for you to maneuver into either the right or left lane or stay in the lane you were driving in. This was compounded with three separate tri-light signals in each lane that either stayed in the green or switched to the red phase, forcing you to brake hard without spinning out of control. This was my baby, and I nailed it every time.

I always had an affinity for driving a 917 Porsche Panzer and flying a WW II P-51 D Mustang. In the early 1970s, the 917 Porsche was king with its monstrous 1,100 HP engine that mastered the Circuit de la Sarthe, better known as France's Le Mans. The 917's top speed is a staggering 246 MPH, and there was no other racecar in its day like it.

When I put the pedal to the metal that last qualifying day in San Pedro's racecourse, I fantasized I was driving the 917 at Le Mans. In reality, I never went above 90 mph before having to brake for the curves and chicanes on our L.A.P.D. racecourse. Just the same, I grasped the principles of pursuit driving along with the science and mechanics of road racing. L.A.P.D.'s driving instructors will be responsible for saving many officers' lives in the coming years.

Our role-playing classes were always fun. An Academy staff member would play the role of a pissed-off citizen who called for a black-and-white to resolve the impossible.

Our role-playing classes mimicked the type of radio calls an A-car would get on a typical day. At least half of your daily radio calls are "415" disturbance calls—family disputes, neighbor disputes, business disputes, and domestic disputes, to name a few. The 415 scenarios were fashioned so that no matter how you and your partner handled it, you fucked it up big time!

In my Academy ride-alongs, I learned that an officer's sole responsibility was to just "keep the peace" for that moment in time so people didn't end up killing each other over a simple disagreement. Put a smile on their faces, get the fuck out of there, and roll to the next war. After handling any radio call, the officer makes an entry into his daily log's disposition section. The typical words for the generic 415 entry read, "Advised and kept the peace."

Less enjoyable, but essential, were the officer survival or self-defense classes. The P.T. staff taught us three types of sleeper, or choke holds. Of all three, the bar arm was the most disagreeable. In our practice sessions, a cadet placed his inner forearm across the suspect's trachea from behind. It locks off the airflow, thereby blocking any oxygen-enriched blood to the brain, rendering the suspect unconscious. In addition to getting knocked out, the clamping pressure against one's throat damaged all the adjoining tissue and left one with excruciating pain and soreness for weeks. This training module was intended to make us acutely cognizant of when to continue or discontinue this technique on a combative suspect. In most cases, when we were forced to use one of the restraints holds, the suspect would capitulate before he was rendered unconscious.

Before we completed this module, I was unfortunately paired with Andy Musaelian, aka "Moose," who was as wide as he was tall. We were practicing the bar-arm that day. You have the "choke-er" and the "choke-ee." The choke-ee sits on the grass with the choke-er kneeling behind him as he applies the bar arm. The choke-ee is supposed to clap his hands just before he becomes unconscious, signaling the choke-er to stop.

Moose was so fucking strong and efficient in that monster technique that I went out like a lightbulb before I was able to signal him to stop. I suspect he got that Hulk-like strength from loading those "big ugly fat fuckers," B-52 D models, during the Vietnam War. Moose once told me that each B-52 had a bomb-load capacity of 60,000 pounds of "get-some." Moose was in the Air Force, but I always thought he was more suited for the Marine Corps.

Moose's "get-some" put me in the "Geek Squad" for a whole week. I was sent to that piss-ant Central Receiving Hospital in Rampart and diagnosed with damaged thyroid cartilage, notch, and cricoid cartilage of the larynx. The Geek Squad was for injured cadets. When a cadet incurred an injury, he would have to stand silently at "parade rest" to the side of the other cadets while they were mangling each other's bodies during the combat self-defense classes.

The chemical agent class was another painful course. I had already eaten that chlorobenzalmalononitrile (CS gas) sandwich three times in the Marines. My first two, fully unprotected exposures were in 1960 and 1961 when I completed the nine-day Marine Corps Devil Pups youth program for ages fourteen to seventeen. We were given an intense overview of what to expect and completed countless drills on how to properly use the gas mask. Once my young Devil Pup brothers marched into the airtight Quonset hut and stood at attention against the rectangular walls, our drill instructor (D.I.) walked up to a small table in the center of the room and ignited the solid CS capsule. The gas immediately engulfed the room, at which time we were ordered to remove our protective masks and sing the first verse of the Marines' Hymn before we were allowed to exit the hut in orderly single file.

We didn't get past "To the shores of Tripoli" before we met our youthful human limit of tolerance. Our skin was on fire, our eyes were burning. Our noses, mouths, and throats were spewing uncontrollable amounts of mucus of all colors. We started coughing and heaving, but continued to sing one word after another. We managed to tough it out and complete the eight-line verse, however unintelligible it was. When we finally got the order to file out, a couple of the young Devil Pups at the end of the queue cut in line to get the hell out of that inferno. They were quickly seized by the D.I. and forced to return to the end of the line and stay in the room for a few moments more.

The effects of the gas can last as long as an hour after exposure and leave your garments with an odious residue. After the Quonset hut gas chamber of hell, we showered and changed. It was truly "old school" back then. It was America's standard of raising our youth, and we were some tough little "mofos."

My third bout with CS gas was some years later when I joined the Marine Corps in 1968. And now again for the fourth time, I was about to eat that CS gas but hoping to get a "by your leave" from our instructors. They were aware that many of us had been trained in and exposed to chemical agents before. They asked, by a show of hands, who had been exposed to chemical gas before. Sergeant Shields smirked and said, "Good, you can tell your civilian classmates just how it's going to feel for hours on end." Our main P.T. instructor, Sergeant Stokes, and a few Academy staff onlookers started laughing.

Evidently, the word always got out when an Academy class was going to have the gas module, and anyone who had the time would try to come by to watch us exit the gas chamber. To be perfectly honest, I would have done the same. In this comical ballet of uncontrollable indignity, a horde of grown young men ran out of the gas chamber, flailing their body parts in all directions and smashing into one another, with all sorts of thick gooey snot running out of every hole in their faces. We didn't give a fuck who was watching. Like everyone else, I ran around flailing my head, arms, and legs, trying to dissipate the gas fumes. And like the three previous times, it was pure hell.

———

In addition to all of the challenging courses, the Academy used arduous hill runs as a tried calculus to expose a cadet's character. Quit on the runs in the Academy, and you were flagged as the type to quit in the field with a suspect in a life-or-death physical struggle.

Our two principal P.T. instructors were Sergeants Jerry Stokes and Rex Shields. Stokes was a six-foot-tall black man with an astonishing resemblance to my old platoon sergeant in the Marine Corps. Shields was a six-foot-two, 230-pound hulk of a man.

One afternoon, Sergeant Stokes told us that we were about to go on a fifteen-mile hill run, a crucible of sorts that every Academy class must complete at this juncture. A couple of years ago, two cadets fell out of that run, were hospitalized for heat exhaustion, and nearly died. We had already done some grueling seven- and nine-mile hill runs this summer, but never a fifteen-miler.

Just before we started, Stokes pointed out a female nurse at the far end of the field seated on a metal folding chair. He told us that she was from Central Receiving Hospital and was here to monitor us and take our vital signs—blood pressure and heart rate—before and after the hill run. This was when nurses still wore those really cool white uniforms, including that funny-looking bonnet. But to be perfectly honest, this was one of the ugliest women any of us had ever seen. She looked like she could kick any of our asses.

We couldn't help eyeing her as we started our warm-up drills. And some of the guys were engaging in that old-school, locker-room talk. "Fuck, look at that beached whale. I wouldn't fuck that with your dick. That's a two-bagger." The shit went on and on, and we were all muffling our laughs and snickers. Stokes was over at the far end of the track field talking to the nurse when we started to get slightly out of hand.

Then we heard one pissed-off scream from behind us. "Get on your fucking faces!" Shit, it was Sergeant Bowers, the Academy P.T. director. No one saw him coming in from behind. "Get on your face" meant assume the up position in a push-up and hold the isometric pose—until the ambulance came. Within a couple of minutes, even the fittest of us started going into uncontrollable body spasms from holding the position. The exceptionally hot weather added to the punishment. But no one dared quit, not even the lesser fit.

I glanced to my right and left and saw my brothers' faces grimacing in pain, beet-red, looking like they were about to explode. Stokes and Bowers got the message and ordered us back into platoon formation before one of us went into cardiac arrest.

I heard some of the cadets behind me snickering again. I thought to myself, oh shit, not again, we're going to be put back down on our faces. The laughter got louder, so at this point I looked back.

Nurse butt-ugly was Sergeant Shields, dressed in a nurse's uniform with a stethoscope wrapped around his fire-hydrant-sized neck! He walked about our ranks and started checking our vital signs. Stokes and Shields had accomplished their most important job—busting our balls. It was indeed a brutal hill run that day, but not a fifteen-miler, just another long nine-miler.

———

As I worked through the library of courses and physical challenges I still had to complete before graduation, I had to contend with my crippling dyslexia that reduced my reading speed. When we began the Academy, we took a series of English grammar and spelling tests to measure those skills. I was the only one in my class to fail them all.

Any cadet that failed any single course three times is washed out of the Academy. By now, I had successfully passed three of the six English modules that I failed on day one, but not before failing two of them twice. I had also failed the spelling test twice and was on my third and last attempt. I was graciously given the opportunity to take the final test at my convenience before graduation day on December 19. I knew I was a breath away from being washed out of Class 8-75 and dealt with endless flashes of sheer terror in my heart and soul. I needed to nail a score of at least 70 percent.

It would have been a Shakespearean tragedy to be washed out of the Academy for failing a fucking spelling test. So, as I prepared for my third and final go, I was writing out forty words taken from a list of the five hundred most misspelled words in police report writing ten times a night—for a total of four hundred words each session! That was in addition to our regular homework.

It was one week before graduation, and our platoon count held at fifty-six. That Monday, I was called into the administrative office and asked when I planned to take the final spelling test. I shot from the hip and suggested Wednesday, three days before graduation. I needed to keep my powder dry and not go completely mad.

"Judgment Day" arrived; it was Wednesday. After morning roll call, I asked permission to leave the class and go to the administrative office. The class knew why and all nodded with a firm and warm look of support. I was shuttled into an empty classroom by one of the Academy staff members.

I was in such a state of... well... there are no words. I don't even recall who the staff member was, although I must have seen him a dozen times. He handed me a single white sheet of paper and a number-two pencil. The fifty words came at me without apology, and I swear, I truly don't recall a single word on that test.

When I completed the spelling test, the proctor took the test sheet and walked out of the room. It was maybe fifteen minutes before he and a couple of the other staff instructors returned. They didn't have to say a word—they had smiles on their faces that extended to their earlobes as they placed the graded sheet on the desk and walked out of the room.

I scored a 97 percent! I sat there in a state of... well, again, I have no words for that blessed moment in time. In retrospect, all I recall is a brilliant white light and absolutely nothing else. All my platoon brothers and the Academy staff were overwhelmed with joy for me. My God, what fine men and what a brotherhood!

———

Our graduation ceremony was Friday, December 19, 1975, at one-thirty in the afternoon. It started with the field review and uniform inspection, accompanied by the L.A.P.D. band and the department's motorcycle drill team precariously maneuvering their big-ass, oil-leaking Harley-Davidson motorcycles on the tiny track field where we had physically mangled each other's bodies for the last four-and-a-half months.

A reporter from the *Los Angeles Herald-Examiner* was there to cover the graduation. Ironically, I was captured in one of the two photographs that was posted with the story on page A-5.

It wasn't until the indoor presentation of diplomas that I saw any of my family members. As I walked up to the center of the stage to receive my diploma from Chief Davis, I spotted my lovely mother and three of my young sisters, Victoria, Teresa, and my darling baby sister

Cristina, sitting on Mom's lap. Cristina was stretching her little neck upward trying to get a look at her big brother receiving his diploma dressed in his Los Angeles police uniform.

My father did not attend my graduation. Our unnatural estrangement began at my birth twenty-nine years ago when I was born in Tijuana, Mexico. At that time, my father, Alfonso Antonio Moreno, was on the run from the federal authorities for deserting his naval unit in World War II. After the war, he surrendered to the federal authorities and spent some years in a federal penitentiary in Terminal Island, California. After his early release, he spent the rest of his life as a crushed and lost soul with an ugly disposition toward his first-born son.

One need not have a degree in the behavioral sciences to understand the psychological complexities and damage that type of relationship has on any offspring. There were twelve children in all, four girls and eight boys (I was the second-born, three years after my sister Irene). We were raised in an 874-square-foot, three-bedroom home in the gang-infested streets of Florencia-13, next door to South Central

On December 19, 1975, I proudly became an Officer of the Los Angeles Police Department. I am on the far right.

Los Angeles. It was the 1940s, '50s and '60s, when America was still sorting itself out from its racist history.

In 1954, when I was attending the second grade at Saint Aloysius Catholic school, I was diagnosed with a rare childhood disease, Legg Calves Perthes, which required the use of crutches and metal braces for the next four years. This physical disability was exacerbated by an undiagnosed case of severe dyslexia and dyscalculia (a difficulty in learning or comprehending language and math). I was branded the dumbest kid in class and forced to repeat the sixth grade. The embarrassment was so overwhelming that I acted out in class in an attempt to distract everyone from my learning disability.

And I paid for it in spades. It was a decade and a half of punishments from the nuns, my father, and the Christian Brothers in high school. My teachers came at me with writing repetitive penances on the chalkboard of "I shall not dos." On occasion, I was slapped across the face or struck on the palm of my open hand with a heavy wooden ruler. It was much of the same in the three high schools I attended before dropping out my senior year, six weeks before graduation.

In 1965, when most Americans were enjoying the era of *A Summer Place,* I was arrested three times—once for burglary, once for armed robbery, and once for felony assault. In the assault arrest, I chose to go through a full-blown jury trial. The trial ended in a hung jury and the case was not refiled.

After high school, I drifted from one meaningless job to another for three years before I enlisted in my beloved Marine Corps and served in Vietnam as a fire team leader and radioman.

A little over a year after I returned to the United States and discharged from the Marine Corps, I attempted the impossible—to become a member of the Los Angeles Police Department. It was a five-year Herculean task in which I overcame nine separate erroneous disqualifications while securing a two-year associate's college degree in only eighteen months. To this day, I hold the record for successfully overcoming more disqualifications than any other Los Angeles police officer, going back to the department's beginning in 1869. I was graduated eighteenth in my L.A.P.D. Academy class. Only in America. Oo-rah!

After the graduation ceremony, I followed Mom home still dressed in my uniform. I wanted to let my neighbor Spanky and the homies see me in uniform. Unfortunately, he wasn't able to attend my graduation because he was very ill with rheumatoid arthritis.

Before I stopped at Spanky's, I dropped in to see my "Asian Pearl," Sakiya, at Nick's little ghetto grocery store around the corner from our home. She was much older now and quite wrinkled, but she was still stunningly beautiful in my eyes. When I walked into the store, she looked up from behind the counter where she stood next to Nick, her husband. We smiled at one another, and she hurried around the counter and gave me a sweet hug and kiss on the cheek.

"Look at my policeman!" she proudly proclaimed. Nick joined his wife and grabbed my hand. The customers all seemed a little confused. We spoke for a short time, then I left. Just as I started to drive away, Sakiya ran out of the store and gave me a tall R.C. Cola, as she had on numerous occasions when I was a child on crutches. I never opened that precious gift, but unfortunately, I accidentally dropped and broke it while moving years later.

Mom pleaded with me to stay a little longer and said she would fix me my favorite meal—round steak and her special home-fried potatoes. I told her I needed to stop at Spanky's and then prepare for work on Monday. That wasn't true; I just didn't fancy being home when Dad got there.

Spanky was seated in that same little dilapidated couch on his porch that must have been there from the time he first moved in a year after our family moved to Lou Dillon. He looked terribly frail but was in great spirits seeing one of the few homies who actually made good. "Corky, I never had any doubt that you would make it," he said, grinning. "You are different from anyone I've ever known; God bless and take care."

Spanky's best friend, an old-school gangster who went by the moniker, "This Way and That Way," was seated next to him and was all smiles as well. He stood up and shook my hand. I thought he would never let go. When he finally released my hand, he rushed into the house and returned with a three-quart bottle of ghetto beer, Brew 102. "*Pendejo* (idiot)!" Spanky yelled. "Corky's the *pinche hura* (fucking cops); show some respect!"

We all started laughing and I told my homies, "I'll fix that!" I removed my shirt and belt, and carefully placed them in the backseat of my car—badge, revolver, and all. About an hour later, some of Spanky's older gangster homies (O.G.s) drove up in their war wagon low-riders, and it was time for me to get the hell out of Dodge. I scurried across the street and gave Mom a hug and kiss, then headed home to my little apartment in Downey.

As I walked in the door to my apartment, I was strangely overcome with a feeling of debilitating weakness. Never in my life had I ever felt so completely physically and psychologically drained. I didn't feel any earned pride, accomplishment, or joy. I just wanted to sleep. I turned on the TV and grabbed a beer from the fridge. After a couple of drinks, I walked into the bedroom and collapsed into a deep sleep. Astonishingly, when I awoke, I glanced at the clock and it was two in the afternoon on Saturday. I had never slept that long in my entire life! I walked into the shower and felt like I was about to faint. It scared the hell out of me!

I thought a long run would get my head right, but after a block or so, I felt like I was going to pass out. I looked around to see if anyone was watching me when I stopped, because all of my neighbors were accustomed to seeing me run along the neighborhood street for years. It was scary and embarrassing. I made my way back to my apartment and just wanted to sleep again. I walked into the kitchen, but I wasn't hungry or thirsty. I went back into the bedroom and slept the rest of the day. I recall it was about nine o'clock when I woke, but I felt just as frail as before. My Lord, was I losing my mind?! The phone kept ringing, but I wasn't in the mood to talk to anyone. Was I suffering from the beginning of a mental breakdown? The thought turned my blood ice cold.

I walked into the living room and sat on the sofa, staring at a blank TV screen. Then it came to me: I was decompressing from the past five years of fighting the most powerful city government in the United States. The City of Los Angeles and the L.A.P.D. were still in the throes of its self-imposed exorcism from its *L. A. Confidential* racist past.

I cocked my head back on the couch and surrendered to the Lord. Then without thinking, I recited the Lord's Prayer.

2
Old School

THE DAY OF RECKONING was at hand. It was Monday, December 22, 1975, and I was off to begin what I was born to do—protect the helpless against that lot that rained hell on the streets of my youth.

Four of my classmates from platoon 8-75 were assigned to Venice Division. I wanted to be assigned to 77 Division, but that sort of chaos would have to wait.

There is a pecking order of street cops within the L.A.P.D. The Praetorians that were assigned to South Bureau were considered the badass hot shots of the department, while our brothers who worked over the hill in the Valley were scoffed at as a bunch of pussies. My assignment at Venice Division didn't have much more esteem than that of Valley Bureau. Venice Cops were looked at as a bunch of burnt-out, beach bunny pussies.

On my drive to the station, I still felt completely out of it. But I trusted that prayer would pull me through this empty abyss. I drove into the parking lot behind the station and identified myself.

There was no formal indoctrination for the four of us who still needed to complete another seven-and-a-half months before we were officially Los Angeles police officers. We were simply directed to the roll-call room and told to have a seat in the front row and "shut the fuck up." When the rest of the day-watch street cops walked in, we sensed a nonverbal distain for the fucking new guys (FNGs), much like in the military.

My training officers, Daniel Hays and Michael Arbore, couldn't have been more vanilla. These irredeemably square white boys had no idea of what was shaking on the dark side of the moon. Both were in their late twenties, a little taller than me, with light hair and brown eyes. Both wore glasses that didn't help their street command presence. Neither were former military, so I lost out on the treasured automatic combat brotherhood. And they both were uncomfortable using tactical language—aggressively screaming profanity-laced commands at suspects in an effort to intimidate them into submission. However, they knew the department manual inside-out and were good, honest policemen. They were the complete opposite to Brophy and Wilder, the consummate street-wise Praetorians I worked with on my Wilshire Division ride-alongs while still in the Academy.

I worked with Officer Hays on my first day. Once we drove out of the station parking lot, I picked up the mic and cleared, "14-A-5 day watch clear, good morning." And once I did that, my two-and-a-half-day funk evaporated!

Hays looked over at me with a look of censure. Should I have asked him if it was OK to clear? Unlike at Wilshire or some of the other hotter divisions, we weren't inundated with a barrage of radio calls, which gave us time to hunt for assholes.

It was colder than hell that morning, so I cranked my window up. Hays looked over at me and said, "Put that window down; you might not be able to hear breaking glass." I thought to myself, what in the hell was that all about? But rightly, I kept my mouth shut and said, "Yes, sir," and would do so for the remainder of my probation. I was never able to form any sort of dialogue or bond with him. It was an extremely uncomfortable situation, and I was concerned about what he was passing on to the supervisors in Team-1 about my performance.

One redeeming thing about getting assigned to "pussy" Venice Division was being assigned to work 14-A-5, the Oakwood area car. The 14-A-5 was the patrol car you wanted if you really wanted to do police work! In the mid-1970s, Oakwood was a mini 77, with constant street robberies, shootings, felony assaults, and hordes of hypes.

However, Hays always headed straight for Ocean Front Walk (the Venice beach strand), 14-A-1's area of patrol. Oakwood was where all the action was, crawling with hypes and burglars at that time in the morning. In the early morning, Ocean Front Walk (OFW) was desolate with no pedestrian traffic, all of the businesses were closed, and it was freezing-butt-ass cold. On one of those typical mornings, Hays punched the accelerator and headed toward one of the newly constructed pagodas on the boardwalk and bailed out of the car without saying a word.

Shit! What did I miss? I ran behind him but only saw a lone female drunk sipping on short dog (cheap bum wine). He snatched her off the ground, wheeled her around, and cuffed her. The whole time I was thinking, what was this all about? She was just a plain drunk, not hurting anyone. Christ, we could have been trolling the Oakwood hood for some hype burglars. Damn, she was just another generic street drunk with wet-butt breath, fleas, scabies, urine and fecal-matter stains all about her lower clothing. Her name was Susan Sanchez, she was forty-four years old—an OFW fixture.

Hays placed her in the right-rear seat of our car. I did the procedural thing by sitting next to her behind the officer driver, and shit, her clothing was still wet from her urinating on herself. On the way to the station, she was nonstop "motherfucking" us to the top of her lungs and splattering me with gusts of her diseased saliva. Once we pulled into the station, Hays looked at me and said, "Well, pull her out."

Damn! I wanted no part of touching that! I needed to search her before locking her into one of the holding cells, while Hays got booking approval from the watch commander (W/C), Sergeant Moreland. I really admired that sweet old-school soul. He looked just like the 1930s character actor Sir C. Aubrey Smith who played the grandfather in the tear-jerking movie, *Little Lord Fauntleroy*. He sported a thick guardsman mustache and had pure silver white hair.

At this time, the L.A.P.D. had few to no female police officers in the department. So I asked one of the female record clerks to witness me as I conducted a cursory search for contraband or weapons. When it came to searching her female area, I used my police baton to brush over her anatomy, then locked her in one of the holding cells while she was still "motherfucking" the world.

I could see the thinly veiled disdain on Sergeant Moreland's face when he wrote out the booking approval for this bullshit arrest, but Hays was clueless. What a waste of man hours and taxpayers' dollars.

—

A couple weeks later, we responded to an ambulance-shooting call in the Venice Canals. Back then, the Canal residents were primarily a bunch of counterculture hippies akin to those in San Francisco's Haight-Ashbury. They dressed like it was still 1967 with multicolored clothing and long, unwashed hair. And they were in no short supply of LSD, methamphetamines, and marijuana (unlike the Oakwood residents who preferred opiates with their grass).

It was a Code-2 call, so we got there in no time. When we arrived, I did the Marine thing and rushed out of the car toward the residence with the shotgun. Hays screamed at me to back off and assess the area before I moved any closer. He may have been vanilla on steroids, but he knew his shit when it came down to it. I was still green and had a great deal to learn.

We cautiously approached the residence. The inner door was wide open. When we looked inside, we could see the Person Requesting (P.R.) standing in the middle of the living room silently pointing to another room. We walked in and checked this strange-looking dude for weapons. His name was Darryl; he was in his late twenties, tall and skinny with disheveled hair down to his ass. He never said a word; he just kept pointing to the restroom.

I walked toward the restroom and saw a ghastly figure lying on the floor in a lake of her own blood. Her name was Laura; she was nineteen years old and nine months pregnant with Darryl's baby.

She had taken Darryl's .357 Magnum while he was out and blew her brains out. It was a very small room with the floor about an inch lower than the rest of the residence, making for a literal reservoir of blood. Her brain matter, skull fragments, hair, and tissues were on the opposite wall, perfectly aligned with her position, sitting on the toilet stool, at the time she shot herself. I heard Hays walk up from behind me and murmur to himself, then he quickly walked off to call the watch commander.

Sergeant Moreland made the standard notifications, including calling for an ambulance unit. The on-call homicide detective was Detective Rick Russell—suave, tall, fit, and sophisticated looking, with a bit of gray in his brown, slightly receding hairline. All the detectives wore nice suits, but Russell was the bomb. He immediately walked up to me instead of Hays, and I gave him a detailed overview of what we had. I followed him to the restroom where Laura's body was. Maybe Hays was just letting me get the experience, or maybe he was just burnt out from seeing this shit time after time.

After about an hour and a half of checking every microscopic detail, Russell called for another black-and-white to transport Darryl to the station so that he could interview him in a proper setting and confirm his story of the shooting. Russell also took the .357 Mag and booked it into custody. He left us there to wait for the coroner to pick up Laura's remains to be transported to the morgue for an autopsy. It was well after our watch before the coroner arrived. Just another busy day in the city, and the dead would have to wait their turn.

Driving home that evening, I couldn't stop wondering if I should have listened for fetal life sounds in Laura's abdomen. I would have had to cut her open to save the baby. I'm sure if I did, Hays would have had a myocardial infarction on the spot and sued the city for a stress pension. It would have been divine to have saved that little innocent soul in Laura's tummy.

———

It was most unpleasant working with Hays and Arbor, but within a few weeks I figured out a cheeky way of getting a different training officer. I normally showed up well before roll call and had the officers' empty locker room all to myself. That way I didn't have to rush, and that gave me an opportunity to walk over to the detective tables to read crime and arrest reports. It paid off big time in improving my writing skills and gave me an edge on suspect intel throughout the division.

After about forty minutes of studying the police reports at the detective table, I would walk into the W/C's office and chat with whomever the W/C of the day was. I would ask the W/C if I could get him a cup of that skank 10-cent coffee from those old-time coffee vending machines. Then just before roll call, I would volunteer to carry the large magnetic duty-board to the roll call room for the W/C. On the way to the roll call room, I'd switch my assignment to anyone other than Hays or Arbor.

My first choice was Officer Rick Mesnard, one of the most knowledgeable street cops I've ever worked with. Rick had bright red hair, freckles, and a whiter-than-rice complexion. He was about five foot nine and 125 pounds on a good day. Rick's forte was dope. He could smell someone taking a puff on a joint a mile away. He taught me everything I knew about the world of narcotics and its unbridled darkness.

By now, I had qualified as a Superior Court-tested expert in possession for personal use and possession for sales in marijuana and opiates (heroin), thanks to Rick's tutelage. And Rick and I were cleaning house in Team-1's Oakwood area with our daily hype arrests. Heroin addict arrests served a dual-purpose: When you arrest a hype, you also take an active burglar off the street.

Oakwood was a cherry orchard of heroin addicts. Every street in the hood had one or two hypes prowling in the early morning hours. Hypes were almost never violent since they were much too sedated to care about anything on earth other than when and how they were going to hustle their next $10 fix. We only had to cruise up and down the neighborhood streets a bit until we spotted one walking like a lost zombie in slow motion.

On this day, we spotted William Wilkens, a black male in his early twenties, skinny as a rail with an unusually big head, squinty eyes, and an exaggerated Afro. Rick had arrested him numerous times before. Wilkens had just left his mother's home on Seventh and Indiana.

Rick picked up the mic. "14-A-5, show us Code-6 at Seventh and Indiana, on a narcotic investigation." That procedural broadcast informed Communications of our location in case the shit went sideways. Normally, when other patrol units heard a Code-6, (self-initiated investigation) they rolled by if they weren't tied up on another call.

We stopped Wilkens, and I told him to assume the position as he had done dozens of time before. He interlocked his fingers behind his head and spread his legs, then slowly turned his back to me so I could check him for weapons.

In this routine and mundane stop, I learned the bitter lesson of complacency. By now, I had stopped and arrested numerous hypes, and it was the same drill over and over again. But this time, it blew up in my face! When I reached up to grab his hands, he wheeled around and struck the left side of my face with his elbow, momentarily stunning me. Then he reached for my gun. Rick went into him with nine "from the sky" (baton blows), preventing Wilkens from tearing my revolver from my holster and killing the both of us. That happens every day in the badass streets of America to our men and women in uniform.

All three of us slammed into the cement sidewalk while we attempted to cuff this asshole. We finally managed to hold Wilkens down and wrestle both of his wrists behind his back. After what felt like an hour of intense street combat, Rick cuffed him. I eased up and slid my right leg next to his head.

Suddenly Wilkens turned and bit into my inner right thigh, just short of my genitals. The pain was excruciating. Once again, Rick went at him with his baton, but now he was beating the hell out of both me and the suspect. I screamed at Rick to stop, then reached over with both hands, grabbed the suspect's Afro, and slammed his head to the pavement. It worked. He lost a few teeth in the process, but fuck him, he would have killed Rick and me if he would have gotten my gun.

By now, a few other patrol cars arrived, but it was Code-4 (all's secure). When we searched Wilkens, Rick recovered twelve multicolored balloons of heroin in a clear plastic baggy from his right coat pocket. That's why he had fought us—he knew he was going to take a long fall in the joint for possession of heroin for sales.

Another unit transported me to Marine Mercy Hospital for medical treatment. That was the first time I was injured on the job, but far from the last. Boy, did I screw up! My complacency could have killed Rick and me if it weren't for Rick's lightening, kick-ass response. I learned so much from him in such a short time.

Cops get dumped on the streets just about every day in America, and the news media and the public couldn't be less interested.

After I was treated at the hospital, I returned to the station and was ordered to take the remainder of the day off and go home and rest. I was still amped up from the arrest, and my leg was hurting from that vicious bite. I've always had an aversion to taking those Dr. Feelgood pain pills. I felt a drive along the beautiful coastline would soothe both my pain and my spirit.

When I got to the intersection of Hermosa Avenue and Herondo Street, which was the dividing point between Hermosa and Redondo Beach, I saw this lovely three-story apartment building on the beach side of the street. It was called Harbor Cove, and it had a Chart House restaurant on the ground floor; perfect.

I drove into the complex, entered the restaurant, and took a seat next to the ocean-side windows. I wasn't appropriately dressed for this upper-class restaurant. But there I sat, wearing a white T-shirt, sneakers, and a pair of one-legged jeans, exposing my injured, swollen leg. When the pretty waitress came over, she looked at me like I was just another Joe-shit-the-ragman looking to get out of the elements and get a handout.

I ordered an extra-large Bloody Mary, celery stick and all. The waitress slowly strolled off to the bar, moving her voluptuous hips from side to side, then looked back and smiled. She was warming up to me. Her name was Pamela. She wasn't very busy that early and we got to talk quite a bit. When she asked me what happened to my leg, I gave her the abbreviated war story and she loved it. I asked her how long she had been working here, and if she lived in one of the apartments. She answered, a little over a year. She told me there were a couple of vacancies, with one-bedrooms facing inward with no ocean view, going for $315 a month. That was just about half of my monthly take-home pay, but what the hell. Pam said she was good friends with the onsite property manager, Victoria, and she offered to introduce us if I was interested.

After I finished that luscious Bloody Mary, I walked into the rental office with Pam and met Victoria. That was an appropriate name for her; she looked like Victorian England royalty in her long butter-white gown with embroidered sleeves. This lady was sophistication at its finest in dress, manner, and speech. Victoria must have been in her late fifties, with soft brown, graying hair and light-blue eyes. She was quite wrinkled, but her wrinkles only added to her graceful aura and timeless beauty.

On the other hand, I looked like I was straight out of Victorian London's East End. Despite my appearance, she treated me like a young gentleman. When I introduced myself, I used my full name, Alfonso, hoping that might evoke some old-world deference. I'd never done that before. I either used Al or Corky.

"Are you interested in joining our community here at Harbor Cove, Alfonso?" Victoria asked.

"Yes, ma'am."

"We have one single room on the first floor and two two-bedroom units on the third floor. Would you like to see them?"

"Yes, ma'am."

We started with the two-bedroom apartments on the third floor, then went down to the single room on the first floor. I fell in love with it straightaway! It was approximately 800 square feet with a replica fireplace in the living room. The walls were painted in a soft white and the floors were carpeted in a light ash-blue. The kitchen was complete with appliances. Each floor in the building had its own washers and dryers. When you exited the apartment on the north or south side, you stepped onto the sand. All of this for $315 per month!

After my tour, we walked back to the rental office and Victoria asked me what I thought. I tried with all my might to dampen my enthusiasm, but I'm sure Victoria saw right through that feeble attempt. I just said, "I'll take the one-bedroom, ma'am."

"You're going to be one of our neighbors now, so please call me Victoria. When would you like to move in?"

"As soon as possible, Victoria."

After I completed my rental application, she noted I was a Los Angeles police officer and a former Marine. She looked up and asked me if I had gone to Vietnam. I told her yes, I served with India Company, Third Battalion, Seventh Marines, in I-Corps (Northern South Vietnam).

Then she looked back down at my application and her eyes teared up. "My only son, Ethan, was killed in Vietnam on April 28, 1967, with your Marines, Alfonso. I understand it was somewhere in the most northern part of South Vietnam, along the DMZ. He was a Navy Corpsman."

It was quite possible Victoria was talking about the same battle my best friend and brother L.A.P.D. Officer Rick Beach was in. Rick's unit, coined "The Walking Dead," was in a series of hellacious battles along the DMZ where Victoria's son was killed. I made it a point not to tell her that. It was much too painful to see her grief for her only child.

When I completed and signed the rental agreement, one thing stood out—the address: 211 *Yacht Club* Way, Redondo Beach, California. Damn, I couldn't help but think just how far I've come—from the murderous streets of 7932 Lou Dillon Avenue to 211 Yacht Club Way.

"Alfonso, consider yourself our new neighbor—that lovely apartment is yours," Victoria said as she handed me the keys. I hadn't even given her the check for the usual first and last month's rent. "I'll wave the security deposit, and you can start moving in at your convenience. Welcome aboard, Marine. That's what my son would have said. I'll start your rent on the first of September." That gave me six free days' rent.

Just as I started to leave the rental office, she reached out and grabbed my hand. "Your leg... did it happen at work?"

"Yes, but I'm OK." She didn't respond, but I could see in her eyes a "please, please be careful." Victoria and I would become special friends in the years to come.

I walked up to my new apartment and turned on the fireplace just to see how it would look and feel. Then I sprawled out on the floor. I had never experienced such security and serenity. My God, that sustained, Herculean effort to get on the Los Angeles Police Department was so worth it. I drifted off into the sweetest nap and woke about an hour later. I was at peace.

I wanted to go out, but felt I needed a shower first. I limped out to my car and saw a parking placard on my windshield. Evidently, Victoria had searched the parking lot for my vehicle and placed it on the windshield.

I drove to my apartment in Downey where I had lived that monk-like existence while attending Cerritos College and the Los Angeles Police Academy for the last three years. I packed all my belongings into my car. I just needed to move out my toiletries, bedding, my sparse wardrobe, a small TV, a radio alarm clock, and a few other items. I made the move in one quick trip and said farewell to no one.

I got along with all my neighbors, but never really got close to anyone because of my hermitlike existence.

I made one quick stop before I returned to 211 Yacht Club Way for a handful of candles; the apartment's electricity was not in service. When I got back into my car, it was getting late, and my leg was letting me know its dislike to my reluctant care for it, but it was a Marine leg and good to go.

By the time I completed the move into my new world, it was well past eleven, but I wasn't a bit fatigued. After neatly placing my scant belongings into my apartment, I showered, and for some strange reason, felt the same type of spiritual cleansing I had experienced in that humble little blue shower stall on Hill-10 in Vietnam. I didn't want to get out of the shower. But it was late, and I wanted to sample the sublime nightlife of living in the South-Bay, Redondo, Hermosa, and Manhattan Beach.

I started walking west on Hermosa Avenue, the main business drag in Hermosa Beach, honeycombed with small-town restaurants, pubs, and boutiques. There was a really cool song that had been released in that magical spring of 1976 that came to mind as I strolled past the little businesses and all the beautiful people. I started singing it to myself: "*Gonna find my baby, gonna hold her tight; Gonna grab some afternoon delight....*"

The pubs were all packed with "Beach Boys" and "California Girls"—God, this was heaven. I stopped in front of this one pub painted in a garish red that caught my eye. It was Fat Face Fenner's Falloon. I stood at the entrance for a moment and looked at the type of patrons I was going to be mixing with for what I hoped was the rest of my life. Yes, yes, yes!

I made my way to the bar and slowly squeezed between a couple of beauties, then called out to the bartender for a drink. The girl to my right looked at me with her deep-blue eyes and a cheeky smile. I introduced myself and she said her name was Susan. She was twenty-four years old, nearly my height, had a lean, athletic figure, and blond hair cut in the popular wedge cut of the day, like Dorothy Hamill. She recently graduated from Santa Monica College with a nursing degree and worked at Santa Monica Hospital. Within a minute or two of our conversation, Susan asked, "Are you a cop?" My God, I was shocked.

Susan and her friend started laughing and said they noticed me when I was standing at the doorway checking everything out before I walked in, just like a cop would do.

It was impossible to carry on a meaningful conversation with all the noise. Susan asked me where I lived. I told her I had just moved into the Chart House, I mean Harbor Cove, about a quarter mile down the street. "I'd love to see it," she said. I told her there wasn't any furniture or anything, but I had a very cool fireplace. "Let's go, but can I see your badge first?" Susan asked. For the first time, I produced my L.A.P.D. shield and it felt so damn cool. She asked if she could hold it, and I told her let's wait 'til we're out of here.

On the way back to my apartment, I realized I didn't have anything to drink. It was just before 2 a.m., and Mickey's Italian Deli on Hermosa between First and Second Streets was still open. One of the very cool things about Susan was that she was exclusively a beer drinker. Great! I didn't have to stress about choosing a decent bottle of wine. I asked her to pick her favorite brew. She reached for two six-packs of Miller High Life and started laughing as she said, "One for you, and one for me."

We were in my new apartment within a few minutes, and I turned on the fireplace for some ambience. It wasn't at all cold that night, but the fireplace cast a pleasing silhouette of us on the opposite wall.

I asked Susan to tell me all about herself while we sipped on our cold Millers right out of the can. She said she really didn't have much of an exciting life story up to now. Her parents were recently divorced. She had two older sisters married to successful businessmen. Her father was a wealthy accountant and she was still living at home with her mother in the upper-class West Side of Santa Monica in a large four-bedroom home. Susan was making pretty good money at the hospital and wanted to get her own apartment in the South Bay, but she didn't have the heart to leave her lonely, brokenhearted mother. She resented her father because he once told her she was a mistake. She described her father as one of the coldest men she ever knew.

Time was flying by, and we were halfway through our sixers and having ever such a lovely time just talking. I must have only interjected once or twice while she was speaking. There was no point in saying anything, I just listened to her soft voice and gazed at her lovely presence. Then all at once, she jumped up and ripped everything off but her bra and blue lace panties, then exclaimed, "Let's go for a swim!" I thought the water must be freezing, but what the hell, yes! She was indeed lean but had a beautiful round, hard, bubble butt.

I couldn't strip in the same fashion. I had stopped wearing underwear in Vietnam. The humidity was much to suffocating for my Johnson and his two mates down below. When I returned to the world (the States), I never wore undershorts again.

I took off my pants and quickly wrapped a towel around myself. We ran through the hallway and exited the apartment by the north exit onto the sand. Fortunately, there wasn't a soul around. We dashed for the water and discarded what we had on. She swam ahead of me like a dolphin. I, on the other hand, was satisfied wading no more than chest deep. Poseidon was in a tranquil mood that early morning, with peaceful ebbs and flows of no more than a foot.

Susan kept asking me to swim out to her, but I was no match for her aquatic prowess. I could hear her gently laughing, then after a few minutes she swam into my arms, wrapped her beautiful long legs around my waist, and started kissing me.

It was a challenge to couple, due to the shifting current, and we both laughed. She reached down and fussed us. She started softly biting my ear and whispered, "Relax, I'm never going to let you go, and it's only going to get better."

The sun still hadn't awakened, giving us some cover when we got out of the water. Damn, Susan couldn't find her Victoria's Secret panties, so, we gave it a Code-3 (red lights and siren) run back to my apartment. We jumped into the shower and made love again, then fixed a makeshift bed on the floor next to the fireplace and slept for a few hours. She had the weekend off, too. At about nine in the morning, I gave her a ride to her car so she could run a few errands and return sometime in the early afternoon.

I had forgotten all about the burning pain in my leg on that magical day of bliss. Once Susan left, I kept having flashbacks about that fucking hype going for my gun.

I instinctively knew that Susan was going to be my second chance after losing Danique.

Susan returned a little after two in the afternoon dressed in a running outfit. She also brought a day bag with a change of clothing for our night out. She was a gymnast and runner in high school and college. Lord! I hit the jackpot! For some reason, I had a strong nostalgic urge to run the hill trails across the street from Cathedral High School, just about a mile from the L.A.P.D. Academy, and I knew Susan would love the idea. She did and lit up like a roman candle at the suggestion.

We drove to Bishop Way north of Broadway and parked half a block down the street from the main entrance of the high school. It's amazing how the memories come flooding back sometimes. I recalled our dancing classes at school where Italian kids danced to Xavier Cugat's rumba with Chinese kids. Partnered soul brothers and Caucasian students shook their booties to Celia Cruz's salsa. Only twice in my life have I ever experienced such unique racial harmony: first at Cathedral High, and then in the United States Marine Corps.

I thought Susan would freak out at the start of the hill run. It was really steep, but she wasn't the least bit intimidated. When we reached the top of the hill, I looked over to see if Susan was OK. This steep start always gave me a measure of my latest victim's fitness and just how hard I could push the person. When I looked over to my right and down, I didn't see her. She was to my left and ahead of me. Damn!

I decided to give Susan the big push—I was going to take her up Big Bertha. It's at the apex of the steepest and tallest hill overlooking Elysian Park, the Golden State Freeway, and the undulating 110 Arroyo Seco Freeway leading to South Pasadena. From the top of Big Bertha, you can see a huge swath of the Valley on the north and much of the cities to the east of Los Angeles. But first you have to get to the top by a very narrow path full of weeds and thorns. It's a ballbuster even for the fittest of runners. If you can make it all the way to the top without stopping, you are one fit *mofo*.

Three-quarters of the way up, Susan bent down and leaned forward. I could hear her gasping for air and coughing up some unpleasantness. But she never stopped until she reached the top. This woman is one fit, intelligent beauty, with rare, deep character I thought to myself.

Funny, my leg was swollen and bruised, but I felt like I could run forever. That's what happens to a man when he is with the right woman.

When we got back to Cathedral, we retrieved our workout bags from the car with a change of clothes and towels. We headed for the empty shower room on campus, but it was locked. Shit. I suggested we could drive to a gas station and take a field shower; Susan was good with that. As we walked back toward my car, I saw Mr. Lee by the gymnasium. He was one of the groundskeepers from back in the day. I affectionately yelled out at him. Unfortunately, he didn't remember me even when I told him I had attended Cathedral in the early '60s. It wasn't looking promising, but I noticed he couldn't take his eyes off Susan.

She stealthily asserted her charm and he warmed up to her in a flash. She asked him if we could please use the shower room, and that we would take great care not to make a mess. He smiled at her and walked us to the locker room. There were no female facilities, but Susan didn't care a lick. We showered together, making haste and taking great caution not to make the slightest mess with a quick "Afternoon Delight."

When we left the gym, I saw Mr. Lee standing just outside the doorway, fixated on Susan. She looked divine in her short white-on-white embroidered minidress that accented her million-dollar legs. She walked over to Mr. Lee and kissed him on the cheek. He looked like he had just won a lottery.

When we got to the car, I asked Susan if she would like to see the historic El Pueblo de Los Angeles, better known as Olvera Street, for a little sightseeing and to get some authentic Mexican food and beer. She reached over, kissed me and said, "I'd love to." We were off.

I parked the car in the same little parking place I've used since 1964 when I used to bring my friends from high school. It was always such great fun for all my crews. We walked up and down the same cobblestone streets that the founders of Los Angeles used in 1781. Susan stopped and read every historic placard as we passed rustic buildings graced with trees and fountains. Susan was enamored with all the arts-and-crafts shops and roving mariachi bands. I suggested my favorite restaurant on the east side of the street in the center of Olvera Street. Like me, Susan wasn't one for ostentation. We had the "Number 3"—three taquitos with guacamole, beans, and a small dinner salad—plus a hard-shell taco and several Modelos to wash it down.

When we got back to 211 Yacht Club Way, we went out to the beach and talked for the remainder of the afternoon and early evening, then returned to the apartment and made love for the rest of the night. Susan left Sunday afternoon after we had brunch and a couple of margaritas. We entered into an on-again, off-again relationship that lasted years. The whole time she never dated anyone else of consequence, but she never pushed the marriage thing. I thought that was a product of her loveless and cold-hearted relationship with her father, like I had with my father.

———

Monday rolled around once again, and it was another day I would never forget. I was assigned to an L-car (a one-man unit) and always loved the total freedom it gave me at the beginning of my police career. My first call was a burglary investigation.

The suspects were long gone, and that's why it was assigned to an L-car. The radio call was in the outskirts of Oakwood where many lower-income Caucasians and Mexicans lived. The residence was a single-family dwelling with two very small bedrooms. I knocked on the door and was welcomed in by a lovely young Mexican couple, both college graduates from Guadalajara. I immediately sensed an aura of intellect and grace. They were also very-good looking. Mariann, a Natalie Wood clone, did most of the talking, with her husband Luis close at her side.

When I asked them what property was taken in the burglary, Luis stepped up and walked me to the back door that led to a very small backyard with no garage. The suspect had used a pry bar to muscle the door lock open. The thieves had taken family heirlooms and the television.

While I was taking the Preliminary Investigation Report, a wonderful aroma filled the air. Mariann was in their small kitchen heating up a cup of *champurrado,* a traditional thick hot chocolate drink. She was fixing it especially for me. On occasion, a victim will offer you a cup of coffee, but you always gracefully decline. I don't recall a single other time I ever accepted a cup of anything; however, the *champurrado* was irresistible. I had two cups.

When I finished the burglary investigation and hot chocolate, I walked out to my car and retrieved the print kit. To be perfectly honest, 99 percent of the time we never attempted to lift prints while conducting a 459 investigation (burglary). We always covered our asses on the reports by writing, "no evidence of latent prints." Management didn't want you spending extra time dusting the entire residence for fingerprints. We were always pushed to get in and out and clear for service. Be that as it may, I got an A in my Latent Print course at Cerritos College and couldn't wait to test-fire my knowledge. In my print class, we not only learned how to lift prints, but also learned how to classify the many types of prints—arches, loops, whorls, radial and ulnar loops.

Luis and Mariann got the VIP treatment for that delicious *champurrado*. In fact, that extra effort resulted in the arrest of two active Venice juvenile burglars, and I received my first of two 1.27s (commendations) for identifying the burglars.

—

Back at the station, Sergeant Moreland asked me to come into his office. He had that usual warmth about him. "Officer Moreno, I want you to know that I'm getting a lot of good feedback from all the supervisors about your good work," he said. But then he took on a stern and commanding look. "Did you ever change your partner assignment when you carried the assignment board to roll-call room for Sergeant Cizin and me?"

Shit, busted! There is no way in hell that I would ever lie to this man, come hell or high water. "Yes, sir, I did," I confessed.

He didn't seem surprised with my veracity. I had no idea what the consequences were going to be, but the greatest fear I had was to lose this man's respect.

He stared down at me for a few moments. Then all at once, he smiled and said that he and Sergeant Cizin knew what I was up to the whole time, and they used to get a chuckle out of it. "Get back to work, Officer Moreno, and keep up the good work. I would have done the same thing, be safe!"

Phew! After that, it was back out to Oakwood, and I immediately headed into the belly of the beast, Sixth and Indian. Within five minutes, I found my mark—one of the countless hypes trolling the hood for his next victim. Sure enough, it was Bobby Yates, a known hype.

When I stopped him, he was clearly "down"—his speech was slow and deliberate, his pupils were excessively constricted, and his skin was cool and clammy to the touch. The injection point on his inner-right arm was red, raised, and oozing a clear fluid. I knew his urine sample would come back positive for heroin.

Yates, like all other dopers, had cornered the market in lying and deceit. "Officer Moreno, I'm clean. I'm on the methadone program and haven't chipped [injected] in months." This was one sorry, lying asshole. The hundreds of track marks on both his arms clearly indicated he was using on a regular basis.

Repeat offenders were put on this worthless program known as "methadone maintenance therapy" (MMT). The truth is that the program was exponentially cheaper than warehousing these assholes in our county jails. I never once met a hype that realized sobriety from the MMT program. It didn't provide the thrill of pushing that needle through your flesh and experiencing that instant euphoria.

I hooked Yates up, and he spewed nonstop lies all the way to the station. When I arrived, he was on the nod and had pissed all over himself and my car. It stunk like the netherworld. Fortunately, there were some maintenance workers at the station that day, and I asked them to industrially clean and detoxify my sled. I placed Yates in one of the less populated holding cells much to the chagrin of his cellmates.

I always sequestered myself when I wrote my crime and arrest reports. I felt uncomfortable having to use my master spelling list in front of my brother officers. When my master spelling list didn't have the word I was looking for, I always could depend on my Cerritos College mistress, Ms. *Merriam Webster*. It took me twice as long as any of the other officers, but when I emerged from my cocoon, my reports were bulletproof.

In my many assignments at the department, I was always struck with the high-caliber supervision. However, like in any other industry, there are always "witchetty grubs" (Australian worm) supervisors. All of us at one time or another would think to ourselves, how did that person ever become a supervisor? On that day, I met my first witchetty grub, Sergeant Lady. I appropriately coined him Sergeant Witchetty Grub, but kept that christening to myself; my bros loved it!

A few minutes before I was done with the Yates report, Sergeant Witchetty Grub opened the door and said he needed to talk to me. I thought he was going to give me some shit about Yates stinking up the holding cell, but he said the prisoner had accused me of stealing $5,000 from him, and he needed to search me. This was a bit annoying, but I understood he was obligated to look into the complaint. I produced my wallet and emptied all my pockets and thought that was going to be the last of it. But the worm was only getting started. He asked me to remove my shoes. Then he asked me to empty my weapon. What did he think? Did I stuff $5,000 dollars of cash in the cylinders of my .38?

Then it got to the unfathomable—he was going to subject me to a cavity search! I told him that I stopped wearing underwear in 1969 when I was in Vietnam, and I was uncomfortable having him look up my ass over the word of a hype who never earned an honest dollar in his life!

I suggested that I would rather submit to a hand search up and around my genitals and buttocks with my pants on, as opposed to the degrading cavity search. I thought that would have been more than reasonable. Fuck! But a hand search wasn't good enough for that grub. I hadn't completed my probation and knew that I didn't have a wheel to stand on. The grub was hell-bent on having a sick look up my private parts, and those three chevrons on his uniform sleeve ensured he could.

I capitulated to the profound indignity and removed my uniform pants. I noticed Sergeant Witchetty Grub had a fiendish look of pleasure as he scanned my naked body. Then he started the generic commands for the cavity search: "Open your mouth wide and wiggle your tongue. Bend down and run your fingers through your hair. Lift your balls and penis. Turn around and lift the right, then left, foot. Wiggle your toes. Bend forward and spread your cheeks."

After all that, I was so sick I couldn't finish my watch. I needed to get the hell out of the station to clear my head. I asked Sergeant Moreland if I could take the rest of the afternoon off. I don't know if Moreland knew what had just happened—I doubt it—but he told me to take all the time I needed.

On the way home, I was trying to make some sense out of what pushed Sergeant Lady to take that unconscionable action. Then I recalled my first field incident with him. I was working the beach car, 14-A-1, with Officer Dave Gossman, my favorite training officer in Venice Division, when we got a call to "see the supervisor at Windward and Ocean Front Walk." It was Sergeant Lady. He had stopped a motorist for a traffic violation and wanted me to write the citation for him. I may have been new to the job, but I knew that I couldn't write someone a traffic ticket unless I personally observed the traffic violation. A traffic ticket is an infraction and must be committed in the presence of the officer for him to take action. So, I respectfully told Sergeant Lady that I was unable to write the citation. Both Gossman and I saw that that really pissed him off!

I advised him of what I had learned in the Academy about such an incident. He squinted his small, pale-blue eyes nestled behind those Coke bottle-thick glasses, then nervously tried to initiate a normal conversation with Dave. After a couple of long minutes, he walked over to the traffic violator and released him without a citation. When we drove off, Gossman looked over at me and said, "Watch your ass with that one." Gossman had a little over seven years on the job at that time and had recently secured a law degree from Santa Monica College. So, whatever he said, I absorbed it as scripture.

The problem is, that grub was one of Team-1's sergeants. It was impossible to stay as far away from him as I would have liked. Gossman was right; Lady got his day of sick reckoning.

—

By July 1976, I was getting near the end of my one-year probation period. I was continually getting high marks from field supervisors and awarded a stream of 1.27s (commendations). At times, I lead the division in arrests and was being partnered up with less productive officers and starting to get some blowback from the older guys. But I was having the time of my life. I had put the body cavity search behind me.

One morning on the way to work, I found myself simulating a vehicle pursuit broadcast for some reason. I picked a vehicle ahead of me in traffic and went through the standard pursuit protocol. Ironically, that morning I was in my first pursuit while working an L-car (one-man unit).

Sure enough, just as I cleared, "14-L-21 day watch clear, good morning," Communications responded, "14-L-21, roger and good morning. 14-L-21, see the man 459 investigation at 403 Brooks Avenue." Enroute to the call, I stopped for a traffic stop at Fourth Street and Brooks Avenue when a white 1964 Chevrolet came to a stop on the right side of the intersection. The driver appeared much too young to have a driver's license. He looked like a gang member. He was stretching his neck upward to see over the steering wheel. When he saw me, he gave me that proverbial, "oh, shit!" look. He panicked and ducked down beneath the dashboard in a feeble attempt not to be seen, but he was busted and knew it.

I advised Communications I was going Code-6 self-investigation on Brooks and Fourth when the juvenile suspect punched the accelerator and turned W/B on Fourth Street. I matched his speed and lit him up. When I got close enough, I radioed the plate in and started the verbal pursuit protocol I had practiced earlier on the way to work: "14-L-21, I'm in pursuit."

Communications (RTO) responded, "All units, all frequencies, stand by, 14-L-21 is in pursuit. 14-L-21, what's your location? The vehicle is a Santa Monica stolen."

"14-L-21, I'm northbound on Rose approaching Lincoln Boulevard."

You find yourself driving at breakneck speed through business and residential neighborhoods and pray that vehicles and unsuspecting pedestrians hear your siren. This is exacerbated when the suspect blows through stop signs and lights with no regard for human life. It doesn't stop there, with the suspect recklessly maneuvering back and forth through multiple traffic lanes forcing other drivers to swerve uncontrollably and slam on their brakes. Above all else, you must manage the overwhelming surge of adrenalin racing through every cell in your body and maintain a calm and composed voice for the RTO to understand your broadcast.

In most pursuits, there are two officers. Your partner handles the radio and broadcasts, allowing the driver to concentrate on traffic. However, when you're working an L-car, you are forced to both drive and communicate with the RTO. Incredibly, the suspect couldn't give a shit about anything other than losing his pursuers as he drives like a soulless maniac with malevolent disregard for human life and property. At this point, I crossed into the city of Santa Monica and a couple of Santa Monica police units joined the pursuit. Suddenly, the suspect locked up his wheels and stopped midblock. This whole time I had been thinking, is the little fuck armed? My heart rate was up, and I did a foolish thing—I left my cover, weapon in hand, and walked toward the driver using loud and shocking verbiage to scare the suspect into submission—it worked.

Using tactical language is not taught in the Police Academy, but I wasn't concerned about trampling on anyone's sensibilities. My intent was to shock this fuck into submission and take him into custody without using physical or deadly force. In the end, my Marine Corps shock tactic worked 99.9 percent of the time. Officer Rick Mesnard and his partner transported the subject to the station, while another unit impounded the stolen car.

When I returned to the station to interview the subject and start the endless reports, Sergeant Moreland walked up to me with an ear-to-ear smile, "Good job, Al. I got a call from downtown Communications to advise me of what a great job you did handling the pursuit without a partner." I felt like I had just hit a grand slam home run—pleasing Sergeant Moreland was next to pleasing the Commandant in the Sky.

I removed the subject from the solitary cell (juvenile and adults must be held separately) and walked him to an interview room in the detective's squad room. He was only fifteen years old and a Culver City gang member. He had one prior arrest for grand theft auto, two arrests for burglary, and one arrest for armed robbery. No doubt those were just the times he got caught.

When I asked him if he wanted a parent or an attorney present while I interviewed him, he looked directly in my eyes, completely uncowed, and said, "Fuck *no homes, no soy puto* [I'm no bitch]." I had grown up with that lot's brutal mentality. I saw my first murder while walking home from first grade while attending Saint Aloysius Catholic grade school. The victim was fourteen years old, a Hickory Street gang member from Watts caught in Florencia-13's turf, and he paid for that infraction with his life. It was a particularly gruesome crime scene. The kid didn't die right away from his multiple stab wounds; he crawled for several yards in a hopeless attempt to get help, leaving a gruesome trail of thick blood behind, knowing he was going to die.

I may have been relatively new to the crime-fighting business, but I instinctively knew that you win or lose an interview with a suspect within the first two minutes. So, you better sauce-out what characteristics—body language, idioms, and vocabulary—you're going to employ with your suspect. I asserted myself at the jump, and this hardass gangster knew he wasn't going to be able to jack me off.

When I started to question him about the stolen vehicle, he leaned back in his chair—all five foot two, 125 pounds of him—and said, "I'm not telling you a fuckin' thing, *con todos respeto* [with all due respect]."

Game over. I walked him back to the holding cell and started the reports. The detectives gave it a second go, but he told them to get fucked as well (with no "*con todos respeto*"). They were able to get a detention order predicated on his lengthy arrest record that included several crimes of violence. An A-car transported him to the juvenile hall in Norwalk.

A few days later, I received another 1.27 for the pursuit. In the 1.27, Communications emphasized the calm and clarity of the broadcast. By August 8, 1976, four days after completing my probationary period, I had received six 1.27s. I was on the fast track for getting into the department's "outstanding" pool—the top 10 percent.

—

One day I was working with a new partner, Officer Barstow. He had about eight years in the department and was ultra-low key. After roll call, we were approached by Sergeant DeAmicis, a former METO Division (the department's badass). He told us he had a special assignment for us. At first, we thought it was going to be a hot detail like a robbery stakeout or something. It was a stakeout, but it sure as hell wasn't anything a street cop would look forward to work. The suspect was Ruth Cumming, one of a horde of unlicensed pedestrian vendors on Ocean Front Walk selling worthless trinkets for a few bucks and pissing off the established licensed business owners on OFW.

DeAmicis told us Ruth was in violation of 103.311 (LAMC), an obscure Los Angeles Municipal Code section for selling secondhand articles without a city business license and police permit. Ruth was on the warpath with the Venice police and had written everyone in city hall complaining that she had been singled out and was being harassed on a daily basis by the police. She claimed her constitutional rights were being violated.

DeAmicis told us that she had been warned on numerous occasions to stop her sales on the boardwalk or she would be cited and arrested. I could see he felt a little uncomfortable giving us this shit sandwich. We were ordered to drive to OFW, find her, and park our police vehicle a short distance from her. Once we saw her make a sale, we were ordered to arrest her, WTF.

We drove up and down OFW for a couple hours and finally spotted Ruth unfolding her little table to place her trinkets on. I had seen her a few times before on the boardwalk and she always seemed congenial. I smiled and she smiled back. She was in her early fifties, petite, and looked like she had spent too much time in the sun, but no doubt she was a looker in her day.

After about an hour, an older couple stopped by her table and bought a little clear plastic trinket for a buck fifty. The crime had been consummated, shit, we needed to arrest her. Barstow walked up to the couple, confiscated the evidence, and got the contact information. He looked back at me standing next to Ruth and told me to handcuff her.

Crap, I felt like a piece of shit handcuffing this sweet lady. I asked her if the cuffs were on too tight. She said no. Then I put her goods in the trunk and we headed for the station. We could have cited her and released her out in the field, but we were ordered to arrest and book her at the station, then release her.

Unseemly experiences aside, I was on fire. By now I received three more 1.27s for outstanding Obs (observation) arrests. In police parlance, "Obs arrests" are self-initiated arrests as opposed to radio-call arrests. The first was for arresting a suspect while on a typical traffic stop that led to an arrest for Possession of Marijuana for Sales. The second was for an Obs arrest of a serial hot-prowl burglar. And the third commendation was for breaking up a professional auto theft ring that ultimately led to the arrest and conviction of the entire auto theft gang.

—

Tuesday, August 17, 1976, was a day that would forever leave this world a little less safe and palatable. Officer Gossman called and told me that Detective Ray Hicks, my dope expert soul brother, was killed while on a drug raid in Inglewood.

Ray and members of his narcotic unit had gathered intelligence on a thirty-one-year-old suspect by the name of Darrell Edward Brooks and his crew for sales of phencyclidine (PCP, also called Angel Dust). The Venice Narcotic Unit compiled enough evidence to secure a search warrant on Brooks's residence. When the officers breached the front door, they ran into a fuselage of gunfire from the suspects in the residence. Ray took a bullet center-mass from a .357 Magnum but somehow managed to return fire and hit one of the suspects before falling to the ground mortally wounded.

After the firefight, Brooks and his crew were arrested for murder and for the possession of narcotics for sale. Ray was transported to Daniel Freeman Hospital in Inglewood, where he succumbed to his wounds. He left a lovely wife and four small children. The narcotic unit seized 167 grams of PCP and 120 grams of marijuana.

Six months later, a Torrance Superior Court judge dismissed all charges against Brooks and his crew for the murder of Ray and the sales of narcotics, citing a glitch in the search warrant. Before joining the Los Angeles Police Department, Ray had served in the Army and done a tour of duty in Vietnam only to be murdered on the streets of L.A. while in further service to his country and community.

Ray's death led to many positive changes in serving dangerous search warrants, including wearing raid jackets and body armor, no doubt saving fellow brothers and sisters in law enforcement from certain death. We've all heard the saying that the good always seem to die first. I truly believe that, and that truism would come back to haunt me years later when I lost my best friend in the department.

Rest in peace, Ray. You were everything that is good in the human condition. You were a sweet son to your parents, a patriot, a loving husband, a wonderful father, and a role model for all men of all colors.

Life's enigma of splendor, horror, and indifference went about its business in 1976. Southern California experienced one of its warmest winters on record that year. The warmest day of the year was November 4 at 97 degrees. December had an average temperature of 76 degrees as opposed to a norm of 66 degrees for that time of the year. Susan and I delighted in that warm weather. It was perfect for our nature-trail runs and meals out at the many charming ethnic restaurants in downtown Los Angeles—Chinatown, authentic Mexican, or Philippe's for the French-dipped roast beef that they've been dishing out since 1908. If we really felt like misbehaving, we'd indulge ourselves at the greasy-spoon Pantry on Ninth Street and Figueroa with some real comfort food like humongous omelets, steaks, or maybe some hotcakes.

My new digs at 211 Yacht Club Way made it impossible not to have the time of my life with all the restaurants, dance clubs, shops, and boutiques. Susan fancied the Red Onion in Hermosa Beach because they played the best dance music of all. She had a terminal case of disco fever! There must have been some cheeky, soul-brother milkman blood in that woman because she could shake her booty on the dance floor. Her favorite group was the Bee Gees.

The Oscar for best picture that year went to *One Flew over the Cuckoo's Nest*. The Super Bowl champions were the Pittsburgh Steelers over the Dallas Cowboys, 21 to 17. The breathtaking final game between the Boston Celtics over the Phoenix Suns, with a score of 128 to 126 after a triple overtime win, had some basketball pundits calling it the greatest championship game of all time.

The 1976 Winter Olympic Games were held in Innsbruck, Austria. The Soviets took the Gold Medal count with thirteen. The only real star for the United States was Dorothy Hamill with a first place in the figure-skating competition. Women around the world copied her wedge haircut. Mom wore that elegant look for the rest of her life, and that made her look all the more graceful and beautiful. The Summer Olympics were held in Montreal, and again, the Soviets swept the competition although American Edwin Moses took out the competition in the 400-meter hurdles, and Bruce Jenner trashed the world's best in the decathlon.

By now, my probationary period was well over. I was preparing to get "wheeled"—a standard operating procedure in which officers are transferred to another one of the eighteen geographical divisions in the department after completing their probationary period. My lord, I had realized the impossible; I was a member of the finest, big-city police department in the world!

On occasion, Susan and I managed to get both Friday and Saturday off. She came over early one Friday and we did what we loved to do—a long beach run in ankle-deep water from my apartment to the Manhattan Beach pier and back. After our run, we returned to my apartment, showered, and made love into the late afternoon. When it came to sex, we were on the same page—it was a "take no prisoners" thing.

This time, after a lovely dinner at the Chart House, we headed for Susan's favorite digs, the Red Onion, only walking distance from my apartment. By now we knew a lot of the regulars and managers. Susan was good for business because everyone enjoyed her sensuous moves on the dance floor, and management liked the security of having a cop around. It was always a great time. However, the next couple nights were an aberration.

After several hours or so of dancing and drinks, some nut behind me stuck his finger into my right upper back. I cringed with pain from the forceful stiletto-like jab and turned to ask him what he wanted. This guy was polluted. He didn't respond to my question, and I didn't recall ever seeing him before. Again, I asked him what he wanted. He just stood there looking at me blankly. After a few moments, I knew this guy was a nut, and we moved a few feet away. About half an hour later, it happened again. WTF?

At this point, I told him, "Do that again, and I'm going to knock you on your ass!" All seemed good when we walked away from him a second time. However, both Susan and I kept our eyes out for that drunk. Sure enough, about twenty minutes later, I saw him walking over toward us from behind. At this point, I had had enough. When he raised his hand once again to prod me from behind, I wheeled around and gave him a thunderous push. He went down flat on his ass. Management ran over and threw him out of the restaurant. I spoke with the manager for a few minutes, and all was well for the rest of the night.

The following night we returned. Susan and I had just entered the restaurant and walked over to the stairway next to the dance floor. We were waiting for a hostess when we heard a slew of screaming vulgarities coming from this big guy standing halfway up the stairs. I looked around to see who he was screaming at when it became apparent he was looking straight at me. He quickly shuffled down the stairs, screaming all the while. I pushed Susan aside and made the determination that there was no way I was going to be able to reason with this asshole.

This craziness made no sense whatsoever. This was two nights in a row in the "Twilight Zone." Then I thought, this guy may have been a friend of the guy I pushed last night. When he got within range, he raised his arms, and that's when I put him down. Management rushed over again with a perplexed look, and after trying to reason with this stranger, they threw him out and apologized to me for the incident. I told them no need; they had nothing to do with these two freaks. However, that was the last of the Red Onion for me and Susan.

—

A couple of weeks had passed, and I had put this unsettling anomaly behind me. It was the beginning of December, and Officer Frank Galvan asked me if I wanted to go to a party in Redondo Beach. I was still considered a boot and was a little surprised when Frank asked me to join him, but I was impressed and grateful.

Officer Coors from Venice and his civilian roommates were throwing the party at an apartment building on Herondo Avenue, just four blocks from my apartment. It was going to be mostly officers from 77 Division, plus plenty of hot babes. I got to the party a bit late that evening, and Susan was working, so I went alone. The place was packed; there must have been at least fifty people in the small two-bedroom apartment, and Frank was right, it was crawling with California beauties. God bless the USA.

At first, I didn't see anyone I knew, but eventually I noticed Frank and Officer Hallett having a drink of Jungle Juice, a mix of punch with every conceivable liquor in it, next to the kitchen. I squeezed through the crowd, and Frank scooped up a glass of that skank devil's brew for me. It tasted like shit.

Frank, Hallett, and I didn't know any of the guys there, but I could tell they were high-octane 77 officers full of bravado. These coppers deserved whatever bravado they emanated since they worked the hottest division in the city. These Praetorians experienced more murder, rape, assault, robbery, and dysfunctional humanity in a week than most other police departments experience in twenty years.

We were all having a great time when Frank pointed out this hot-looking Asian babe. She was petite with long, shiny, jet-black hair, boobs as big as Bombay mangos, and a tanned silky complexion. Damn! Why not—I walked up to her and asked her for a dance. She took my hand and told me her name was Helen. *Oorah*, game on!

After a few dances, it was obvious that she fancied me. Time was flying by, and I hadn't noticed Frank or anyone else for that matter. I had hit the long ball and was just about to ask Helen if she wanted to go to my place for a drink. Just then, Frank walked up and told me some guy, not a cop, was getting into his face. I told him I had his six if he needed me but to let it go and push for one of the babes that were all around. It was a time for love, not war. When Frank walked away it seemed all was going to be alright. Helen suggested the Chart House for a drink, and I was more than good with that.

We were trying to sneak out without saying good-bye to anyone when Frank walked back up to me and asked me to follow him to the restroom; Helen followed from behind. I thought this was going to be an opportunity to chill Frank out for good.

We made our way through the crowd up to the restroom. There were a couple of guys standing in line. Unbeknown to me, one of the guys was the one whom Frank was at odds with. Within a few moments, Frank and the guy started chipping at each other, and I made the mistake of trying to be the peacemaker. The guy told me to get fucked. It was obvious he had more than his fill of Jungle Juice. He became increasingly belligerent and I tried to leave, but not before he stuck his finger in my face. I put him down straightaway.

Unfortunately, this dude was the brother of one of the 77 officers. All at once, everything went sideways.

An undisciplined phalanx of bodies rushed us through the narrow hallway, then into a bedroom, throwing punches every which way at me and Frank. It was pure mayhem. I curled up and bent forward to avoid taking blows to the face. Then one of the guys in front put his forearm around my neck and tried to choke me out. It was something a cop would do in this type of situation.

Shit! I was in a major hurt-lock and I was about to be put out. A few seconds later, I heard one of the other guys shout, "Is he out yet?" Precisely at that time, I forced my body to go limp, hoping the officer would release the chokehold; it worked. As he released the chokehold, I slowly slipped forward, and just before hitting the deck, I grabbed the front bottom of his pants and jerked back with all my might. He tumbled back against the wall next to the bed and smacked the back of his head on the wall.

I turned right and left and put the other two guys down. Then I noticed the guy who was putting the boots to Frank run out of the bedroom. All was at an end at this point. I saw Hallett standing at the bedroom doorway holding back a couple other 77 officers. One of them was holding a leather sap. I could see that their blood had cooled after watching me reverse the tables on the three lying on the floor.

Hallett and I helped Frank to his feet, and we slowly made our way to the living room. Everyone looked stunned. I guess they were surprised that I was walking out of the bedroom, as opposed to being carried out!

We took Frank to his car, and I told Helen I wasn't up for the Chart House. She understood, and we went to my apartment for a memorable evening after that senseless bullshit.

Fortunately, I was born with a natural pugilistic talent and was forced to hone that skill defending myself and my seven younger brothers and four sisters from the ruthless gangsters in the Watts Barrio. In 1966, when I was twenty-one years old, my older sister Irene met Ralph Gutierrez. He was good friends with Aileen Eaton, one of the most influential boxing and wrestling promoters in Los Angeles.

Although Irene was married to Jake, I could tell Ralph really fancied her. On numerous occasions, Ralph treated Irene, Jake, and me to ringside seats at Aileen's main venue, the fabled Olympic Auditorium. After the fights, we were off to the Danna Room for dinner and drinks. It was a high-class restaurant in Los Angeles where all the winners celebrated their victories. One of those nights, Ralph told me Irene had mentioned that I was quite the street fighter. He suggested that I consider giving the fight game a go and asked me to meet him at the Main Street Gym in the midst of L.A.'s skid row.

After watching several matches at the Olympic, I knew if I gave it a go, it would require nothing short of a full court press and a lifetime commitment of pure training. Boxing isn't a team sport where one of your team members could watch your six or save your ass if you needed a hand. Boxing is an individual sport that requires total and dedicated commitment!

I knew I was the perfect prototype for that sort of life, and I had all the natural tools and instincts to be a credible contender in the welter- or middleweight division. I had the speed of a welterweight with the natural punching power of a heavyweight. I was a person of color from the barrio, poor as a church mouse, and stupid as hell with D and F report cards all through grade and high school. And if that wasn't enough, I had an arrest record. In short, I was fucked for life!

One afternoon, I met Ralph at the Main Street Gym and walked up to the second floor above the old Adolph Theater. At the entrance, the marque read, "Main Street Gym 318 ½: World-Rated Boxers Train Here Daily."

When I walked in, I was immediately overcome with the pungent odor of sweat streaming off the fittest bodies I had ever seen. Every one of them was fixated on the same dream of becoming the next world champion in their division and extricating themselves from a world of shit just like the one I was brought up in.

Ralph was already there, standing by the seedy office. A bell went off, and everyone in the gym stopped their workouts. A minute later the bell went off again, and all returned to their workouts. Ralph pointed to the dressing room where I could change into my workout gear. When I walked in, I marveled at the dingy, malodorous locker room. In these hallowed halls, modern-day gladiators like Rocky Marciano, Floyd Patterson, Smoking Joe Frazier, Sugar Ray Robinson, and Muhammad Ali changed, showered, and bled here. Damn!

After absorbing the wonder of the locker room, I returned to the workout area for a session of hitting the big bag. I learned most of one's punching power comes from your legs, including jabs, right and left crosses, hooks, and power punches; I was a quick study. It came naturally to me. In a few months, though, I realized that my heart wasn't in it. I eventually weaned myself from the endeavor. I was born to be a cop, not a prize fighter.

The day after the fight at the party, Frank asked me if I had submitted my 15.7, a report that must be filed anytime an officer becomes involved in an off-duty incident. I completed the report in excessive detail and submitted it to Sergeant Moreland. I knew there was going to be an investigation.

Weeks went by, and then I was informed that I was going to be wheeled to Hollywood Division. I was looking forward to the change. Hollywood wasn't 77, but it was a freakazoid place to work, and busy as hell.

A couple of weeks before I transferred out, I was called out of the field. "14-A-5, come to the Station Code–2." I was working with Mesnard that day, and he told me that type of call means one of two things, and neither of them are good—someone in your family is dead, or someone in management is going to take a huge dump on you. I walked into the watch commander's office and was met by Sergeant Larry Rye, who told me the Captain wanted to talk to me.

Sergeant Rye was the most intelligent sergeant I ever met on the job. He was an expert in officer safety, explosives, and terrorist groups. He told Mesnard to get a cup while I met with the new Venice C.O., Captain Burk. He had just been promoted from Lieutenant in 77 Division to Captain and was assigned to Venice Division as our new C.O. The word was out that Burk was a decent and honorable man with a reputation for caring for his men. So, I hoped I would get a fair decision from the Hermosa Beach fight.

While we walked to the captain's office, Sergeant Rye could see that I was stressed. He grabbed me by the arm and said, "Al, I'm not supposed to tell you this, but Captain Burk thought it was great that you kicked some ass." Rye told me that I was going to get a five-day suspension for being in the fight. I told him I didn't start the fight, I just finished it, and I thought that was unfair because I was trying to stop a fight in the first place. Rye said, "Al, take the five days, or you're going to piss off the powers upstairs."

Unfortunately, I saw it as a matter of principle—a flawed logic that would cost me dearly months later. I told Captain Burk I was going to contest the recommended suspension and demanded a Board of Rights. Burk wasn't pissed off, but I could see that he knew I would pay dearly for my stubborn inexperience.

A few days later, I received my first-ever Los Angeles Police Department rating report; it was a big disappointment. I didn't make the "Outstanding" rating pool that I had worked so hard for. However, I achieved the next best, "Excellent," with the word "Plus" typed directly under the word "Excellent." It read in part: "Since completing his probation, Officer Moreno has developed into an effective street policeman. His enthusiasm for the job motivates him to be among the top producers in Team 1."

The fact of the matter was, I wasn't much good at the things most men were good at—working on cars, plumbing, carpentry, or electronics, to name a few. But I was a natural-born Praetorian. I loved the feeling of helping others who were unable to save themselves from the human darkness in this world. I'll nail an outstanding rating next time!

3
Hollyweird

FEBRUARY 13, 1977, was my first day at Hollywood Division. And again, I lucked out—I was assigned to the seediest and busiest part of Hollywood, Team-63. Our car designation was 6-A-27. The patrol area was Franklin on the north, Santa Monica Boulevard on the south, Normandy on the east, and Highland on the west.

I was partnered up with two of the best street cops in the division, Officers Dave Ballweg and Mel Arnold. Unlike Venice Division, there weren't any lulls between radio calls. That prevented the officers from asserting preemptive strikes on the bad guys with little time for "Obs" arrests.

The beat of 6-A-27 was a real eye-opener back in 1977. Hollywood and Sunset Boulevards were crawling with pimps, hustlers, petty thieves, rundown businesses, filthy single-room porn theaters, and the ubiquitous prostitutes, female and male. On any given day, there were a couple hos working every block, and at night the number increased.

Child prostitution was rampant along the boulevards. There were large groups of juvenile runaways, boys and girls from all over the United States. Eventually, they would be pressed into selling their bodies to survive on the street, then graduate to all sorts of depravity under the auspices of their pimps and street thugs.

The male prostitutes had their own geographical hot spots, starting at Western on the east, running all along Santa Monica Boulevard, to West Hollywood, and up and down Highland Boulevard. To mentally survive the day-to-day debauchery, we embraced a form of socially unacceptable black humor while dealing with society's throwaways.

The biggest laugh of all was watching the dumbass tourists on Sunset and Hollywood Boulevard trying to spot a movie star of consequence.

In 1977, the L.A.P.D. had a little more than 6,700 sworn officers with virtually no females working patrol. The city had an estimated 2.8 million souls. Between the barrage of radio calls for service, we were expected to write at least one "greenie" (traffic ticket), or you'd have your boss up in your ass. Traffic enforcement was a must. Besides forcing the public to drive in a sane and responsible manner, it also drew in a great deal of income for the city coffers.

My first night out on patrol with Officer Ballweg was a roller-coaster ride of human depravity. It was one family/boyfriend/girl-friend/business/neighbor dispute after another. Fights, "Man Down," officers requesting backups, and on occasion, "Officer Needs Help" calls. And after all that, you were expected to go home to the little woman and chill with little Dick and Jane like you just returned home from a round of golf with the boys. Most of society is profoundly clueless! After watch, I couldn't catch my breath from the adrenalin racing through my body, but God, I loved it!

Sometime later, a couple hours before the end of watch, Dave made a sudden stop on Hollywood and Western between calls. I had no idea what I missed. He walked up to this fine-looking soul sister, wheeled her around, and handcuffed her. He looked over at me and said, "Put Jackie in the car." Dave said he needed to get off on time, and this arrest would ensure that.

On the way back to the station, I picked up the radio and advised Communications that we were going "time and mileage," the standard broadcast when transporting a female arrestee, just as I learned when I worked with Brophy and Wilder on my Academy ride-alongs. After I made the broadcast, Dave started snickering at me. He told me that Jackie-Lee had a shitload of prostitution warrants. But why was he laughing at me? When we arrived at the station, I informed Communications and walked Jackie-Lee inside, then put her in a holding cell.

The whole time, I noticed everyone in the station was having a good laugh. Sergeant Finn, the W/C, took me aside and said, "Moreno, you don't go time and mileage on male suspects."

What the hell? Jackie-Lee was a drag queen? Be that as it may, Jackie-Lee was as fine as frog's hair. He/She was a little taller than me, with nice shoulder-length hair, big beautiful brown eyes, a small cute nose, full lips, and a movie star smile. He/She had small breasts and narrow hips, but great-looking long legs and a great-looking butt. I know women, and she couldn't be a he. She was dressed in a low-cut skimpy white blouse and cut-off pants. I couldn't get my head right over this. The only way I would believe Jackie was a man was when we stripped searched her at Jail Division downtown.

We took Jackie to the misdemeanor booking section to process her into custody on the first floor. The first-floor booking lobby was packed as usual with your generic filthy, diseased, loud, obnoxious, smelly, flea-carrying drunks and assorted other shit-bags. When we walked in with Jackie, all the drunks exploded into nonstop howls and disgusting catcalls, while pulling on their shackles. The stench of their unwashed bodies and minds was hideous.

I handed Jackie's property to the jailer on the other side of the screen, then started the strip search. Shit, Jackie didn't seem to mind a bit. In fact, she was enjoying all the attention. Jackie took her shirt off, revealing thin shoulders and tiny breasts. When I told her to take off her shorts, Jackie slowly wiggled the shorts down her long legs, shimmying and bending forward with a devilish smile. She stood up and straddled her legs open.

Then it happened! Jackie-Lee's giant schlong fell forward from its rear-tucked position between his buttocks. Damn, it was a man! The room full of drunk arrestees blasted out sick cries of communal laughter. I didn't know how to act for a moment. I found myself looking at his face, then looking down at his penis, back up, then back down. I just couldn't put this shit together.

On the drive back to the station, I could see that I had made Dave's day. He couldn't stop smirking and laughing. "Get used to it, Al! Welcome to Hollywood Division."

Within three D. P.s (28-day deployment periods) of working with Dave and Mel, I had accelerated into one of the top-producing officers in night watch and received a couple more 1.27s working with these two old school "Keepers of the Gate."

Susan and I were seeing less and less of each other. We both loved our work and were extremely dedicated to advancing our careers. Susan was working toward earning whatever other college course credit she needed to work as a surgical nurse. We were working different shifts. But when we got together it was still magic. We had so much in common, and that made us not only lovers, but the best of friends. All the while, neither of us ever delved into each other's affairs.

I was also seeing Helen more and more because she lived in a studio apartment at the Gallery apartments, my new home on Second and Hermosa, in Hermosa Beach. The three-story apartment building was enormous, just six blocks from my old place at Harbor Cove. The Gallery was the next best thing to the Kingdom of Heaven. The tenants were middle- to high-income professionals with a handful of cops and firemen. The center courtyard was the meeting hub for all the tenants with a large pool and a Jacuzzi next to the pool. The women at the Gallery were not only hot, but intellectually stimulating as well. Nirvana! I was all in.

I lived from paycheck to paycheck and never saved a dime. I had little faith in tomorrows at this point in my life. I had seen more death than most men—from my childhood in the barrio, where life was precarious at best, to the wholesale slaughter of men, women, and children in Vietnam, to now working as a policeman and witnessing humanity maim and murder itself. I was profoundly aware of just how fleeting and capricious life really is. So I embraced the 1,440 minutes of every precious day. A life of always living close to death gives one a hypersensitivity to the majesty of nature's four seasons— spring's rebirth, carefree summers, the glorious panoply of autumn's colors, and winter's life-giving rains.

—

One afternoon at roll call, I was handed a subpoena. It seemed that I was spending half of my life at 211 West Temple Street, L.A.'s criminal court building, but this subpoena had a different address, 312 North Spring Street—it was the Federal Court House in L.A. One of the defendants on the subpoena was me, the other two were the City of Los Angeles and the L.A.P.D. The plaintiff was Ruth, the sweet lady I was forced to arrest for selling trinkets on Ocean Front Walk while I was working Venice Division. Ruth had refused to secure a city business license, but she engaged a clever attorney and claimed that the Venice police and the City of Los Angeles singled her out for harassment and were violating her human and constitutional rights.

It was a humbling experience walking up the steps to the federal court building on that first day. The city attorney thought Ruth was clearly in violation of the statutes under which she was arrested, but I still had a sinking feeling as I sat at the defendant table in the courtroom. Why wasn't my partner, Officer Barstow, included in the lawsuit? The only redeeming thing about this industrial shit sandwich was that it was a civil suit, not a criminal case, so if Ruth won, I wasn't going to federal prison.

Ruth's attorney had some unique arguments against the statutes, otherwise why would he spend his time and a great deal of money bringing this action against the city? By the end of the first day, the jury, mostly comprised of women, had been seated. The judge gave the jury instructions, and Ruth's attorney began with his opening statement. At the outset, he admitted that Ruth had violated section 103.311 of the Los Angeles Municipal Code, selling articles without obtaining a city business license and failing to obtain a police permit. However, he went on to outline how those two draconian sections violated Ruth's human rights and prevented her from gainful self-employment.

Occasionally, I glanced over to the jurors to assess their reactions while Ruth's attorney pleaded her case. They were spellbound. At the summation of his opening statement, he cited one of Clarence Darrow's poetic verses: "You can only protect your liberties in this world by protecting the other man's freedom. You can only be free if I am free." I knew right then it was all over for the city, and I was scared to death.

The city attorney attempted to emphasize that Ruth had callously violated the government's statutes. She should have never used the word "government"—colossal mistake; that word represents suppression of the people! Then the city attorney went on to accuse Ruth of unlawfully refusing to pay the meager annual business license fee while the rest of the merchants paid their yearly fees.

Ruth's "Clarence Darrow" subpoenaed every city business entity in Los Angeles and intellectually disarmed them piece by piece with his eloquent and imaginative arguments. At the end of this six-day trial, Ruth's attorney closed his argument with another of Darrow's brilliant missives: "I have never killed a man, but I have read many obituaries with a lot of pleasure." The jury ate it up.

After only a couple hours of deliberation, the jury returned with a $50,000 verdict for Ruth. Fortunately for me, when Ruth took the stand, she looked directly at the jury and said, "Officer Moreno was very nice to me; he even asked me if the handcuffs were on too tight." Lord, that single unsolicited statement saved my ass.

———

It was such a relief to return to work, even though I was still showing up at least an hour before roll call and digging through the crime and arrest reports on the detectives' table.

Dave and Mel were moved to morning watch, and I was working with several different partners. Every once in a while, you are partnered up with the perfect partner—in this case, it was Officer John Gamble. John was a little younger than me with six years on the job. He was about my height, fit, and motivated. John's report writing was impeccable, and with his tutelage, I perfected my crime and arrest report writing.

We were on a roll, making one Obs arrest after another in between the hail of radio calls, and we loved every minute of it. One night, John and I were patrolling Western Avenue between Hollywood and Santa Monica Boulevard looking for a suspect who had been terrorizing small business owners all along that corridor with armed robberies, resulting in the shooting of one merchant. John spotted him—he was carrying a large television, headed toward a pawn shop. When he saw us, he freaked and dropped the TV on the sidewalk and headed back toward an alley. Busted!

We stopped him just before he reached the alley to question him about the TV His name was Clarence. He started stepping all over his dick with one lie after another. Before we hooked him up, we walked him back to the discarded TV and had him place it in our truck. I asked records to run the serial and model number of the TV and run Clarence for wants and warrants. Records informed me the TV was stolen in a Hollywood burglary, and Clarence was wanted for a parole violation.

We hooked him up and drove to the station for booking approval, writing the reports and booking the evidence. It turned out he wasn't the robbery suspect we were looking for, but we took this cheese-dick thief off the streets for a few days.

While John and I were writing the Arrest and Evidence Report, we heard a loud commotion on the other side of the main hall where the three suspect holding cells were located. We ran toward the commotion and saw a suspect kicking the shit out of four officers just outside the holding cell. Officers Chester and Nelson had just arrested the man for being under the influence of PCP.

PCP was first brought into the medical world in the early 1950s as an anesthetic but was soon removed from use because of its hallucinogenic side effects. In the mid-1970s through the '80s, it became the drug of choice in the barrio and hoods because it was cheap and had a long-lasting demonic high. In addition to the psychedelic effect, it made users impervious to pain and somehow gave them extraordinary strength. On the street, phencyclidine was principally sold in two forms—sprinkled onto mint leaves and rolled into a joint or as a liquid dip cigarillo. People smoked the shit and went bat-fucking nuts.

The combative suspect was finally overwhelmed and put into a holding cell, but not before he injured all four officers. After we completed our reports, it was off to Glass House to book Clarence. It was a weekend night about 10 p.m., and the Hollywood Freeway traffic was busier than usual. Halfway there, we heard an Officer Needs Help (O.N.H.) call broadcast. It was Nelson and Chester, what the hell? They had left the station with their PCP suspect minutes before us. So, we knew they were still in their police car. I've never heard of an O.N.H. call broadcast from inside a black-and-white before.

Evidently, while they were transporting the suspect, he slipped his cuffed hands from behind his back under his legs, freeing him to reach over and rip Chester's .38 revolver from its holster. During the struggle for the gun, the suspect wiggled under Chester and pinned him to the roof of the car with his feet. The suspect stuck the barrel of the gun into Chester's gut between his thick leather utility belt and body armor. Chester had the presence of mind to grab the cylinder of the revolver, thereby preventing it from rotating to fire. Chester knew that type of gunshot wound would splatter his guts all over the car.

Meanwhile, Nelson was trying to maneuver the car out of the heavy traffic to stop and help his partner. By now, the lactic acid in Chester's body was weakening his grip, and he saw the cylinder turning to the right to fire. After what seemed like an eternity, Nelson managed to get the car out of traffic to the shoulder of the road.

When Nelson reached the right-rear door to aid his partner, he reached for his revolver, but somehow he had dislodged it from its holster when he dashed out of the driver's seat. There was no time to run back for the gun, so he reached down to his ankle holster for his back-up two-inch .38. With no other means of stopping the suspect from gut shooting his partner, Nelson stuck the muzzle of his weapon into the suspect's face and pulled the trigger.

The whole time this was happening, the radio mic was somehow keyed on the floorboard allowing everyone to hear the nightmarish chain of events, including Chester's cries for help and the sound of the gunshot.

We were the first unit at the scene, and the condition of Nelson, Chester, and the suspect raised the hair on the back of my neck. Chester and Nelson's uniforms and faces were drenched in blood from the exploding head shot.

The contact shot to the suspect's right eye caused overpressure to the suspect's cranium, blasting the left eye out of the socket and leaving it hanging by the optic nerve halfway down his chest. The backseat and rear window of the car were covered in blood and brain matter from the exit wound.

Police work is much too often spiritual as well as physical carnage, and our modern-day gatekeepers mentally pay for it for the rest of their days. God help them and their families.

After we tucked Clarence into bed at Glass House, we got back to the station. It was another three hours before I got home. It's impossible to describe or relate the difference from one moment to another in police work. One moment, I was experiencing the horrors of this night, then within a few hours, I was back home in Hermosa Beach having a glass of wine in our courtyard Jacuzzi and talking to Brandy and Cherry, flight attendants for United and TWA. There were three other guys in the Jacuzzi as well whom I hadn't met before. They were talking shop about their day in their air-conditioned office making sales calls and pushing pencils for eight hours. And no, I wasn't about to blow their minds and share my night of death with that gentry. Brandy and Cherry knew I was a copper and caringly asked how my day went. I simply said all was cool and changed the subject.

One of the salesmen mockingly asked me how many tickets I wrote today. I just looked at him and the other two and evasively murmured "none," and they left it at that. I got to know them later; they weren't a bad lot.

I sat in the Jacuzzi well after they all left and finished that lovely bottle of wine. It was just before dawn when I went to bed, and then it was back to work that early afternoon with my brother gatekeepers.

—

A few months had gone by, and I was totally dialed into my new assignment at Hollywood Division. It was controlled mayhem with all these Hollywood coppers busting their asses off, putting it all on the line for people they've never met. This lot loved the intensity that came with their work.

The personnel complaint from the Redondo Beach apartment party was finally adjudicated. I was notified by a Mr. Peepers look-alike, Lieutenant George Knop, that my Board of Rights for the fight incident was scheduled for the end of June 1977. Lieutenant Knop was the acting commanding officer for Hollywood Division while Captain Hickman was on vacation. He was the only supervisor at Hollywood whom I kept a wide berth from. I sensed when I first spoke to him that he had a primal enmity toward me for some unknown reason. However, Lieutenant Phil Sadlier, my team lieutenant, and Lieutenant Norris, aka Lieutenant 187 (California Penal Code section for murder), had my six. No one dared call Lieutenant Norris by his moniker, but we all knew he liked it because it made him feel like a badass.

By now, I had come to appreciate the wisdom in Sergeant Rye's and Captain Burk's advice to take the five-day suspension. A Board of Rights could mean a much greater penalty if things went sideways for me. And the department damn sure didn't appreciate having to muster a time-consuming and expensive Board of Rights for some cheeky police officer contesting a piss-ant, five-day suspension. I've always put a premium on principle; however, in this case, I should have mitigated my intrinsic ethos. It was too late now to reverse my request for the Board.

I called the Los Angeles Protective League for advice, and they told me to talk to Sergeant White to see if he would act as my defense counsel for my Board of Rights. White had worked as a defense rep for years and knew the drill. I met with him a few times to prepare for the Board, and he told me it could go either way. It was your generic "he-said, she-said" type of case and would be adjudicated on the "Preponderance of Evidence"—a legal term meaning the case required much less proof for a conviction compared to a criminal proceeding.

An L.A.P.D. Board of Rights is comprised of three captains or above in rank. The three captains must leave their everyday assignments to serve on the Board, which doesn't endear the department to the accused.

The Board's judicial rulings are guided by a cursory Department Board of Rights manual that outlines the procedural dos and don'ts to guide the Board's actions and rulings.

The department's prosecutor is called the *advocate*. He is normally a sergeant assigned to Internal Affairs Division. At a later date, I would come to learn that this system is endemic with corruption and violations of policemen's rights. The three captains and the advocate are not law students, attorneys, or seated judges—they are cops.

A few days before the Board convened, Sergeant White and I went to Glass House where Internal Affairs Division is headquartered. The accused picks three Board members from a coffee can containing the names of the department's upper management to serve on the Board of Rights. If the accused picks an individual who the officer knew and had a previous issue with, he has the right to discard that individual and pick another name. I picked Captains McGarry, Nielson, and Tucker. Sergeant White gave me an approving nod and I took his advice.

On the first day of what turned out to be a two-day Board of Rights, I walked to the fifth floor and entered a small room in Glass House where the Boards are convened. When the three captains entered the room, everyone stood up like in any civil or criminal proceeding. Captain Tucker was the Chairman of the Board. He told everyone to be seated, then asked the department's advocate and the accused rep if they were ready to proceed. All answered in the affirmative. Just then, I got a case of dove-balls and knew I had really screwed up by not taking the five-day suspension. After a brief introduction, the Chairman read the charges:

> *Count 1: On December 5, 1976, at approximately 0130 hours, at 415 Herondo Street, Apartment #142, Hermosa Beach, California, you, while off duty, without provocation, physically assaulted Richard Mabee.*

> *Count 2: On December 5, 1976, at approximately 0130 hours, at 415 Herondo Street, Apartment #142, Hermosa Beach, California, you, while off duty, without provocation, physically assaulted John Camron.*

> *Count 3: On December 5, 1976, at approximately 0130 hours, at 415 Herondo Street, Apartment #142, Hermosa Beach, California, you, while off duty, unnecessarily became involved in a disturbance, which caused members of another law enforcement agency to respond.*

> *Count 4: During the year last at the Red Onion restaurant located at 655 Harbor Drive, Redondo Beach, California, you, while off duty, after being involved in a physical altercation in which you identified yourself as a Los Angeles police officer, failed to notify the department.*

After Captain Tucker completed reading the charges, Sergeant White and I looked at one another a bit confused. There were four individuals who went at me and Officer Galvan that night, and we expected six counts, not four. Evidently, two of the 77 officers managed to evade being identified and were not named on the personnel complaint.

Sergeant White was right; it turned out to be a "he said, she said" affair. The 77 officers told their disingenuous side of the story, and the much smaller group of Venice officers told our side. Ironically, it was the testimony from Helen, the girl who I met that night and subsequently dated for a while, that nailed me. She mentioned that the guy I put down extemporaneously uttered, "Why did you do that?" Helen left out the part about him sticking me in the face with his finger.

Just as Helen made that statement, Sergeant White nudged me with his foot—I was toast. Helen was the last witness in the proceedings. Captain Tucker excused everyone while he and the two other members on the Board left the room to deliberate their verdict. They were back within the hour.

The Board reached a unanimous verdict:

> *Count 1: Guilty.*
>
> *Count 2: Guilty.*
>
> *Count 3: Guilty.*
>
> *Count 4: Guilty.*

In the Chairman's guilty summation, he credited Helen's testimony above all. He reasoned that Helen was an independent witness as opposed to the parties involved, thereby giving her testimony a great deal of weight. And yes, he emphasized the one sentence in Helen's testimony, "Why did you do that?" It sealed a guilty verdict.

Captain Tucker referred to that single sentence as *res gestae*, a Latin legal term for a "dying declaration." Not that the guy I put down was dying, but he was no doubt temporarily stunned, and that utterance was interpreted as unblemished, thereby giving credence to the idea that I struck the first blow without provocation. That was not how it really went; however, I clearly understood the logic and unbiased reasoning in the Board members' minds. If I had been one of the Board members, I, too would have arrived at the same conclusion and joined in their guilty verdict.

Then came the "Come to Jesus" moment; I was suspended for twenty-two days without pay. I recall the very first thought I had when the verdict was read—*It will take years for me to get into the department's outstanding pool.* As it turned out, standing up for one's "principle" can be a double-edged sword.

I wasn't going to sour out and blame the department. There is a higher bar of conduct for those in law enforcement, both on and off duty. When I got home that night, I made several calls to my brother officers to set me up with off-duty, armed-security details that paid substantially better than the department did.

I had to be extremely careful—when you are on suspension, they take your shield and firearm from you. However, I was living from paycheck to paycheck and needed the income. I was able to get twelve days off work, and I spent the rest of the time with Susan when she was able to get away from her job.

———

As if the twenty-two-day suspension wasn't enough, when I returned to work, Lieutenant Mr. Peepers, the mother of all nerds, was still the acting commander in Captain Hickman's absence. After roll call, he summoned me to his office and hit me with a bombshell. He couldn't get over my 15.7 report of the altercation. "You describing yourself as some sort of mythical superhero, beating everyone up single-handed!" he laughed.

I felt that I had served my time and placated the department with the twenty-two-day suspension, but this grub wasn't satisfied. Evidently, with his vanilla-on-steroids life and myopic philosophy, he just couldn't understand a "boys will be boys" fight. He reassigned me from p.m. to day watch for maximum supervision and ordered me a special psychological evaluation with Doctor Herman Schwerte, a Beverly Hills psychiatrist. I wanted to vomit.

I told him, "Sir, with all due deference, that is a waste of taxpayer money." I made double sure to measure my tone, body language, and words when I spoke to this shit. I wasn't about to give him what he wanted and hoped for, which was losing my temper and going nuclear. God, I knew he was hoping for that!

This was bullshit; I had already gone through extensive psychological evaluations from 1970 to 1975 just to get in the department. I ultimately took the Minnesota Multiphasic Personality Inventory

(MMPI) test four separate times, the Rorschach test four times, and I was examined by both a private psychiatrist in Downey and the department's psychiatrist. I also went through an exhaustive psychological evaluation at the Hecker Clinic and took a series of additional psychological tests, including the Wechsler test, the Thematic Apperception Test (TAT), and just about every other psych test in modern psychology.

I couldn't help but think this was a setup, that the Beverly Hills psychiatrist was a company man bought and paid for by the department who was going to serve me up well-done. I was frantic, what was I going to do? I did a little research on my own and found out the department had just incorporated a Psychological Behavioral Department with an in-house psychologist. So, why was Lieutenant Knop sending me to Beverly Hills?

I decided to preempt all this by seeing Doctor Martin Reiser, the department's new shrink, with the hope that he would be fair and honest. I made sure to take all the documents from my previous psych evaluations with me. When I met with Dr. Reiser, I could tell that he was seriously pissed off at Lieutenant Knop for putting me through this cruel and shameful gauntlet. But he was afraid to jeopardize his new position, so he was measured in his support. After his exhaustive evaluation, he assured me that he would write a positive report and hopefully that would put this matter to rest.

When Lieutenant Knop received the report, he was even more pissed off that I did this on my own. He never relented. God, I was screwed.

The following morning, I drove to Beverly Hills for my meeting with Dr. Schwerte. His office was beautifully furnished in mahogany furniture with oil paintings of distinguished-looking gentlemen on the walls. I was stunned when I saw three gorgeous lithographs—one of the "Boston Strong Man," John L. Sullivan, the last of the bare-knuckle boxers; another of James John "Gentleman Jim" Corbett, the father of modern-day boxing; and one more of Jack Johnson, the "Galveston Giant," and the first African American heavyweight boxing champion. This doc was a boxing fan of the first order!

However, he did not look like a man who was interested in anything other than reading deep cerebral books. My God, this poor man was terribly ugly. He was about six foot, three inches and skinny as a rail—his suit looked like it was two sizes too big for his frail frame. His face was long with sunken cheeks and a much-too-small nose holding up coke-bottle glasses. His hair was curly but very thin. But, his voice! It had a perfect cadence—soft, yet strong—with flawless diction. It reminded me of the 1940s A-list actor with that Stradivarius voice, James Neville Mason.

He walked around his desk with an athlete's gait and gave me a solid handshake, then asked me to have a seat. "Why are you here?" he asked me. I really didn't understand his opening question. I mean, we both knew why I was here.

I answered, "Lieutenant Knop ordered me to see you, sir."

His response was even more bewildering: "You're being evasive, Mr. Moreno."

What the fuck? I wasn't there more than two minutes, and it was already going sideways. But I had brought my ace-in-the-hole, my psychological evaluation documents. To my horror, he told me that he didn't want to see them. "Why don't you really tell me why you're here, Officer Moreno?"

I thought to myself, it's all over at this point, so just go with the simple truth and speak from the heart. And I wasn't going to hold back on my street language with this man. I figured that if he loved the primal sport of boxing, he wouldn't be offended by some imperfect street patois.

I told him that last December I attended my first-ever police party in Redondo Beach and got into a fight. The fight was the consequence of my trying to be the peacemaker between one of my brother Venice officers and an obnoxious drunk. My effort failed, and I ended up fighting the drunk, and then my partner and I were bum-rushed by three 77 officers and another person. I ended up kicking the shit out of three of the four that came at us.

"That's the long and short of it doc, an old-school 'boys will be boys' fight."

I noticed a faint twinkle of "Oorah!" in the doctor's eyes as he listened—thank you, Lord!

I continued: "After the fight, I was charged with Conduct Unbecoming an Officer (C.U.B.O.) and received a five-day suspension from my Captain in Venice Division before I transferred to Hollywood Division. I did not initiate the fight, so I thought that a five-day suspension wasn't fair, and I requested a Board of Rights. The Board found me guilty and I received a twenty-two-day suspension."

"How do you feel about the suspension, Officer?" Dr. Schwerte asked.

"Doc, I was raised in the barrio and have a PhD on how unfair life can be at times. Yes, I took a heavy broadside, but that isn't going to deter me from becoming one of the best officers the department has ever seen. I did my brick time [suspension] and when I return to work, I'm going to work even harder than before. I love my job more than life, and I am the best at what I do!"

"Officer Moreno, please tell me a little about your life before you got in the department."

"I was raised on the mean streets of South Central Los Angeles in a family of fourteen in a matchbox of a home, under 800 square feet. When I was in second grade, I was diagnosed with Legg-Calve-Perthes on my left hip. It required me to walk on crutches for two years, then a full-length metal brace on my left leg with an elevator shoe on the right foot for another two years. All through grade and high school, I was a D and F student due to an undiagnosed case of dyslexia. It was all a bit overwhelming, Doc."

"After I dropped out of high school in 1965, I was arrested three times within a year. The first arrest was for burglary; we stole a surfboard. The second arrest was for a bullshit P.C. [probable cause] armed robbery, and the third was for felony assault."

"What were the circumstances in the assault arrest?"

"A sweet female friend of mine was being relentlessly harassed by three drunks and she asked me to help her. I told the three to leave her alone, and the fight was on; I put one of them down hard."

"Mr. Moreno, were you found guilty of any of these arrests?"

"No, sir. However, I own some culpability in the burglary arrest. I was with a group of surfer buddies, and two of them took a surfboard from a garage, and we were all arrested."

Then I went on about my Marine Corps Vietnam experience. By now, I saw some indication of exhaustion on the good doctor's face. I knew that I needed to close before my hour was up. I started my summation with my successful eighteen-month push for a two-year degree in Administration of Justice at Cerritos College, and told him I made the Alpha Gamma Sigma honor society.

"How did you accomplish that, Mr. Moreno, with your dyslexia?"

I gave him the abbreviated version. I met a college counselor who was doing a paper on learning disabilities and was sweet enough to spend some extra time with me and tutor me. After a few sessions with her, I grasped and refined a study regimen that worked, and I remembered everything I read. However, my reading was still painfully slow.

I concluded my story with the unbearable hell I went through for five years, fighting the General Manager for the City of Los Angeles, the L.A.P.D. Personnel Division, and the endless fraudulent medical disqualifications from Central Receiving Hospital. Then at last, I spoke of realizing my lifelong dream of becoming a Los Angeles police officer.

By now, Dr. Schwerte looked totally exhausted. "Was it all worth it, Officer Moreno?"

"Yes, Doctor, I love my work more than life itself."

"We are done here, Officer," he said. "Go back to work and please be careful. I'm sure you will have a wonderful career with your Los Angeles Police Department."

I stood up and respectfully walked to the side of his beautiful mahogany desk and reached for his hand. He stood up from his elegant chair and gave me a firm, long handshake. I looked over to his fighter's lithographs before I released his hand and said, "John L. Sullivan is my favorite." He gave me a warm smile. This was a rare man of letters with a warrior's heart.

By the following deployment period, I was back working p.m. watch with my professor of report writing, Officer John Gambill. Our team was getting a lot of GTA (grand theft auto) calls in those days. As usual, I arrived early for work and poured over the crime and arrest reports at the detective table. In this case, it was the "hubcaps" table (detectives who work stolen vehicles). I analyzed an obvious pattern of the thefts: They were generally occurring between 2230 and 0300 hours.

The hot zone for the GTAs was within a four- to eight-block quadrant between El Central Avenue on the west, Van Ness on the east, Fountain on the north, and Santa Monica Boulevard on the south. There had been some scant witness sighting of the GTA suspects, but nothing of tangible value. The "wits" (witnesses) described the suspects as a pair of Mexican juveniles. Not much to go on, but better than nothing.

John and I needed to change our watch to 1900 hours to 0300 hours. Those were shit hours to work, but it was a must. It worked! From September 9 to September 24, John and I made three Obs arrests for GTAs. My analysis was spot-on; all three arrests were within the quadrant I had mapped out. The first was on the corner of Banner Avenue at El Central. Two juvenile Rebel gang members had just broken into a vehicle and punched the ignition. They were just about to drive off when John spotted them. When they saw us, the passenger ducked down and the driver froze in place. John and I blocked their exit with our vehicle and drew down on them with our .38 and shotgun, using our vehicle doors for cover in case of a firefight. We never said a word to one another throughout those first moments. Our actions were as one, like that of a Swiss watch. It was just that way with John and me.

The following night just before we went end of watch at 0300 hours, we saw a vehicle almost hit a parked car. The two occupants in the front seat were struggling with each other. When we lit them up (red lights) and pursued them, the vehicle didn't bolt, nor did it stop. It just continued to roll. We couldn't have been traveling more than 20 mph the whole time. Then the passenger threw out two handguns.

I turned on the siren and advised Communications that we were in pursuit. By now, we had a couple of backup units behind us, and we advised Communications to have a unit recover the two guns. The suspects slowly continued on for about another block, then pulled over. We ordered them out at gunpoint and instructed them both to exit from the driver's side and get on their faces.

It was another pair of Rebel gang member. They had stolen the cars for a planned drive-by shooting at their nemesis, the Clanton-14 gang. The two guns were fully loaded and traced back to a Santa Monica burglary.

One of the coolest things that night was when Lieutenant Sadlier rolled up on our arrest scene. I'll never forget the look of pride on his face; that was a keeper.

On the way back to the station, John asked the homies why they were struggling with each other in the vehicle. They said they were fighting over who got to drive the stolen sled. We all started laughing, and John told them that's why we lit them up. We may have gotten a flicker of humor from this arrest, but we knew these two young monsters were off for a night of premeditated cold-blooded murder.

Our first pair of car thieves, Hector and Estupido (dumb), were released to their parents from the station once we completed our reports. It was a crime against property, so we were unable to secure a detention.

Loco and Big Joker, our second pair of car thieves, were an entirely different matter. They both had long rap sheets for violent crimes, including attempted murder. The stolen guns and GTA arrest that night gave us the authority for a detention. Loco was all of fifteen years old, and Big Joker was sixteen. They were just getting started in their life of terror.

Our final GTA arrest that month wasn't a nefarious gang member out for a night of murder, but a modern-day Bonnie and Clyde white couple in their midtwenties. The female suspect was a sort of Faye Dunaway look-alike. They weren't really car thieves; they were "tweakers" (methamphetamine addicts) looking for anything to steal and sell for a fix. We found them carrying a car battery down the street while screaming at each other.

When we Obs'ed them, we thought what in the hell were they doing carrying that big-ass car battery at 11:30 at night? We stopped and separated them for questioning. Bonnie spilled the beans. She was still higher than hell and began making incriminating statements. I tried and tried to get a word in edgewise to read her her Rights.

No chance; she went on about how fucked-up and inept Clyde was when they were trying to steal a car nearby. She looked back and pointed to a vehicle with its hood still partially open. She said that after they broke into the vehicle through the passenger window, Clyde punched the ignition to hotwire the car, but couldn't figure out which wires to match to start the engine. So, they opened the car hood and settled for the battery. She was seriously pissed off at Clyde! But her statements nailed them both for attempted GTA and theft. Bonnie was put to bed in the hotel "Sybil Brand" (the Los Angeles County Jail for women), and Clyde was booked into custody in the Glass House (L.A.P.D. city jail).

The rash of GTAs was over. John and I received three 1.27s for our labors.

The following day, I was shocked when I read my first rating report form Hollywood Division after taking that twenty-two-day suspension. It read:

> *Officer Moreno is one of team 63's best police officers. Numerous comments in field supervisor's logs, commendations, and comments from area investigators indicate the quality and quantity of his arrests and investigations. His reports reflect thoroughness and knowledge. He is an aggressive and innovative officer who will relentlessly pursue a crime problem in the team area. Moreno is constantly making suggestions to improve the crime picture in team 63. His suggestions reflect careful thought, planning, and feasibility. A portion of the recent decrease in GTA activity in the team area is a direct reflection of his labors. He is a loyal dedicated officer who will accept any task or assignment. During the rating period, he worked three different watches with equal effectiveness. He is possessed with a great deal of common sense and street knowledge. Additionally, his Spanish ability makes him even more valuable. He enjoys police work and his enthusiasm toward the job and the department is a morale builder to those around him. He presents an outstanding appearance and is in top physical condition. He is on a regular workout program and his latest PFQ was at level V. An off-duty personnel complaint prior to his transfer to Hollywood resulted in a twenty-two-day suspension during the period. However, his attitude, demeanor, and performance before and after have been so superior as to warrant this Outstanding rating.*

Signed, Sergeants Vern Dandridge, Terry Cunningham, and Lieutenant Phil Sadlier."

My God, I received my first "Outstanding" rating report!

—

September of 1977 is a month that I'll never forget. It all started with another busy night in Hollywood. John and I planned on having a few beers after watch at the Short Stop on Sunset at Sutherland, a watering hole about twenty minutes from our station. The Short Stop was always packed with women of all kinds who fancied dating and marrying cops. We called them "war brides" or "camp followers." Many of them ended up marrying their warriors.

It was about an hour before the end of watch, and we had just cleared for service with Communications from three radio calls only to be given the standard three more in a row. Perfect, these were all 415 dispute calls that would carry us to the end of watch with no overtime, barring an arrest.

We were stopped southbound on Argyle at Hollywood Boulevard. I was picturing a cold icy beer when a citizen ran up to my driver's side screaming at the top of his lungs, "There's a man on Hollywood Boulevard chasing people with an ax, knocking out storefront windows, and hacking up cars!" Shit! The first thought I had was no cold ones tonight.

I figured the suspect was probably going to be long gone before we got there, leaving John and me with multiple attempted Assault with a Deadly Weapon (A.D.W.) reports on citizens he was trying to hack up, and a shitload of vandalism reports to write until the sun came up. We didn't bother asking for a description; I mean, how many guys were there on Hollywood Boulevard trying to kill folks with an ax?

John informed Communications to reassign our radio calls, and we requested backups for a "possible 415, man with an ax on Hollywood and Argyle." I wheeled westbound onto Hollywood and no sign of the crazed suspect, but holy shit—there were numerous broken storefront windows, one business after another. Then I thought again;

A.D.W. and vandalism reports for the next eight hours. I suppose John was thinking the same thing.

I drove slowly past Vine Street toward Ivar, and it was much the same—broken storefront windows with citizens running frantically all about. It was a Thursday night, and the Boulevard was packed with shoppers and tourists. Once we passed Ivar, there were groups of witnesses on both sides of the street yelling and pointing toward Cahuenga Avenue. I'll be damned, the suspect was not G.O.A. (gone on arrival) this time. Oorah!

The suspect was a male Caucasian in his early twenties, about six foot and skinny, with long blond hair halfway down to his ass. He was dressed in a white T-shirt, white pants, and sneakers, standing on the northeast corner of Hollywood and Cahuenga, blasting out the windows of the First Security National Bank.

I drove to the center of the intersection and we bailed out of our car, but not before John put out an Officer Needs Assistance call: "415 man with an ax on Hollywood and Cahuenga." The blue wave (police backup units) started cascading in with sirens blaring toward our location. I drew my worthless .38 and assumed my war face. John had my six with the shotgun just to my right rear. I stopped at the apex of the northeast corner, inches from the curb, and assumed a firing stance. The suspect had his back to me and was still blasting out the bank windows. I screamed at him using "tactical language" (street vulgarities) in an attempt to cow him into submission to drop the ax so I wouldn't be forced to cap a round in his ass.

It's amazing how one's brain can calculate tens of variables all at once. Time moves at warp speed in situations like this, but you can still sauce out all the variables in a nanosecond.

I was calculating the suspect's every move, but at the same time, all of my senses were extremely cognizant of everything around me, including an Air-6 (police helicopter) hovering overhead, illuminating all below. I could hear my brother officers screaming at the onlookers to stay the fuck back while they were forming a human perimeter. As Air-6 closed in with its piercing rotor noise and wash, it momentarily reminded me of being back in Vietnam.

Incredibly, all those distractions did not interfere with my calculations in dealing with the ax-wielding madman. I knew precisely what kind of a shot I had to make if he turned and rushed at me—it would have to be a heart/lung shot, or a clean shot just above the eyes to bring him down straight away—nothing else would work because of the inefficient knock-down power of the .38 revolver. Just then, the suspect wheeled around, holding the ax over his head in a striking position. I held my position and tried to verbally scare him into submission. No luck. His face was bloodied from glass fragments, and he looked possessed. All at once he screamed out, "Shoot me, shoot me! God wants me to do this; this world is fucked up!"

He repeated the same thing over and over and took a couple steps toward me. I instinctively evoked the USMC B.R.A.S.S. firing system: breathe, relax, aim, slack, squeeze. All Marines are taught this firing system on the rifle range. I held my fire but was ready to shoot. By now, it was apparent that I was not going to be able to scare or reason with this suspect. He was hell-bent on murder or dying.

Shit! This fuck was "dusted" (under the influence of PCP). He was just a few feet away, and I could smell the telltale odor of ether emitting from his person, along with that crazed glassy-eyed stare. That changed everything; dusters can tolerate unbelievable pain, including a fusillade of bullets, before they can be brought down. No wonder I was unable to scare him.

Time was running out, and I needed to secure this damn thing before he bolted into the crowd and started mutilating innocent bystanders and officers. He started walking westbound across the street, facing me the whole time. I mimicked his every step until he stopped at the northwest corner in front of a shoe store. Good, the store was closed and there were no innocents behind him in case I was forced to fire. He still had the ax over his head in a striking position while looking directly into my eyes. I was confident I was going to be able to do what I needed to do when he went for it. He took that glazed stare away from me now and looked over to his right, then moved his right leg as if he was about to bolt into the crowd of onlookers.

I needed to fire now or risk losing the kill shot. I started to B.R.A.S.S. the round off when he torqued his head back toward me and stepped forward to plant that ax in my skull!

God, I didn't want to kill this human being, but he was sure as hell about to end my life. The ax started to come down when I fired, but instead of putting the round into his heart or face, I lowered my weapon and fired at his right leg, just above the knee. It was all so fucking surreal. I felt the kick from the .38 recoil. I saw the flash of fire from the muzzle of the .38. I saw the impact of the round go through his right leg and make a small dark hole on his white pants followed by a gush of blood on his jeans. My Lord, he didn't go down, nor did his face show any reaction to being shot.

I precisely wheeled my weapon to the left leg and fired a second round, just above the knee. Again, I felt the recoil of the shot, saw the flash of fire from the muzzle, and the dark spot of the bullet on his pant leg, followed by another gush of blood against his white jeans.

Astonishingly, his response was no different from when the first shot went through his right leg. I fired a third round back at his right leg again. It was another through-and-through hit. He slowly looked down at his legs and finally went down. My brothers swarmed him on the ground, and after a short struggle, cuffed his hands behind his back. Dear God, it was over.

The suspect was twenty-year-old Eric Vincent Bell. After he was cuffed, he continued to struggle, rolling from side to side. It occurred to me just then how masterfully John and the other officer handled their actions throughout this shooting. They demonstrated profound restraint and respect for human life by not firing at the suspect after my first shot when he didn't go down. It could have been a mess.

Within minutes the R.A. (rescue ambulance) arrived, and the paramedics started treating Bell's wounds with the assistance of half a dozen officers holding him down. Bell never stopped struggling while he was being treated and placed onto the gurney. He was placed in the R.A. unit with three officers holding him down while he was transported to the General Hospital's jail ward.

John and I were separated and transported to the station. When we arrived, we were put into separate rooms to be interviewed by R.H.D. (Robbery Homicide Division's) Officer Involved Shooting team. I recall there was an endless stream of well-intended officers and supervisors coming in one after another with ten-cent cups of skank vending machine coffee while I was waiting for R.H.D. to arrive. After thanking them and drinking about six cups of that shit, I was saved by Sergeant William Hall from the O.I.S. team.

We went over every single event that occurred from the time the citizen approached our car and told us about the man with the ax, including who transported us to the station after the shooting, and whether we spoke to anyone about the shooting at the station. After being interrogated for about four hours, John and I were told to get into our civilian clothes for the walk-through portion of the shooting investigation. We were transported to Argyle and Hollywood Boulevard where the citizen had told us about the man with the ax. We meticulously worked our way to the northeast corner of Hollywood and Cahuenga, where it all concluded.

It was a little after 9 a.m. when I finally got home. I was still amped to the max!

I was scheduled to return to work for p.m. watch that afternoon, so I needed to get some sleep, but I was still emotionally running at Code-3. I took a long hot shower, hoping that would chill me out to get some sleep, but no deal. Fuck it; I grabbed a couple of sixteen-ounce cans of beers and walked to the Jacuzzi. Needless to say, I was the only one in the Jacuzzi at that time in the morning.

Brandy, the United stewardess, walked by the Jacuzzi with a "what the fuck?" look. She was on her way to work at LAX. She stopped and started laughing, "You okay, Al?"

"Couldn't be better," I said. "Just worked a little overtime and felt like a cold beer and a Jacuzzi."

"If I wasn't going to work, I'd join you." Bam! I was in with Brandy. She was of Dutch heritage, like Danique, although Brandy looked quite different—full figured, with short blond hair and blue eyes. "I'll take a rain check on the Jacuzzi, Al, maybe tomorrow. I live in apartment 235."

—

I really wasn't looking forward to going back to work because I knew I would be assigned to some administrative task for the next few days until the department completed their initial review of the shooting. When I returned to my apartment, I called the station and asked Sergeant Finn for a "Special" (accumulated overtime hours). "No problem, Al, good job last night." I had two scheduled days off after the Special, which gave me three full days off to decompress.

Within a week, John and I were back on the street. For the next few days, the *Los Angeles Times* published articles on the unique shooting. Never before in a L.A.P.D. Officer Involved Shooting had an officer shot an armed suspect in the extremities by design—in this case, the suspect's legs. That is not taught in the Academy or in in-service training.

In one article, Tendayi Kumbula, *Times* staff writer, wrote:

> *The motive for Bell's window breaking was unclear. However, last Nov. 26, his roommate John Blasingame, 26, also of Hollywood, was fatally shot by police in the same area with Bell at his side. Blasingame had used an American flag wrapped ax to destroy at least 18 large business establishment windows in the 6400, 6500, and 6600 block of Hollywood Boulevard. In that incident, police said Blasingame was shot after he ignored orders to drop his ax and advanced toward an officer with the ax raised. He was killed instantly by a police shotgun blast.*

The *Times* received several letters praising the way I handled the Bell shooting compared to this previous incident, among many others. Citizen, Mr. John Scott Coen wrote, "At a time when policemen's actions in violent confrontations with suspects are being scrutinized, Moreno's performance was a breath of fresh air. It should remind all of us that behind that gun stands a man with a brain and that the two can work together for an intelligent application of police procedures."

Mr. Greg Howell of West Los Angeles wrote, "A relative rookie has done more for the Los Angeles Police Department public relations than anything I can recall. Officer Moreno deserves a citation of some sort."

A few weeks later, I received a subpoena to appear for Bell's preliminary hearing at the Criminal Court building downtown. I spoke to the D.A. out in the hallway before the proceeding, and she said she had already spoken to Bell's public defender about this matter and they came to some agreement. She also said there were only two other witnesses who were going to give testimony, a couple of citizens who were just feet away from the shooting. They were called first for their testimony while I waited in the hallway for my turn.

When I walked in the courtroom, it was unusually empty except for a few older citizens seated in the back of the courtroom. I was sworn in and then saw Bell seated next to his public defender. He looked indifferent to the proceeding; he was just looking around as if he were in a restaurant waiting to be served when he was being charged with multiple counts of felony vandalism, including attempted murder of a police officer.

The D.A. started with her questions, and I answered them in a slow, deliberate way. Bell's public defender only asked me four or five easy questions, and it was over. The judge looked over at me and told me I was excused, but not before praising my actions for that night.

When I stood up to exit the witness stand, a gray-haired chubby old man dressed in a black suit starting walking toward me. The judge admonished him to stop and contact the D.A. or the public defender outside if he had any statements as to the proceedings. He stopped just before the gate and said, "Your honor, Vincent is my son, and I want to thank the officer for not killing him." His sweet statement was infused with tears streaming down his cheeks. The judge relented from his stern admonishment and advised the old man to please wait outside should I want to talk to him.

Before I left, both the D.A. and Bell's public defender thanked me as well for my actions that night. Bell just looked at me with an apathetic stare. When I exited the room, Bell's father was next to the doorway in the hall. I was somewhat uncomfortable about talking to him, but that all evaporated when he reached over and took my hand. "Officer Moreno, I know my son wanted to kill you that night, but you shot him in the legs instead of killing him. I want to thank you for sparing my son's life. I called Mr. Montenegro's office [one of L.A. city's councilmen] and asked him to give you an award." I was overwhelmed with this sweet soul's words. I advised him that I didn't need any award; I just felt blessed and gifted to be able to do what I did that night.

A few days before my testimony, I was approached by one of my Team 63 supervisors, Sergeant Terry Cunningham. He patted me on the back and asked me if I would consider taking the "Medal of

Valor" award under the table. Terry went on to say that the department was in a state of angst and consternation as how to deal with this unique O.I.S.. The department needed to consider the legal consequences in the future if they awarded me the Medal of Valor. Would that subject the department to relentless liabilities in future O.I.S.s? My actions in this shooting might set an impossible and dangerous precedent for all future O.I.S.s. The public and enemies of law enforcement would forever ask, why didn't the officer shoot for the suspect's arms or legs?

That made all the sense in the world to me. I sincerely thanked Terry for that thoughtful overture but declined the offer. I told him that the award wasn't really important to me. To spare a single human life is to save the universe from collapsing on itself, at least for the moment; that's what was in my heart.

Unfortunately, sixteen years later, there was a dreadful epilogue to this story. I had just walked into my flat and turned on the television, then started for the kitchen to grab a cold beer, when a news flash caught my ear: "A man with an axe in Hollywood was fatally shot by L.A.P.D." I listened in disbelief. It was Eric Vincent Bell again. This time, he took a bullet to the heart and was killed.

I called R.H.D. to confirm the shooting—was it a different Bell? I told them my story and they faxed me a copy of the L.A.P.D. press release, which read:

> On Saturday, January 15, 1994 at approximately 2:30 a.m., the Los Angeles Police Department was notified of a burglary suspect inside the bank of America, 6300 W. Sunset Boulevard. Hollywood area uniform Officers Bennet, 33 years of age, 3 ½ years with the department and Chase, 33 years of age, 6-year department veteran, responded to the location.
>
> Upon the officers' arrival at the location, they observed Eric Bell, 36 years of age, seated inside the Bank. The officers noted one of the glass-entry door windows shattered. When the suspect observed the officers outside the bank, he stood and walked in their direction. Bell was armed with a large ax. As Bell reached the doors, he raised the ax and broke out a second glass door. The officers repeatedly ordered the suspect

to drop the ax; however, he was unresponsive and maintained his grasp of the ax.

Bell then stepped out of the bank, raised the ax, and walked directly toward Officer Bennet, who fearing for her life, fired one round from her 9mm service pistol.

Bell sustained a gunshot wound and fell to the pavement where he was taken into custody without further action.

Bell was transported to Cedar-Sinai Hospital where he failed to respond to medical treatment and death was pronounced. Detective R. H. Karlson, Officer-Involved-Shooting Section, Robbery-Homicide Division.

4
Out of Body

AFTER MY MOVE from 211 Yacht Club Way to the Gallery apartments six blocks away, my life was a dream come true every day of the week. And it served as the perfect therapy of sorts from working L.A.'s crime-ridden communities. My neighbors weren't uptight and pissed off at the world. You didn't have to look over your shoulder when you left the house. You didn't hear police and R.A. units frantically racing back and forth blaring their sirens throughout the day and night. The homes and businesses were right out of a Norman Rockwell painting. The small shops and restaurants were always a delight to visit. And of course, there was the ocean with all its majesty. Lord, how so incalculably different life in Hermosa Beach is from sections of L.A. just miles away!

The summer of 1977 brought us another escape in the form of the movie blockbuster, *Star Wars,* with its unique and unforgettable characters. Susan was a big *Star Wars* fan. I thought it was cool but got a little tired of it after she pressed me to see it with her three times. However, there was an enormous payoff for placating my sweetheart's taste. We were driving back to my place on Second Street after that third viewing when I spotted a car in one of the many used-car dealerships on the Pacific Coast Highway (PCH).

This car was out of this galaxy, like Han Solo's Millennium Falcon. We snuck in to have a closer look. It was a 1968 Aston Martin DB-6, Superleggera Mark-2. She had a white-cream complexion and the curves of a supermodel, with chrome spoke wheels. Her interior was in black leather with two bucket seats and an ample rear passenger seat. The steering wheel was on the right side and with a four-speed stick-shift, which meant shifting with your left hand, but no worries—I was a quarter British on Mom's side from her daddy, Grandpa Adams.

I was at the dealership early Monday morning before it even opened. The Aston Martin didn't have a price placard on it, but if it wasn't crazy priced, I'd work all the off-duty gigs I needed for her hand.

"You have good taste, young man," said Mr. McMillian, the owner.

"I've never seen anything so beautiful, sir."

"Let's take it for a spin, young man! It's right-hand steering; do you think you can manage it?"

"Yes, sir. I have some British roots." Mr. McMillian started laughing.

I mounted her, turned the ignition switch, and heard the three Smith carburetors kick in. It was like listening to the seductive nymphs in Homer's *Odyssey*. I had to have her!

Within a mile or two on PCH, she and I were like two young lovers fused as one. When we returned to the dealership, I noticed a pin on Mr. McMillian's lapel—a First Marine Division Marine Corps pin. Oorah!

He told me he had been an officer in the Korean War. I told him I was with India Company, Third Battalion, Seventh Marines, in Vietnam. He responded, "*Semper Fi*, Marine." Now I knew I wasn't going to be screwed on this purchase.

"So, how much, Mr. McMillian?"

"I'm sacrificing it for $7,999."

My God, even with all the off-duty security gigs, I'd have to move out of my beautiful loft apartment. Maybe I could move into a smaller unit, like Brandy's studio.

We walked into his office and took a seat. Before he sat down, he walked over to a coffee vending machine like the one at our station, and oh shit, he bought two cups. He handed me one and took a huge gulp of his, without cream or sugar. Damn, old-school hard Corps.

He looked up and said, "There's powdered cream and sugar over there if you like." I always put copious amounts of both in my joe, but told him I drank my coffee black. The joe was as skank as the coffee at the station, but I made like it tasted as good as the finest Columbian brew.

"What was your M.O.S [job] in the Corps, Mr. Moreno?"

"0311 [infantry], sir."

"It's yours for $7,500."

I about fell off my seat. "Can you please give me a couple hours, sir, so I can drive downtown to our police credit union to see if I can get a loan?" I asked.

"Police?"

"Yes, sir."

"My Dad and grandfather were policeman. You can have it for $7,200."

I was out the door in a flash and drove Code-3 to a credit union. The loan officer was a sweet elderly lady; she told me I qualified for the loan, but it would take a few days to process the paperwork. I emphasized the exigent circumstances of getting the check today and told her the whole story about the Aston Martin. "Let me talk to our loan manager," she said. She returned in about ten minutes with a check for $7,200.

I bought the car and named her Lady Aston. Little did I know that by 2018, Lady Aston would be worth between $400,000 and $1 million.

I took her out for a long drive along the coast and headed for Point Vicente Bluffs in Palos Verdes where Danique and I had spent treasured summers together spear fishing in those lovely secluded coves. All my senses seemed to be intensely awakened, like when I was walking point in the jungles of Vietnam.

The aroma of the fine leather seats, the humming of the three Smith carburetors kicking in, the sound of the robust waves crashing along the shoreline created a sense of being in Valhalla.

As I continued down the narrow two-lane highway, a song from the newest Fleetwood Mac album, *Rumours*, "Never Going Back Again," played. I thought to myself, what did I do to deserve all this?

When I got to the end of the peninsula on Twenty-Fifth Street, I stopped at a liquor store and bought a bottle of Christian Brothers Champagne and a plastic cup, then headed back along the narrow two-lane-weaving peninsula road toward Hermosa Beach, but not before stopping at the cove Danique and I once favored.

By now, some construction development was eating up the pristine field on the ocean side of the road. At that time, there were no sidewalks or lots for parking on either side of the street; you just drove onto an empty field out of traffic. I parked Lady Aston and headed out through the beautiful field toward the cliff edge, cautiously made my way down the 200-foot cliff, and sat along a suitable rock near where Danique and I used to stack our diving gear. The breakers were a little rough by this time, and I was occasionally kissed with sweet salt water from the crashing waves. I was in nature's chapel.

I popped the cork of the champagne and poured a cup. But before I took a sip, I poured a toast onto the rocks in honor of my fallen Marine Corps brothers. One of my two best friends, Chuck LeBosquet, was vaporized by a 155-mm artillery round while taking a break on an operation in the Barrier Islands south of Da Nang. One thing that always stood out about Chuck was his beautiful rose-blossom complexion.

Another dear friend, Martin Regan, was in-country for only about six weeks when he was killed. He and I were called out of the field to attend a three-day radio school. We got to know each other quite well. After completing the course, we went out that night with our squads as radiomen for the first time. Somehow, a Claymore that his fire team set out on an ambush went missing, and while they were searching for it, their squad's second fire team came up on them and took them for NVA (North Vietnamese Army). Regan was hit on the back of the neck with an M-79 round, blowing his head completely off.

Tom Hofer was another new Marine in-country, killed within three weeks. He was ordered to walk point while we were on Operation Oklahoma Hills, a multibattalion operation in the mountainous jungles of the Que Son Valley. Many sections of the jungle were thick canopy, making it a heaven for NVA sniper teams. Tom was shot through the heart by a sniper. Another Marine and I assisted the Corpsman in applying a compression bandage to his chest, but he was gone. We couldn't get him choppered out due to heavy enemy fire, so we carried him in a body bag the rest of the day and night. All through that long hot day, we kept dropping him as we slipped on the wet thick foliage. We felt horrible when we continually dropped him like that.

And here I was sitting in this lovely setting, drinking champagne, dating a beautiful lady, living in Hermosa Beach, driving an Aston Martin, and my Marine buddies are DEAD at seventeen, eighteen, and nineteen years old. You could go completely mad trying to figure this all out. Why wasn't it me instead of them?

But this was a time for happiness, not remorse and dread, and I am 100 percent certain that Chuck, Martin, Tom, and the rest of my buddies would put their size-12 jungle boots where the sun doesn't shine if I didn't snap out of my shit. *Semper Fi,* my brothers, see you soon for a cold one.

On my drive back home, a sweet sense of inner peace came over me, no doubt coming from my brothers on the other side. It was really late when I got home, and I slept like a baby. I had three days of R & R at hand and was going to party down like there was no tomorrow! It was only days before Christmas, in the height of winter, but the weather was most congenial just the same. So, I called Susan to see if she could get a few days off. I told her I had bought the Aston Martin and was about to test fire her on a drive to Ensenada, Mexico.

Susan had never been to Mexico. She called some of her friends to cover her shifts, and we were off. Our first stop across the border was at El Nido's restaurant in Rosarito Beach for one of their signature humongous steaks and some margaritas. The restaurant is located at the end of the main drag on the ocean side of the street. When you enter the restaurant, you are immediately overwhelmed with the sweet aroma of their botanical garden in the main dining room to the left, or you can walk straight up to their U-shaped bar for drinks, fresh chips, and salsa.

We were hungry and thirsty, so it was the garden room. Susan didn't have a hint of makeup on, but she looked ravishing, turning heads wherever we went. Her hair was still very short and bleached from our California sun. I had only recently noticed a faint patch of freckles across her small button nose and high cheekbones. Intelligence fused with beauty—a 10 on the female Richter Scale. We ordered some margaritas to start with while we waited for our Porterhouse steaks, which came with baked potatoes and dinner salads.

There were only a few couples dining at this time with a handful of patrons at the bar. By the time our steaks were ready, we had gone through a couple of margaritas and a large basket of chips and hot salsa. The Porterhouses were so large that they exceeded the borders of the large dinner plates, and the baked potatoes needed to be served separately. There was only one thing missing—the mariachi band. Our waiter said they normally start coming in after five o'clock.

I couldn't take my eyes off Susan during dinner. She looked so incredibly sexy dressed in a light-blue sleeveless top, tight jeans, and powder-blue loafers. The whole time I was fantasizing about having unrestrained sex and exploring new naughty positions once we got our room in Ensenada.

There was no way we were going to finish that meal fit for kings, so we called for the waiter to take our plates. He returned in five minutes with two large margaritas. At first, I thought it was an "on the house" thing. That's not uncommon in some of the nicer restaurants, and good for business.

It wasn't on the house; he pointed to a large patron seated at the far end of the bar in the next room. Damn, it was Max! He kicked my ass in an arm-wrestling match inside Hussong's Cantina years ago, just before I shipped out for Vietnam in early 1969.

I waved for him to join us, and the party was on; the three of us got on great. It was as if we had been in constant touch for the last eight years. We were at the restaurant for hours catching up on everything of significance in the years past. Tragically, Max's father had been murdered in a robbery while on a business trip to Guadalajara. Max started to tell us the story, but didn't go into much detail other than saying it had something to do with his father's cheese business in Ojos Negros (black eyes), a town about an hour east of Ensenada known for its epicurean cheeses.

We told Max we were headed to Ensenada and had made reservations for two nights at the Hotel Bahia in the middle of downtown. He invited us to stay with him and his mom on their 400-acre ranch in Ojos Negros. I graciously declined, but told him we would drive to the ranch the following day.

By now it was well into the late afternoon and getting dark. What a great way to kick-off our stay in Mexico. Max penciled a detailed map to his ranch, and we went our separate ways after a stiff double Tequila shooter.

On the forty-five-minute drive south to Ensenada, I put the pedal to the metal at 130 mph while the sun was setting. Susan and I couldn't keep our hands off our pleasure zones. It grew to a crescendo when Susan got totally naked and straddled me in between the steering wheel. It was a menage a trois—Susan, Lady Aston, and me.

At the hotel, our room overlooked the center courtyard with a view of the pool. After a warm shower, we were off to the legendary Hussong's Cantina about a half-mile walk from the hotel. The atmosphere in winter was totally different from that of a summer visit. Many of the shops were closed early, but the experience was much more authentic without all the gringos mucking about.

Once in Hussong's, I saw that nothing had changed. The floors were still coated in sawdust and discarded peanut shells, forming a second-layer floor. The bar walls were still adorned in the drawings of drunk tourists from several years' past, including my old girlfriend Claudette's. Different mariachi groups were coming and going. Best of all, El Jefe—Alberto—was tending bar with his exact crew. And it was very cool to again see Pedro, the shoeshine boy hustling his hand-applied spit-shines for fifty cents. These jobs are coveted, and the lucky ones who got them stay for life.

Susan and I walked to the bar, and I wishfully hoped Alberto would recognize me after all these years. The bar was somewhat busy for a winter midweek night, and it took a few minutes before the bartender worked his way toward us. He took a hard look at me and exploded with a big smile of delight. Susan had her back to me at that time, looking at all the drawings on the wall. Alberto yelled out, "Senorita Claudette!" Oh shit. Susan turned, and they stared blankly at each other in a moment of confusion, but then smiled.

Alberto looked over at one of the bartenders and barked out, "*Dos margaritas!*" We chatted a bit and then he got a little busier, allowing Susan and me to take a table. It got pretty warm in no time from all the people coming in and milling around. Susan and I removed our coats, and that's when she started to attract some fans, just like Claudette had back in the day.

A few drinks later, Susan asked me about Claudette. It was such a great story, I left nothing out—including the part when half the bar marched out of Hussong's in the middle of the day for the little chapel just down the street from the city jailhouse after Claudette proposed marriage to me.

"Did you get married?" Susan asked hesitantly.

"No," I told her, "just before the 'I dos,' we both came to our senses and headed back to Hussong's."

Susan couldn't stop laughing. "Is that why Alberto called me Claudette?"

"Roger that."

The rest of the night was a slow burn of fabulous margaritas, an occasional shot of Tequila, fresh-salted peanuts, interesting conversation with various patrons, and listening to mariachi music. My God, life doesn't get better than this!

Damn, Susan could drink, but she always managed to maintain her grace and composure. I knew in my heart that she was the one. She possessed the intellect I needed in a woman, star-like beauty, independence, and a love of physical fitness and faith. What more could a man ask for?

When I thought of losing Danique to the Los Angeles Police Department because I wouldn't go to work for her wealthy father Jos in the shipping business, it sent a cold dark sensation through my spirit. I knew exactly what I had given up for the L.A.P.D.—a lovely hilltop home overlooking the Palos Verdes Peninsula, some phenomenal half-Dutch children. Susan was truly the ultimate blessing, and I was not going to throw away my second chance this time around.

It was closing time and we were about to walk out, but not before Alberto asked Susan if she had ever had Mezcal. Susan looked at me for council, and I assured her she would love it. Alberto opened a new bottle and pointed to the grub floating on the bottom. He poured the three of us a double and fished out the worm.

"Senorita Susan, it is a custom for the prettiest lady in the cantina to eat the worm for her man, and then take the shot." It seemed that all the men in the bar gathered around us just then. The moment of truth was at hand. Shit, Susan grabbed that wet, slimy little worm and chewed the hell out of it before she downed her shot. We left Hussong's with everyone's admiration and respect.

The first thing I did when we returned to the hotel was call the station. I was a bit apprehensive because it was morning watch and I didn't know any of the sergeants who worked that watch. But the God of Specials was with me; Dave Gossman, my favorite training officer from Venice Division, answered. He was recently promoted to sergeant and transferred to Hollywood from Venice. I got the Special, so I was good till Saturday. Dave and I planned to catch up when I returned. I told Susan if she couldn't get Friday off, she would have to call in sick. She was all in.

Remarkably, neither of us had a hangover the next morning. And again, the weather was most congenial. I asked Susan if she would wear her white jeans for me; she looked spectacular in those tight pants. We headed for my favorite "huevos rancheros" restaurant, down the street from our hotel. Susan loved it. After breakfast, she wanted to do the girl thing, a little window shopping. Then she had a hankering for a Bloody Mary. I knew the perfect spot: a two-story outdoor bar at the harbor fish market about a half-mile away.

When we got to the fish market, we were immediately taken by the gamy scent of the perfectly stacked shelves of the fresh catch of the day. It was around noon by now, and we enjoyed our crow's-nest view of the harbor while drinking our Bloody Marys. We watched fishing boats of all sizes coming and going into the deep-water Ensenada Harbor. It started to get a bit windy and cold, but those Bloody Marys made us oblivious to the coming Christmas chill.

We were a bit hesitant about leaving Ensenada for Max's ranch in Ojos Negros because we were having such a great time. I decided to call Max and tell him we were going to miss it this time around and asked him to join us for dinner that night. He graciously understood and said he would meet us at our hotel at about 8 p.m.

Susan heard of the "La Bufadora" (geyser) from one of her girl-friends and suggested we have a look-see. It's one of the largest marine "blowholes" in North America. The scenery was glorious on the seventeen-mile drive through Punta Banda Peninsula to the Bufadora. There were white puffy cumulus clouds whisking by like we've never seen before, adding to the visual lustfulness. We stopped halfway to buy corn-on-the-cob from a sweet lady with her three children playing about. She was using this enormous black caldron to cook her corn, which were the size of loaves of bread.

We wondered how this petite lady hauled this enormous pot out here to the middle of nowhere, in addition to a large stack of wood.

There was absolutely nothing around for miles. The corn was so large, we just bought one; it was wonderful with butter and salt and only 50 cents.

When we got back into the car, Susan called out to the children and handed the eldest a $20 tip. That's probably what this woman made in a month. When we drove off, I saw her through the rearview mirror make the sign of the cross with her little ones at her side.

When we arrived at the Bufadora, it brought back such great memories of when I was with Claudette and her sister Lulu just before I left for the killing fields of Vietnam. The parking lot was just about empty. We walked along the cobblestone path to the blowhole. It was gushing full force from a raging winter sea. Some of the geysers were well over a hundred feet high, and the noise was akin to a thundering locomotive sprinting down the tracks. At one point, we got a little too close and were drenched. That was enough of the Bufadora.

We made off for one of the little mom-and-pop restaurants around for some shelter and warmth. I knew exactly which one I wanted to revisit—Miguel's, the one Claudette and I went to in 1969.

Magic—Miguel and his wife were still there, selling their home-made seafood dishes. They recognized me and said, "*Dios te bendiga, no te mataron Vietnam.*" ("God bless you, they didn't kill you in Vietnam.")

Miguel's wife took my hand and said, "*Lo siento, no Mezcal.*" We all started laughing. I shared the inside joke with Susan later that night. Miguel and his wife really warmed up to Susan. They asked in Spanish if she was "the one." My Spanish ability didn't go much further than, "drop the fucking gun and get on your face," but I managed to tell them I was thinking about it. Miguel's wife counseled me, "*Ella sera la esposa perfecta*" (she would be the perfect wife). I looked over at her and nodded. Miguel brought us an abalone and shrimp cocktail with some warm tortilla chips and salsa. After a great afternoon with them and some wonderful Mexican beers, we needed to head back to the hotel and get ready for a night out with Max. We left with a heavy heart and received an industrial strength hug from these two special human beings.

It was a crisp, windy, pitch-black night when we got back to the hotel, but that just added to the heavenly adventure. We met Max and his sweetheart, Alicia. They made a striking couple. Max at six foot four, lean and good-looking, and Alicia, taller than me, with long straight black hair down to her waist and the look of a Spanish aristocrat. She worked in land development and real estate and spoke fluent English.

Max recommended an Italian restaurant two blocks east of Hussong's. He and the owner, who was originally from Rome, were good friends. The restaurant was arguably the finest in all of Ensenada. I couldn't take my eyes off the walls, adorned with fine paintings of ancient Rome.

Peter, the owner, came to our table and greeted Max and Alicia. They were regular customers. Max made the introduction, Peter took Susan's hand and kissed it lustily as if I weren't present.

Peter noticed that I kept staring at his beautiful paintings, and he gave us a cursory history of the pieces. They were large oils from Rome. He pointed to the first. It was the only one I recognized, the Colosseum.

The next oil was the Temple of Jupiter Optimus Maximus, the oldest temple in Rome, with Etruscan architecture. Peter lost himself while describing the pieces. He started throwing his arms about, his face contorted with emotion and love. He knew and loved ancient Rome. He pointed to another on the opposite wall, stopped and gestured for one of the waiters to bring a bottle of wine and a large basket of warm sourdough baguettes, then continued. He said this one was his favorite, the Aqua Appia, the Romans' first aqueduct, built in 312 BC by the brilliant Gaius Plautius Venox and Appius Claudius Caecus. "Without water," he exclaimed, "there is no life!"

Peter's Mexican wife Martha scurried over and took him by the sleeve and said in poor English, "Leave these poor people alone!" He caught himself and apologized. Personally, I was enjoying the history lesson. When he walked away, Max and Alicia said he does that every time they bring someone new to his restaurant.

Max wanted to know all about what it was like being a policeman in Los Angeles. I really didn't want to get into that subject matter, fearing it would bring a negative atmosphere into such a lovely night. I managed to change the subject and asked Max to tell us all about his farm in Ojos Negros.

Alicia took the reins from here and described Max's business. A Swiss Italian by the name of Pedro Ramonetti Bonetti once came to the area and bought a 260-acre plot to produce cheese. Four generations later, it continued to prosper and was eventually sold to Marcelo Castro Chacon. The cheese is produced almost exclusively by free-grazing Holstein cattle in the rich unfertilized pastures.

Alicia raised her crystal glass of 1977 vintage Tuscan wine slowly toward her long nose and looked as if she were about to have an orgasm. When she was done making love to the bouquet, she lifted the wine up to the light to examine the hue. Finally, to everyone's relief, she took a sip of the damn wine and quietly whispered, "Such eloquence, balance, and complexity."

Susan nudged my foot with her shoe. We didn't believe Alicia was trying to be a pompous ass. She was just being herself, a lady of culture and stature. But unbeknown to her, Susan and I were simple good old-fashioned USA beer drinkers. Actually, the wine was exquisite, and Susan asked if it could be purchased in the States. I about fell over when she said that.

Max was right, the food was gourmet. We started with an appetizer of fried calamari and a dinner salad with warm sourdough baguettes. Susan and I had the linguine in a tomato-based seafood sauce. Max and Alicia had a fine pasta in a white creamy garlic sauce. Susan and I did not order any beer that night.

Susan talked about her work as a nurse at Santa Monica Hospital. Max spoke about his all-encompassing job as a cheese producer, as well as a little about his sisters, Teresa and Magdalena. Alicia talked about her business and how she felt about America (mostly favorable). Again, I kept my work on the down low.

I knew it was coming; Max went into the recent murder of his father, Maximillian Sr. I knew he wanted a professional and independent review of the homicide. He was convinced that the police investigation in Guadalajara was a sham, and he was probably right.

Max suspected that his father's lifelong friend and former business partner, Jorge, hired a hit man to murder his dad. Max's father and mother were a well-to-do family from Guadalajara. A couple years after they were married, Max Sr. bought the thriving cheese business in Ojos Negros with Jorge, his lifelong friend he's known since grade school. They went into the business as equal partners.

Max Sr. and Jorge ran one of the most successful businesses in the Valley. Then the inevitable happened—a protracted business dispute regarding pasteurization. Ojos Negros is known for not pasteurizing its cheese. The cheese makers feel it ruins the natural flavor. That's why it can't be sold in the United States.

Jorge was vehement about changing their cheese production to pasteurization. It would allow them to sell the cheese in the United States; it would triple their sales. Max Sr. was equally passionate about not breaking with tradition and refused to change. Eventually, Max bought Jorge's interest in the business. Later, they became bitter enemies.

Jorge's life drifted to the dark side with alcoholism and narcotics. He returned to Guadalajara and started hanging out with the town's mobsters. A few years later, he returned to Ojos Negros and pleaded with Max Sr. to take him back in the business. Max knew Jorge had lost his soul, and letting him back would destroy everything.

Jorge told Max Sr. he was a dead man, and that's the last they saw of him. A short time later, Max heard that Jorge had fallen in with the Sinaloa drug cartel.

It was at this time that Max Sr. was preparing for a business trip to Guadalajara. Before he left, Max Jr. had a premonition of dread and told his father to be extra careful. Max Sr. cautioned Max Jr. not to share his concerns with his mother, since her health was starting to fade.

Max's business trip was scheduled for three days. When he didn't return, the family became frantic. Max Jr. and his mother Patricia flew to Guadalajara the following day. They pleaded with the authorities for help, but knew that it fell on deaf ears. After several weeks of coming up empty, they needed to return to the business in Ojos Negros. A week later, the family was notified that they found Max Sr.'s bullet-ridden body in a secluded field in the city's outskirts.

I told Max that I agreed with him that it was most likely Jorge who orchestrated the hit, absent of any other information. That's when Max's face turned to primal rage and revenge. Susan and Alicia were pensively stoic the whole time. I needed a moment with Max alone, and we excused ourselves for a short talk outside.

I told Max that he would have to kill the whole Sinaloa cartel if he pursued what was in his heart. I assured Max that fuck would get his in the end.

"Think of your mother, think of Alicia, and think of the rest of your life."

Max teared up. "I know amigo, thank you."

We walked back into the restaurant to be with our beautiful ladies. After dinner, Max took us to a few cool clubs. It was about 1:30 a.m. when we called it a night and said farewell to Max and his lovely sweetheart. That was the last we'd ever see one another.

—

When I returned to work after that dream of a trip, John and I continued to crush it along with two of Team-63's badasses, Howie Silverstein and Dale Erwin. Howie was five foot nine on a good day and about 145 pounds soaking wet, but he had titanium reproductive organs and was someone you wanted to have at your six when things went sideways. Dale was six feet, 185 pounds of no nonsense, an unrepentant street cop with about six years on the job. We were all on the same page and had a great time working together.

The department's image was under relentless attack in those days. A news blitzkrieg was spearheaded by Channel 7 News, L.A.P.D.'s nemesis back in the day. Their ratings encouraged them to pour tritium into the explosive relationship between the department and the barrio and hoods, including those who made a profitable living by trashing the community's Praetorians.

A key example of this was a recent Officer Involved Shooting; Channel 7 broadcasted that a suspect was shot only once in the field but reported that when he arrived at the hospital, he had multiple gunshot wounds. The insinuation was that the two officers in the R.A. unit shot the suspect several more times enroute to the hospital. The fact of the matter is the suspect was shot once with a single shotgun round, resulting in several entry wounds from the pellets.

Then there was the Hollywood morning watch scandal involving four officers who were stealing high-end stereos, speakers, record players, and the like from local businesses. Their M.O. was to break a business plate-glass window with a slingshot, thereby setting off a

Code-30 (burglary alarm). The call went out to an alarm company; the alarm company forwarded the possible break-in to L.A.P.D Communications. In turn, the possible burglary was assigned to a black-and-white patrol car to investigate. If the call wasn't assigned to the police thieves, they would get on the radio and inform Communications they were within a minute or two from the call. It worked every time.

Upon arrival, the officers informed Communications that it was a burglary and the suspects were gone on arrival (G.O.A.). Then they stuffed the stolen merchandise into the trunk of their police vehicle. Once they completed their crime, they followed police protocol, contacting the owner, who secured the premises by boarding up the broken glass. Later, they transferred the stolen merchandise to their personal vehicles.

I didn't know them and don't recall their names, but those officers sure as hell made an impossible job more difficult by playing into the hands of those who chronically complained about bad cops and police corruption. It turned my stomach. I wondered, what turns a good cop into a bad cop? Or were those sorts just intrinsically evil human beings? If so, how did they successfully pass the comprehensive background investigation and the psychological inventory assessment?

As a police candidate, your background phase includes interviews with your entire family tree in addition to your childhood and adult friends and everyone you've ever dated. The background investigator also looks into your grade, high school, and college records and teachers when available. They continue on to check your employment and financial records. They examine military records and any law enforcement contacts and arrests. Then they check your driving record. They look for any history of drug or excessive alcohol use. Hell, even if you lived out of state for a few months, your background investigator flies out there and makes inquiries.

Then there are the "moral turpitude" clauses. For example, if you lived with a female out of wedlock, you were considered of "low character" and disqualified (God knows that's not the case these days).

Finally, there was the extensive psychological assessment that included the 566-question Minnesota Multiphasic Personality Inventory (MMPI) test. It screens for any mental health or clinical issues. In addition to the MMPI, the police candidate takes the Rorschach test.

Finally, there is the sit-down with a psychiatrist. I can't imagine any better vetting!

The best theory I ever read about why cops go rogue was in an article titled, "Bad Apples or Bad Barrels," dated August 2006 in *Psychological Science*. Two psychologists, Eric Wargo and Philip Zimbardo, spoke of the phenomenon:

> *Even the most depressing studies of human weakness can actually be inspiring. There will come a time in your life when you have the power within you, as an ordinary person, as a person who is willing to take a decision, to blow the whistle, to take action, to go the other direction and do the heroic thing. That decision is set against the decisions to perpetrate evil or to do nothing, which is the evil of inaction.*

Doctor Zimbardo concluded with a thought from Alexandr Solzhenitsyn, the Russian poet imprisoned under Stalin: "The line between good and evil lies at the center of every human heart."

—

The first night I worked with Dale Erwin was a keeper. He was driving and I was keeping books. We were working 6-A-27, Team-63's go-to car. That one night, I saw more Hollywood celebrities then the whole rest of the time I worked Hollywood. That night, I also witnessed and admired what our courageous firefighters do day after day after day.

When we cleared for service, Communications gave us the normal three calls as usual, "6-A-27 handled a 415 family dispute at 715 Saint Andrews Place, apartment 406. A 390-down possible drunk, on the southeast corner of Fountain and Ardmore. Possible narcotics suspects on Harvard between Delongpre and Fountain. Suspects are described as two male blacks in their late teens; no further description."

"6-A-27, roger."

When we arrived at Saint Andrews Place, there were a couple of neighbors sticking their heads out of their doors. "She's kicking the hell out of Bert again," one said. Dale had been here several times before and told me to watch out for the wife and twin teenage female daughters. We stood to the side of the door and knocked with our batons. Bert's wife, Margrett, answered the door. She was about 40 years old but looked like 140. She had been drinking and started at us with, "Get the fuck out of here; you're trespassing; I know my rights." I immediately noticed she was toothless and her lips were flapping in the air while she was motherfucking us and spewing chunks of cheesy shit out of her mouth. Bert was seated on the filthy living room couch next to Thelma and Lucy-Bird, their twin daughters.

The girls were dressed in cut-off jeans up to their ass with tiny T-shirts, leaving nothing to the imagination. Thelma was looking at me and my partner with teeming hate in her eyes. Lucy-Bird was looking at me with lustfulness and a twisted smile. Bert's face was black-and-blue from Margrett kicking the shit out of him.

I was trying to calm Margrett down with no success, when Dale shook the walls with a "Shut the fuck up, Margrett, or I'm going to haul your fat, toothless ass off to jail!" Margrett took a seat on a chair next to the couch and was quiet as a church mouse. Dale said, "Bert, do you want me to arrest Margrett?"

"No, Officer Erwin," he replied. "I love my wife; she just got a little upset at me."

Dale warned, "If I get another call here today, all of you are going to jail! Do you all understand me?"

All in unison, like a classroom of third-graders with sweet smiles on their faces, Margrett, Bert, Thelma, and Lucy-Bird said, "Yesssssssss, Officer Irwin."

We kept the peace and got the hell out of there and rolled to our second call. There was no evidence of a 390-down suspect on Fountain. We advised Communications and started off for our third call when a hot shot came out:

"Any Hollywood unit, identify and handle, 415 Man with a Gun, shots fired, at Western and Sunset."

Shit, we were only minutes away. I looked at Erwin and he screamed at me, "Buy it!"

"6-A-27, show us handling the shots-fired call."

Communications, "Roger."

Dale was on it, and we were there in a heartbeat. The intersection of Sunset and Western was completely empty of traffic, but there were numerous onlookers at each corner hunched down and pointing to the armed suspect standing dead center in the intersection. The suspect was a male Caucasian in his early seventies with disheveled gray hair holding a long-barrel shotgun. Fortunately, for him, the barrel was pointing downward.

We came in from the west on Sunset Boulevard and stopped at the marked crosswalk in the number-one lane, then took cover behind our vehicle doors. The suspect turned and faced us; I continually ordered him to drop the gun via our P.A. system and put an Officer Needs Assistance call out. Again, and again, I broadcasted, "This is the Los Angeles Police Department, drop the gun! Lie face down and spread your arms and legs!" The suspect did not comply.

Then it struck me. Damn! It was Frank Faylen, who portrayed Dobie Gillis's dad, Herbert T. Gillis, on the show, *The Many Loves of Dobie Gillis*. He was a prolific character actor in the Golden Age of Hollywood. I loved that show along with millions of Americans.

I kept ordering suspect Faylen to drop the gun, but he continued to mill around, refusing to drop the weapon. Like so many other previous experiences with armed suspects, I knew he was an eye-blink away from forcing us to use deadly force. But shit! I wouldn't be able to live with myself if I killed Dobie Gillis's dad.

Just then I screamed over to Dale, "It's Dobie Gillis's dad!"

Dale said, "Fuck that; if he doesn't drop that fucking shooter, I'm going to cap a round in his ass." Obviously, Dale wasn't a Dobie Gillis fan.

By now, several units had arrived and cordoned off the intersection with their police vehicles. This whole thing was morphing into a classic "contagious shooting" situation in which once a single officer fires a shot, it triggers a similar firing response from all the other officers at the scene.

I continued to order the suspect to drop the shotgun, knowing that if he started to raise the barrel, it would be all over in an instant. After what seemed to be an eternity, he dropped the shotgun. I told him to step five paces to the right, away from his weapon, lay face down, and spread his arms and legs. Thank God, he complied. We cautiously approached him. I covered the suspect while Dale cuffed him. We did it without firing a shot! This could have ended badly with endless deadly possibilities.

When Dale raised the suspect to his feet, I looked around and saw the steely look on all the officers' faces. They, too were critically aware of how this could have ended. But, thousands of times a day in the United States, officers walk that razor's edge and put their lives on the line when they check their fire.

After we put Faylen in the car, several victims from an apartment building on Western came up to us and told us that the suspect fired several shotgun blasts into their apartment building. Faylen owned the building and apparently became enraged when some of the tenants were chronically late for their rent.

Another unit took the multiple crime reports while we transported Faylen to the station. We charged him with numerous counts of 246 P.C. (Shooting into an Inhabited Dwelling). The whole time we had him in custody, he continually uttered the same words, "Thank you for not killing me." He refused to make any other statements once we advised him of his rights. We transported him to the Glass House, booked him into custody, and returned for more.

———

Communications: "6-A-27, handle a 211 (robbery) at 339 Sycamore." I thought to myself, that's a residence? I'd never received this type of call before. Normally 211 calls are either for a business or individuals, not a residence. This must have been some sort of V.I.P. thing.

The home was an opulent two-story, old-English brick house. I took the shotgun and Dale trailed behind me. When we got to the front door, it was slightly ajar. Before we entered the home, we called for some backup—God only knew how many armed suspects and what carnage might be inside.

Once a couple of units arrived and took a corner on each side of the home, Dale and I made for the entrance. I pushed the door open with the muzzle of my shotgun. Once inside, I was overwhelmed with its beauty. The living room had hardwood floors with dark-brown varnish, and there was an enormous fireplace at the far wall. There was a black wrought-iron spiral staircase on the southeast corner leading to the second floor. Once we cleared the first floor, we started for the staircase. If there was death in this home, it was upstairs.

Dale and I stood and listened for a minute before heading up the steps. Just then, a beautiful apparition appeared at the top of the staircase and gracefully made her way down, followed by some skinny white dude with an exaggerated Afro, barefoot, and wearing a multi-colored silk robe. The woman was in a lovely negligee that left little to the imagination.

I looked over at Dale. "I know I've seen her before."

Dale whispered, "Dumb shit, that's Stevie Nicks and Lindsey Buckingham of Fleetwood Mac."

Stevie walked within a foot of me, "I'm sorry officers, we must have left the front door open. We were really tired and went right to bed." Then she moved even closer. "My, that's such a big gun, officer. What kind of gun is that?"

I got into my Marine Corps shit. "Ms. Nicks..."

"Call me Stevie."

"It's a pump-action, model 37, Ithaca 12-gauge shotgun."

"Can I see the bullets?" Stevie asked. I unchambered a single round and handed it to her. She seemed enthralled. I went on telling her that this was a double-aught, high-base magnum round with nine .32 caliber pellets in each round.

Then I did the unthinkable. "Can I have a kiss?" I asked Stevie. Dale looked like he was about to fall over.

She looked into my eyes, leaned up, and gave me a wet kiss on the cheek. "Thank you, officers," she said.

Dale didn't get a kiss. We said our good-byes and left. Buckingham never said a word; he just stood by the base of the staircase the whole time. Dale told me that he grinned when I asked Stevie for a kiss.

At the end of our watch, Dale told me he was going to buy me all the beers I could drink at the Short Stop for having the balls to ask Stevie for a kiss. Oh, hell yes, Short Stop here we come! It was a Thursday night, and the bar would be crawling with good-looking camp followers.

—

For a moment, I let myself actually think about getting off on time and drinking some cold beers with my bros, but then reality set in. Air-6 (police helicopter) came over the air and requested the fire department for an apartment fire just minutes away from our location at 1601 Wilton Place. We bought the call and when we arrived, we saw a two-story duplex engulfed in flames and bellowing toxic, thick black smoke. Several neighbors were outside and told us that there may still be some residents trapped inside.

The fire department hadn't arrived yet. We pounded on the first-floor front door and assisted a Mr. Fraser, who was collecting his family to exit the building. We ran inside and helped evacuate his family. Mr. Fraser frantically repeated that he was unaware if the family upstairs had escaped. By now, the smoke and fire were making their way into the upper floor. We needed to run up the stairway to check the upstairs unit for residents, but this was going to be a real challenge. The stairway was filling with dense smoke.

Dale and I knew that at any time the whole structure was going to go up in flames, and we didn't have any protective gear or breathing equipment. However, if there was a family up there, it was sure death if we didn't get them out. Dale and I gave each other the "fuck it, let's roll" nod and headed up the smoked-filled steps. We were unable to see the top of the stairs through the smoke, so we used the walls on each side to guide us. When we got to the top, Dale was coughing, gagging, and screaming for the occupants to come to the door. There wasn't a sound coming from inside the apartment. I thought, if there were anyone inside, they were probably dead by now from smoke inhalation. Dale looked and sounded like shit, and time was running out.

Fuck it. I pushed Dale to the side and kicked the front door in. The apartment was engulfed with smoke. We found a Miss Stowell inside and started to usher her down the stairway when she told us that there were additional people in the apartment. What the hell?! After we got her to the apartment exit, we ran back upstairs. Once inside, we found a Ms. Cohen and three-year-old Erick Stowell. Dale grabbed the baby and I forcefully grabbed Ms. Cohen. Blessedly, we got them outside before everything was consumed by the smoke and fire. By this time, the fire department had arrived.

Dale started to vomit and told me that his lungs felt like they were on fire. The fire department was hard at work knocking down the blaze, but there was no Rescue Ambulance (R.A.) on scene. I shoved Dale into our car and rolled Code-3 to the hospital. He was treated for smoke inhalation and didn't return to work for several days. I felt like shit but didn't feel I needed treatment and came in the next day for some more. God, I loved my job!

———

It was my first day working with Howie. He had a natural gift for witticism and comic relief regardless of how hectic and dark things got at times.

After a dozen or so typical calls for service, nightfall had set in, and the bad guys came out to go to work in earnest. The radio blared, "6-A-27, 459 [burglary] there now at 939 Western; your call is Code-2."

"Fuck-en-A, let's get a burglar!" Howie shouted. I couldn't help but laugh when he said that. He had this devilish grin on his face like a cheeky third-grader. He wasn't the best driver I've ever ridden with, however. In fact, he scared the hell out of me. Later, I christened him, "Code-3 Howie." A couple of weeks later, I received a single-day suspension for driving like Howie while transporting an ex-con arrestee to the Glass House.

We got to the burglary call in warp speed. It was a furniture store on the corner of Western and Barton. Howie and I looked through the large front window on Western Avenue and found no visible evidence of a break-in, then we walked around the corner to Barton to check the side of the building to confirm yet another bogus Code-30 (burglary alarm). We were just about to return to our car when Howie spotted a suspect squeezing through a tiny window on the southwest corner of the furniture store. The suspect saw us and panicked, then ran for his freedom.

Howie may have been great at the one-liners, but I trashed him when it came to foot pursuits. The suspect turned northbound at the first intersection and fortunately ran out of steam by the time he got to the end of the block. I always enjoyed a good foot pursuit. When I came up within an arm's length of the suspect, I shoved him from behind. He went down like a ton of bricks, then sat upright after his inglorious tumble. I screamed at him to prone-out face-down, but he refused to comply.

Later, I learned he didn't understand a word of English. He was a Mexican in his late teens, about five foot six, skinny as an orphan. Lord, he was one of the most pathetic-looking souls I ever arrested.

After refusing to comply several times, I smashed the side of his face with my open hand and he started to cry like a five-year-old. I immediately felt like the biggest piece of shit in the world! Why did I do that? He wasn't doing anything to challenge or threaten me, but I smashed him across the face just the same. Howie came over and cuffed him. All the way back to our car, he was whimpering like a puppy and looked scared to death. I trailed Howie and the suspect back to our car and thought to myself, it is but for the grace of God that I wasn't born to this lost soul's lot.

My Spanish was shit, but I could understand enough to communicate and take crime reports. It turned out the kid was an illegal alien from Mexico. He, like most others, was here in this foreign land looking for some work to send some money back to his family. This was his first trip to the States, and he was lost and starving. He hadn't had anything to eat in days, that's why he broke into the building. By now, I was about ready to eat my gun because I felt so bad.

I told Howie to drive to this killer hamburger restaurant on Sunset. I was going to get this lost soul a double burger with fries and a big-ass malt before we took him to the station. I uncuffed our suspect and watched him go through that burger and fries like a buzz saw.

I kicked plenty of ass on the job when an asshole needed it, but that was the first and only time I ever did anything I regretted that much. I still cringe to this day when I think about that incident.

After we booked the suspect, we requested Code-7 (meal break) and were stunned when Communications OK'ed our request. The Code-7 angels must have been around; my old friend from Venice Division, Rick Mesnard, recently transferred to Hollywood, also got an OK. We met at that same great hamburger joint. It was so damn cool to chat with my red-haired Venice buddy again. We all planned to meet at the Short Stop after watch for some serious beer drinking, exchanging war stories, and maybe getting laid.

Strangely, Rick went on talking about the ongoing war between him and his team leader, a guy we only knew as Lieutenant 187. Shit, I got on great with him and felt he was one of the best supervisors in Hollywood. Evidently, the Lieutenant, who headed Hollywood's narcotics unit, was *complaining* about Rick making more big-time narcotics arrests than the rest of his unit combined.

It got to where the narcotics lieutenant demanded Lieutenant 187 make Rick stop making any more narc arrests! I reckon management has management's back and thinks to hell with the blue-suiters (patrol cops) on the street! Lieutenan 187 told Rick that his primary responsibility was to handle calls for service because he was working patrol.

Not too far in the future, I would hear a similar argument from the mother of all Lieutenant Witchetty Grubs, Lieutenant William Lynch, commanding officer of OCB CRASH, the department's first-ever specialized gang-suppression unit.

Our forty-five-minute Code-7 flew by; it was time to go back to work. I remember having this strange ominous feeling when Rick got in his black-and-white and started to drive off. He looked over at me and smiled with that youthful freckled faced. God, he was a treasure.

I rarely saw Rick again. He was reassigned to morning watch by Lieutenant 187. Some months later, I heard some crazy unsubstantiated rumors about Rick. In one story, Rick broke into 187's Porsche and placed an overfed turkey in it. The turkey defecated all over the beautiful interior, which needed to be replaced at a punitive cost. Another rumor was that Rick somehow managed to arrange a substantial bimonthly deduction from Lieutenant 187's paycheck to the United Negro Fund. Then I heard Rick left the department for some police department in the San Diego area. San Diego scored; Rick was the best narc cop the department would ever see.

—

Howie and I were looking forward to the end of watch, but that thought of debauchery was short-lived. Three beeps came over the net. It was a Code-3 call: "Any Hollywood unit, identify and handle a 415 Man with a Gun at 606 N. Lucerne Avenue."

"Man with a Gun" is the ultimate radio call; it's life or death, and I had a unique talent in handling these highly volatile calls without using deadly force. Mesnard's specialty was narcotics. Rick Beach was the master of the department when it came to Obs GTA arrests. Howie was the master of the one-liners, and he was second-to-none when it came to chilling out the troops.

I grabbed the mic and looked at Howie before I bought the call. We both knew it would mean overtime and no Short Stop. Howie said, "Do it, partner."

The call was in the south end of the division, so it was a long Code-3 run. The RTO continued feeding us information during our Code-3 run. "6-A-27, be advised the P.R. (person requesting) is the suspect's wife and stated the suspect is armed with a handgun and stated he is going to kill a cop... the P.R. advised that the suspect is a Los Angeles County coroner."

The residence was a single-family dwelling with a large front lawn leading to a raised porch. Howie and the other officers took cover at the apex of the southwest corner of the residence. I sought cover on the northwest side of the home and drew a bead on the armed suspect with my shotgun.

The suspect was a large white male appearing to be in his early fifties wearing a heavy lumber jacket. His hands were in his coat pockets, and he was looking straight ahead with a fixed gaze. He was seated on the porch in one of two chairs next to the front door. I could hear someone shouting from inside the residence; it was the suspect's wife pleading with her husband, "Please don't shoot them; do what they tell you to do!" These screams went on and on the whole time.

I ordered the suspect to fall to his knees and very slowly remove his hands from his coat pockets, fingers extended, then lie facedown, arms and legs extended. He refused to comply; instead he stood up, turned to me, and said, "I'm going to kill you." There was stunning resolution in his face and words.

I had all the right in the world to pull the trigger at this precise moment, but I checked my fire. Again, a million variables raced through my mind. I could feel the adrenaline surging through my body, but at the same time, I felt a sense of calm and complete control. I didn't want to die. I kept thinking, what if he bolts back inside the home and starts shooting his family? Or what if he turns and hysterically starts firing at my brother officers? He continued to disregard my commands and took a couple more steps toward me.

At this point, I made the mental commitment that if he removed his hands from his pockets, and I saw he was holding the firearm, I was going to fire dead into his chest. I also concluded that if he cocked his wrist upward inside his coat pocket, he was a dead man.

Just then, I saw Howie mount the porch from the other side. I knew he was going to try to rush the suspect from behind and hit him like a middle linebacker. The problem was he was exposing himself to a deadly situation. If I had to fire, he would no doubt get hit with part of the shotgun blast. I chambered a round in the shotgun and moved the barrel upward for a headshot, hoping to miss Howie if I fired.

I started screaming as loud and fast as I could to distract the armed suspect from hearing Howie coming up from behind; it worked! Our skinny-ass Henny Youngman morphed into Dick Butkus and tackled that enormous suspect off the porch onto the lawn. It turned out the suspect wasn't armed; it was a "suicide by cop" attempt, though back then these types of incidents weren't identified by that phrase, and we never received any training in the Academy or in service training about that type of phenomenon.

We took the suspect into custody for a 5150 Welfare and Institution code. It's a mandatory three-day hold in a county mental health facility where the subject is evaluated to determine if he is a danger to himself or to others. We returned to the station just in time for end-of-watch. Perfect, Short Stop here we come.

While I was changing from my uniform, Sergeant Dandridge came up to me and told me my father had been admitted to Martin Luther King Hospital and to get there as soon as possible. I knew my father was the ultimate old-school hard-ass and would never consider seeing a doctor or going to a hospital. It had to be something really serious.

—

Sergeant Dandridge followed me to the hospital's intensive care unit; he was a dear man. Mom and the kids were all stuffed in a small room. Most of my brothers and sisters were there huddled around Mom and crying. Once I entered the room, Mom reached out and took me by both hands with tears streaming down her cheeks. "Corky, your Dad is dead." The cries and whimpers from everyone intensified.

I've seen so much death by now, but this time it was family; it was my father. I didn't have the luxury of allowing myself the natural emotions that one experiences in a time like this. I needed to be strong for Mom and the kids. It was impossible to convey any word or thought that would calm Mom and the kids' grief at this moment. It was a time for tears and lament, a time for spiritual exorcism to drive out the dark specter of losing someone who created you.

Minutes later, when one of the doctors walked in, Mom lost it. She grabbed the doctor's white uniform coat by the lapels and screamed, "You let him die! You told me he was going to be alright! You told us to go home and he would be alright in the morning! You just left him out in the hallway to die!"

I had no idea what Mom meant when she said the "the hallway." Once things calmed down a little, the doctor asked me to step outside. He told me that Dad was admitted by ambulance earlier in the evening to the emergency ward complaining of chest pains. They were able to stabilize him and instructed the family to go home because in their judgment, he was going to be alright. Later that evening, he had a massive heart attack and expired.

The doctor asked me if I would like to see Dad. He cautioned me that there were still tubes and medical aids all about his body that hadn't been removed yet. I told the doctor I needed to see my dad just the same. The doctor escorted me to a room where Dad was and excused himself so I could be alone with my father. Dad was on a narrow metal-wheeled table with a white sheet up to his abdomen, his upper body fully exposed. There were tubes coming out of his mouth and numerous I.V.'s attached to his arms, and there was blood everywhere.

For the first time in my life, my father looked at peace—that perennial look of dread and despair was gone. Right at that moment, I felt a celestial reprieve for Dad. He was finally relieved of his earthly constant guilt for that single mistake he made as a young man back in World War II when he deserted his naval unit. I can't imagine what it must have been like for him, fighting those demons of being accused of cowardice in a time of war. That one act irrevocably destroyed his entire life, and he never came to terms with it. Nor did he ever try to explain his actions to his three Vietnam veteran sons.

All through my life, our relationship was one of brutality, rejection, and estrangement. He never once demonstrated any interest in having a loving relationship with his firstborn son. Be that as it may, at this time I only felt love, compassion, and forgiveness for my father.

I told Mom that I would take care of everything and drove her home. We arrived at that gang-infested barrio on Lou Dillon Avenue where Mom and Dad had raised their twelve children.

I asked my twenty-three-year-old sister, Terry, what Mom was screaming about to the doctor in that little room. Terry told me that when Dad arrived at Martin Luther King Hospital, he was examined for his chest pains in the emergency room, then wheeled out to the hallway with no further emergency care. Minutes later, an attendant removed his oxygen mask to use for another patient. He was in the hallway for hours before he was moved to a packed room with other patients. Hours later, Mom was instructed by the doctors and staff to go home. When Mom and the kids got to the house, she received a call telling her that Dad had taken a turn for the worse and she should return straightway. When Mom arrived back at the hospital, he had already expired from a massive heart attack.

Those bungling, incompetent fucks put a heart patient in the hallway for hours without care! The hospital's medical staff and management were wholly inadequate, resulting in countless deaths like that of my father's. The 1972 opening of Martin Luther King Hospital was viewed as a victory for Civil Rights and a source of pride for the black community of South Central L.A. But in a short time, it came to be viewed by sober minds as a place of deathly peril for the resistance and was coined "Killer King" by the community.

Mom was heartbroken. She had recently lost her father, Grandpa Adams, and now her husband of thirty-seven years. Granted, Mom's marriage to Dad was not one of wine and roses, but they walked through the gates of hell for their children and did the best they knew for all of us. It was one crisis after another for Mom and Dad, and when a couple walks through that fire, it creates a bond of mythical proportions.

I didn't want to burden Mom with any of the funeral arrangements when she was in a state of complete loss. Fortunately, my first stop was talking to Monsignor Gannon at Saint Aloysius. All twelve of the little Morenos attended Saint Aloysius, and the Monsignor knew both Mom and Dad. This gentle soul was heaven sent. He walked me through the entire process with genuine care and direction.

Four days after Dad died, it was all set: His funeral Mass was held at Saint Aloysius and the church was filled to capacity. Mom and Dad both came from huge extended families, and everyone attended. At the very last minute, I had to add four additional motorcycles for the motorcade to Resurrection Cemetery in South San Gabriel.

This was all a blur to me, running around from here to there. I don't recall speaking to a single relative the whole time. But I do have one memory that stood out. After the prayer ceremony at the grave, I sat next to Mom in the hearse. Once the vehicle started driving away, Mom bolted forward in an uncontrollable surge and reached for the door, screaming, "Fonsie, Fonsie!" (which was short for Alfonso in Spanish). I swear I could see Mom's spirit leave her physical body for a flash. In the coming years, I would see that phenomenon again and again from grieving family and friends of murdered victims.

Mom wanted to leave and go with her love, but it wasn't her time yet. She would have to wait.

5
Scorched Earth

IT WAS SUCH A JOY to get back to work after all of that incalculable lament. I was back with my favorite partner, John Gamble, and we were tearing it up. By now, I had accumulated twenty-six commendations and had become one of the top producers at Hollywood Division.

But I needed to leave the armpits of the department (patrol). I started studying for the upcoming Policeman III test. One needed to be a two-striper (P-III) to qualify for any specialized unit. I had my sights on Metropolitan Division (METRO), the department dragon-slayers. No radio calls for that lot; they specialized in handling major crime within the city. Once in METRO, I planned for a spot in S.W.A.T., but that would take another three to four years, at best.

I may have just been working patrol at this time in Hollywood, but it was a joy to work with some of L.A.'s best cops, and there was plenty of excrement to clean off the streets. Unlike the five divisions east of Hollywood in Central Bureau next door—Rampart, Central, Newton, Northeast, and Hollenbeck—there was little to no gang war in Hollywood. On occasion, there would be a flare-up between Barrio Westside Rebels 13 and Clanton-14. Clanton was an old-school Hispanic gang with roots that dated back to the 1920s. It originated on Clanton Street, but the city fathers changed the street name to fourteenth Street to downplay the existence of the gang and its crime. The city government did the same thing not too long ago when they changed the name of South Central Los Angeles to South Los Angeles. That didn't change a damn thing—ask the residents!

I had finally learned my lesson about not planning on getting off on time, but just the same, I'm a hopeless optimist.

I met Maria Elena at the Short Stop a few weeks before Dad passed away. She was a business major attending UCLA on a student visa. She was from the gorgeous city of Playa del Carmen, about forty-five minutes south of Cancun, Mexico.

She was a bit short, but had a drop-dead gorgeous figure. She spoke good English and was from a well-to-do family. Of all her blessings, she had the prettiest long hair I had ever seen on a woman: It was really thick and light-brown with streaks of blond, no doubt from European ancestry. She was very fair skinned, with lovely brown bedroom eyes and full lips.

Maria Elena had an apartment up the hill south of Sunset Boulevard, not far from the Short Stop. I was supposed to meet her and her roommate, Matilda, also on a student visa from Playa del Carmen, at the Short Stop after work.

Although John was recently married to a beautiful lady, he still needed an occasional night out with the boys for an exorcism of sorts to drive out dealing with Satan's children. We were both set on doing whatever it took to get off on time that night.

At 1920 hours, we got a Code-3 call. It was an ambulance shooting at the corner of Normandy Avenue and Hollywood Boulevard! This call was the perfect formula to get off on time. The victim was a nineteen-year-old, heavily tattooed Clanton gang member who took six bullets to the legs and was bleeding to death. It was a retaliation drive-by shooting by the Rebels, a Hollywood gang. The victim had shot two Rebel gang member a few weeks earlier.

The victim was visiting his girlfriend who lived in an apartment on Normandy. When they walked outside, two Rebel gang members were lying in wait down the block on a motorcycle. When the victim and his girlfriend walked toward Hollywood Boulevard, the suspects drove alongside of them and opened fire. Miraculously, the female was not hit.

John radioed for an R.A. unit and put out a crime broadcast while I attended the victim. If I couldn't somehow stop the bleeding, he was going to bleed out and die. Fortunately, a neighbor ran over to me and handed me some towels. The most serious of his wounds was a hit to the femoral artery on his left leg. The other gunshot wounds were mostly through-and-through "meat shots." I applied pressure to his inner leg and managed to arrest the hemorrhaging until the R.A. unit arrived.

John jumped into the R.A. unit with the victim to take a dying declaration in the event that he died enroute to the hospital. A couple other units arrived and put the crime scene on ice to secure any evidence and locate witnesses. The victim's girlfriend was transported to the station to be interviewed, and I rolled to the hospital to join John.

Damn, no Short Stop, no Maria Elena, and no cold beers. WTF!

The victim was transported to General Hospital for the multiple gunshot wounds and would receive the best treatment one could get in the United States. The doctors at General dealt with gunshot wound victims on a daily basis and became recognized as the best in the business. In fact, the US military has sent their doctors to General Hospital for a tour of duty to learn how to treat similar wounds on the battlefield.

Our victim went directly into the operating room, and shortly afterward one of the doctors came out and told us that he was going to make it. Damn, they're good! There was no point in hanging around to get a statement from the victim. His name was Juarez, aka Smiley, and he had an extensive violent arrest record. He refused to tell John who shot him, and he sure as hell was going to get his pound of flesh when he got out.

We headed back to the station to interview the victim's girlfriend since she was also a victim of an attempted murder. Her name was Lucy—sixteen years old, a high school dropout, pregnant, and a heroin addict. But, unlike 98 percent of gang-related shootings, Lucy cooperated with us. In the world of "La Vida Loca" (the crazy life), it is verboten to cooperate with the police and can be a death sentence for those who do. Lucy identified the two shooters as Aztec and Huesos (bones), both Rebel gang members.

The standard protocol for officers working patrol is to only conduct the Preliminary Investigation Report (P.I.R.). The follow-up investigation is handled by the detective. However, on rare occasions, an officer can get permission to continue the investigation if he can persuade his bosses that he's got hot leads. I told my boss, Lieutenant

Sadlier, what we had on the two shooters. We were confident we could make an arrest.

I knew there was a specialized unit in the Glass House that worked gang intel and statistics—Investigative Support Division, (I.S.D.) Gang Activities Section. I thought there may have been a possibility that they had the Rebel gang members' monikers on file. John and I drove to the Glass House and met with Detective III, Suarez, head of the specialized intel unit, and two of his Detective IIs, Douglas and Hinds. These three L.A.P.D. O.G.s were an impressive lot. All three had over fifteen years on the job. They were dressed in tailored suits and their appearances were impeccable. These old guards had seen it all hundreds of times and were the go-to source for the history of L.A.'s street gang anarchy.

I told Detective Suarez what I had. He asked John and me to have a seat while his crew went through the files (all police records at that time were in hard copy). A few minutes later, he returned with two coffees for John and me. We were bewildered why a man of his stature would bother to treat us with such respect. Shit, we were merely P-IIs. While we drank our coffees, we filled him in on the details of the shooting. I knew what John was thinking: He was thinking what I was, wondering why two lowly piss-ant blue-suitors were getting the VIP treatment from the likes of this legend.

Eureka! Douglas and Hinds found an extensive file on Aztec and Huesos. They were both only sixteen years old, with no real jail time, but already had lengthy rap sheets for violent crimes. These two, like some other select gang members, had a high-dollar attorney on retainer paid for by their drug sales and other crimes. Now we had a positive ID on both of these two young thugs and were off to their known street hangouts. John and I were surprised when Suarez, Douglas, and Hinds joined us. Their time on the streets dealing with this shit was long over. However, they no doubt were infected with our enthusiasm, and it gave them an opportunity to get out of the office.

Their intel was spot on. We found Aztec and Huesos and the semi-auto .32 caliber used in the shooting in Aztec's waistband.

The two suspects were with a couple of their homies smoking dope and drinking beer in an abandoned property at 700 N. Ardmore, next to the Hollywood Freeway. They were all so high that when they spotted us approaching them, they all started laughing and assumed the position (felony prone, facedown on the dirt). John and I cuffed and arrested them for the attempted murder.

We had no problem getting a detention order for the two. We booked them at Eastlake Juvenile Hall for two counts of attempted murder, possession of a stolen gun, and felony possession of marijuana. The .32 had been taken in a Rampart burglary. Sergeant Gene Ingram wrote John and me up for a big time 1.27.

A couple days later, I got a message in roll call that Detective Suarez needed to talk to me. I thought it was about our arrest of the gang members, but no—Suarez had heard about an opening in Operations Central Bureau "CRASH" (an acronym for Community Resources against Street Hoodlums), L.A.P.D.'s first-ever specialized gang-suppression unit.

The gang-suppression unit wasn't a new concept. In 1973, Lou Sporrer, Deputy Chief and Commander of South Bureau, created TRASH—Total Resources against Street Hoodlums. He anticipated the unrestrained growth and carnage between L.A.'s South Bureau's black gangs, the Bloods and Crips. However, the gang unit was principally limited to 77 Division.

Operations Central Bureau CRASH, started in late 1977, primarily addressed the Hispanic gang wars in Central Bureau's five divisions: Northeast, Hollenbeck, Central, Rampart, and Newton. Newton Division was an exception to the other four divisions. It was exclusively populated with blacks with a few Hispanics. Newton's gangs were a relative new phenomenon in the division. The homies called their street gangs "Sets." Sets were composed of one street gang after another with ostentatious gang names but were no less as ruthless as their Hispanic counterparts. The Bloods and Crips were just forming, but mostly in South Bureau.

Unlike Newton, many of the Hispanic gangs were formed as far back as the 1920s. The Hispanic community had had carnage on their streets for decades and successfully petitioned the City of L.A. to convince the federal government for a three-year financial grant to form a forty-man specialized gang-suppression unit. OCB CRASH was born. In the coming years, CRASH officers and detectives would save thousands of lives—from Hispanics murdering Hispanics and blacks murdering blacks—even though many of them hated the police who put it all on the line for them on a daily basis.

The commanding officer of the unit was Lieutenant William Lynch. He had well over twenty years on the job at that time and was well connected with upper management; that's how he got this sweet assignment.

Lieutenant Lynch reported directly to the Bureau Commander, Robert Vernon, with no one in between. This was highly suspect and had never been done before. The standard protocol for a specialized unit is always headed by a captain with a lieutenant as his subordinate and a few sergeants.

I called the CRASH unit and got an appointment to meet Lieutenant Lynch a few days later. In our meeting, he said he received a call from Detective Suarez who highly recommended me for the opening spot in the unit. His forty-man unit was comprised of the finest detectives, sergeants, and street cops on the Los Angeles Police Department. Lieutenant Lynch personally handpicked every member of the unit after meticulous and thorough vetting.

Lynch said his CRASH unit was going to create an unprecedented intelligence dossier of every gang and gang member in Central Bureau. The intelligence files would include each gang's territory and identify every individual member by name, moniker, tattoos, where they lived, and the make and model of their vehicles. This would be achieved by arresting the thugs for the slightest infraction. Anything short of an arrest in the field, the CRASH officers would complete Field Interview cards (F.I.), and when possible, I-cards, which gave the officer many more entries for additional intel information. When possible, the CRASH officers would also take photographs of the gang members and their tattoos in the field.

In effect, the CRASH unit had declared war on L.A.s street gangs and were going to use a scorched-earth policy to bring order and peace to the communities that they had wreaked terror and mayhem on for the last fifty years.

At the end of our meeting, Lieutenant Lynch advised me that he was going to interview fifty seasoned officers from across the department for the single opening. He said I would be notified one way or the other in a couple weeks.

I was born for this assignment and wanted it desperately. But I was concerned about several aspects of the Lieutenant's strategy. His enforcement policy failed to address the very lifeblood of these gangs—the gangs' narcotics trade that extended far beyond America's borders. And his insular strategy failed to include extortion, human trafficking, prostitution, counterfeiting, and money laundering. And most concerning, Lieutenant Lynch never even mentioned the three "Godfathers" of these ubiquitous gangs: the Mexican Mafia, or *La EmE*; the Black Guerilla Family, which managed all the black gangs in the United States, including the Bloods and Crips; and the Aryan Brotherhood that ran and managed the white supremacist thugs throughout the United States.

Lieutenant Lynch was wholly unsuited for the enormous task at hand. However, I wasn't about to make any suggestions at this juncture, but his ignorant and insular knowledge and strategy were destined for failure! I may have been just a lowly P-II worker-bee, but I was raised in between Florencia-13 and Watts, two of L.A. County's oldest and most vicious gangs. Spanky, This Way and That Way, and Sniper and their merciless homies lived right across the street from my family on Lou Dillon Avenue. After twenty-two years of living in that pit of crime and mayhem, there was little I didn't know about the "La Vida Loca."

If the city fathers genuinely gave a damn, the unit should have been comprised of two hundred CRASH officers at the outset. The department should have completed an exhaustive analysis of the city's gang culture and history, buttressed by a central, national, and international intelligence organization that shared intelligence with local, state, and federal law enforcement agencies throughout the United States—that would have nailed it from the jump!

These forty CRASH officers and detectives were the equivalent of Achilles Myrmidons. But the forty were going up against 450 gangs with an estimated 120,000 gang members. This lot were brought up on the murderous streets of East L.A and South Central, and most Americans were clueless and unable to comprehend what the forty were going up against! Most alarming, the forty would never realize the essential support from the community or the press.

—

A couple weeks later, Lieutenant Sadlier called me into his office and told me I got the spot in the CRASH unit. Oorah!

My first day in the CRASH office was a bit of a shock. The unit was located in Hollenbeck Division's boiler room downstairs. It couldn't have been more than 400 square feet. The commander, detectives, street cops, and two secretaries all shared the cramped boiler room. There were three benches lined up against the east wall with metal shackles to chain our arrestees to while the CRASH officers completed their arrest reports; what the hell?

As I had done for all my previous assignments, I showed up at least an hour before roll call to pour over crime and arrest reports. It gave me an overview of the Bureau's gangs and served as a priceless intelligence source that paid off big time in the field. On that first day, I met Officer Dan Hart, aka Poppin' Fresh or Pillsbury Doughboy. He also showed up for work earlier than most to make coffee for the Bros. He gave me a cursory overview of things and warned me to maintain a high arrest recap! The unit was all about arrest numbers, not the quality of arrests.

The CRASH officers came from all over the department and had one thing in common—they were the department's upper-10-percent performers from the "Outstanding" pool. These men had an intrinsic talent for police work. They were highly motivated and not concerned about working ceaseless overtime. They were street hard, and most important, *temperate*.

The CRASH officer uniform of the day was slacks, a dress shirt, a tie, and a sport coat. The dress code couldn't have been more impractical for our assignment. Sneakers, jeans, a T-shirt, and a raid jacket would have been far more suitable. Our vehicles were dual-purpose unmarked cars; that was one thing the unit commander got right.

Many in the neighborhoods in Central Bureau initially welcomed the CRASH intervention. However, there were some who saw law enforcement as their perennial enemy, and ironically, they were the ones who called and needed us the most. Peek deployment for our CRASH unit was only twelve cars to work the five divisions in the

Bureau. However, having twelve cars deployed was the exception to the rule due to officers Injured on Duty (I.O.D.), sick days, regular days off, court time, and vacation time. The CRASH unit didn't have enough personnel to deploy a day watch, so we exclusively worked p.m. watch from 1500 hours to 2345 hours.

Normally, the unit was deployed in two forces. The bifurcated force worked two of the five divisions, in whichever two divisions the gangs were killing each other the most. The two divisions got six two-man CRASH units. The other three divisions would have to fend for themselves. For example, if 1st Flats and 4th Flats were gunning each other out of existence in Hollenbeck Division, half the CRASH units worked there. The other CRASH units worked a similar scenario in another one of the five divisions.

Our CRASH officers handled anywhere between one and five shootings per night. In between scraping the bodies off the streets—including those of innocent children and adults who were caught in the crossfire—we stopped every gang member we could lawfully detain to build our intelligence dossier. And all of this senseless and inexcusable carnage rarely made the daily news because it was the same old shit day after day.

I worked 4 CRASH-3 with John Ayila on my first night out. John was a super street cop, so I mentally memorized everything he said and did. Right out of roll call, an ambulance-shooting call came out from Cuatro Flats (4th Street Flats gang) in Boyle Heights. The shooting was at a Laundromat on fourth Street, west of Soto Street. We drove into the parking lot and were told by numerous onlookers that a kid had been shot several times.

The victim was a sixteen-year-old nongang member who took two 12-gauge shotgun blasts to the stomach, blowing his intestines out of his abdomen. Amazingly, he was still alive and hadn't gone into deep shock yet. When I knelt next to him in a futile attempt to render aid, I felt his warm blood soaking into my uniform pants at the knee. John rushed back to our car to request an R.A. unit and put out a crime broadcast.

The kid's name was Tomas. He told me he was doing the laundry for his Mom when he was approached by a couple of gangsters. It was raining that day, and both of the suspects had long raincoats on. They asked Tomas where he was from. Tomas told the suspects that he was not in a gang and was attended Roosevelt High School. The shooter grinned at Tomas and opened his raincoat, revealing a sawed-off double-barrel shotgun, then screamed *"puta"* (bitch), and opened up on Tomas with both barrels. Tomas was blown through the air and landed halfway out the Laundromat's rear exit door.

While I was talking to him, he kept trying to raise his head to look at his wounds, and every time I forced his head back down. I knew if he saw his guts splattered every which way, he would most certainly go into deep shock and die. Just then, Tomas's mother, Eveline, and his two little sisters, eleven and thirteen years old, showed up. They lived a block away from the Laundromat in the Aliso Village projects, an enormous government public housing complex that looked like a WW II death camp. His mom and sisters were screaming out of their minds when they saw Tomas. John had his hands full trying to calm and restrain the three.

It seemed like an eternity before the R.A. arrived. A neighbor ran up and took the girls away. Tomas's mother knelt on the other side of him and held his hand. Somehow, Tomas held on. He said that after he was shot the shooter walked up to him laughing and identified himself, figuring Tomas would take that information to the grave. "I'm Apache, *puta* from Cuatro," he said. "And you're going to die."

I told John what Tomas had just told me, and John put out a supplemental crime broadcast. Within minutes, my old Cerritos College classmate Carey Ricard, working Hollenbeck's 4-A-71, recognized the suspect's moniker. Within fifteen minutes, Apache and Spider were cuffed and in the backseat of Carey's car.

Finally, the R.A. unit arrived and we rode with Tomas to General Hospital. The good news was he would survive, but he would be a quadriplegic for the rest of his life. While Tomas was being treated, I told his mother that I could arrange for a Hollenbeck unit to pick up Tomas's father. Eveline stared at me with tears streaming down her cheeks as she told me that her husband, Edwardo, left the family years ago.

How in God's name was she going to support her three children, I thought. She could see that I was concerned, and I suspect she felt comfort in talking to me. She told me she had been working seven days a week washing and ironing clothes for her neighbors and cleaning houses with the aid of her daughters on the weekends and school breaks. She also cooked and sold tamales on the weekends to make ends meet.

After his father left, Tomas pledged to his Mom that he would take care of her and his little sisters. Besides going to school full time, he was working odd jobs after school and on the weekends. Eveline told me that he was a straight-A student and was applying for a college scholarship. But today's satanic act would forever change this family's world into an uncontrollable vortex of hardship and despair for the rest of their days.

My CRASH brothers and I saw similar horrors play out in the barrios and hoods of Los Angeles on a daily basis with no end in sight.

When we left the hospital, John looked over at me and said, "Partner, you need to change your pants." I looked down and saw Tomas's blood caked all over them. We returned to the CRASH boiler room where I fortunately kept a spare pair of jeans and shirt in my locker. I threw the blood-soaked clothes away. There was no way in the world that I would ever want to wear those again even if the cleaners were able to remove all the bloodstains.

Once we left the boiler room, I grabbed the rover (handheld radio) and informed the other CRASH units working Hollenbeck that we were clear. Poppin' Fresh (Officer Danny Hart) and his partner, Juan Villanueva, advised us that they were working Rose Hills, one of the smallest gangs in Hollenbeck located north of their deadly adversaries—El Sereno, Clover, and Big Hazard. Of the three, Big Hazard seemed to have the biggest hard-on for Rose Hills, and on this night, Big Hazard was going to "get some." A Rose Hills gangster had sold a Big Hazard gangster a shit kilo (low-grade grass) of marijuana, and they were homicidally pissed off.

For payback, four Big Hazard gangsters, two males and two females, drove to Rose Hills armed with a .45 caliber semi-auto. Officers Mark Fuhrman and Ted Severns broadcasted that they heard several gunshots coming from up the hills in the public housing project.

The two CRASH units combed the projects for possible victims and were hailed down by a witness in his late sixties. He pointed to a pickup truck that had been shot up all to hell and told the CRASH officers that the passenger had been shot several times. He described the shooters' vehicle as a light-gray 1950s Chevy with four suspects, two males in the front and two females seated in the back. The inside of the pickup was covered in blood. The volume of the blood on the floorboard indicated that the victim probably bled-out and was dead.

CRASH Officers Rick Lane and John Holcomb, two of the best officers in the unit, knew exactly where to fan out and hunt for the killers. They spotted the suspect's vehicle speeding down Mercury Street toward Huntington Drive and alerted their other CRASH brothers. Once Rick and John saw their backup units rolling in, they stopped the four suspects and ordered them out at gunpoint.

The male suspects were searched for the gun, but neither of them were armed. However, one of the two female suspects, in her early twenties and extremely obese, kept moving her legs and wiggling her big ass. They cuffed her and secured her legs with a strap and transported her to General Hospital for a female genital search. The doctors recovered the .45 caliber semi-auto from her birth canal.

It was 4:30 in the morning before we went end-of-watch on my first day. "Welcome to CRASH, Al," John said as I walked out to my car.

On my drive home, I thought about what a phenomenal lot these CRASH officers were. I had worked multiple crime scenes before, but not like this. They were working these crime scenes like Mozart wrote his symphonies, without a single correction.

———

After about six months in the unit and studying everything I could get my hands on from the detective's desk, I was coming into my own and felt a great relief that I was carrying my share of the load.

One day at roll call, the Bureau's Commander, Robert Vernon, told us our unit had far exceeded his expectations and was well on its way to completing its intel dossier on the Bureau's gangs. Of all the unit's challenges he spoke about that afternoon, one thing blaringly stood out. Commander Vernon shocked us when he proclaimed, "I want you to understand that I know what you are up against, and I want to assure you that I have your back. I know that in some cases, your language and use of force will exceed that of working in any other specialized unit in the department. But don't worry; when and if you have to walk that razor's edge, I've got your six."

At the close of his roll call, he informed us that we were leaving Hollenbeck's boiler room for our new CRASH headquarters in Glass House. We walked out of that room with a sense of confidence and security that we wouldn't be thrown under the bus if and when we were forced to exceed the normal boundaries of talking to and dealing with the kind of gangsters who would slit your throat in a heartbeat, though we were aware this didn't mean taking unprovoked measures, either.

Within a couple of weeks, we were in our new digs—Parker Center (the Glass House) Headquarters of the Los Angeles Police Department. We had a new Chief of Police, Daryl Gates.

This chief had a totally different philosophy than his predecessor, Ed Davis. Gates's officers were going to use preemptive policing tactics—stop, investigate, and arrest the thugs before they unleashed their chaos and brutality on our citizenry. This was heaven-sent to his Praetorians out on the streets—we finally had a boss who understood what real police work was all about.

This one night, half of our unit was assigned to "Shoot-en Newton Division." White Fence and 38th Street gangs were at war once again. The other half of the unit worked "Rampages," the nickname for Rampart. Two clicks (affiliate gangs) of Westside 18th Street, Pico Union and Shatto Park, were gunned down the previous night by the Harpys. Of all the gangs in L.A., Harpys was at the top of the murder scale at that time.

Once in Newton, John and I saw four uniformed patrol officers rushing into an abandoned garage on Forty-First Street and Long Beach Avenue across the street from the railroad tracks. We stopped to assist the officers and ascertain if it was a gang-related caper.

When we walked into the garage, we found a fourteen-year-old kid who took a bullet to the mouth with a 9 mm. There was another kid in the garage standing with one of the officers. He was twelve years old and said he was a friend of the victim. One of the Newton officers recovered the weapon, poorly hidden under some old newspapers and empty beer cans on the dirt floor. Fortunately, the R.A. unit was here within minutes. As the victim was being placed on the gurney, John spotted a small tattoo on the victim's hand between the thumb and ring finger. It was a White Fence gang tattoo. John and I told the patrol units, it's a gang shooting, CRASH will handle it.

What was striking about this shooting, besides all the blood and gore, was that the other kid showed no emotion over this blood-soaked crime scene. Any normal twelve-year-old would be freaking out of his mind. We transported the kid to our new CRASH office, and John tried to contact his parents with no luck. After about an hour and a half, the kid went from witness to suspect when he admitted he was "Diablo" from 38th Street Peewees.

I had never arrested anyone so young and so indifferent about being in police custody for his age. He was an angelic-looking child and didn't appear to be a day over nine years old.

At this point, it was time to advise him of his constitutional rights. I made sure to speak in a slow and methodical manner so he understood every word I said. His real name was Carlos, but when I called him Carlos, he stopped me and insisted on being called Diablo (devil).

"Diablo, do you know what it means when a police officer reads you your constitutional rights?"

"Yes, I seen it on television all the time."

"Well, I am arresting you for attempted murder, for shooting your friend."

"He's not my friend; he's from White Fence."

"Okay, Diablo. You have the right to remain silent. If you give up the right to remain silent, anything you say can and will be used against you in a court of law. You have the right to speak with an attorney and to have the attorney present during questioning and have your parents here as well. If you desire and cannot afford one, an attorney will be appointed for you without charge before questioning..."

"...I know all that stuff!"

"I'm not done, Diablo. Do you understand each of these rights I have explained to you?"

"Yes."

After I read Diablo his Rights, I also conducted a "Gladys R" questionnaire, which is used to determine if a child under fourteen years of age understands the difference between right and wrong. After going through the questionnaire with Diablo, it was crystal clear that this little monster knew the difference.

I asked him how he got the gun, and he told me the whole story and never blinked an eye. The gun belonged to his mother's live-in boyfriend. Diablo took the firearm from under the pillow where he kept it. Miguel, the victim, had a sister in Diablo's class at school, which is how they knew each other. Diablo walked to Miguel's house and showed him the gun, then told Miguel to come to the empty garage to "shoot some cans."

The more this little monster talked, the more the hair on the back of my neck stood up. He had planned the shooting out in detail. I could see Diablo was getting to the climax of his story—his eyes grew larger, his face turned a shade redder, and his lips started to salivate.

"When we got to the garage, I told him to stack the cans up so we could shoot them," he recounted. "He picked up a bunch of cans and stacked them up on the other side of the garage. When he turned and looked at me, I shot him in the face."

"Did you feel bad when you shot him?"

"No—fuck White Fence. They always shoot my homeboys."

After the interview, I advised one of our four sergeants, Sergeant Karl Kenerson, what I had. He told me to contact an Intercept Officer (an on-call county juvenile authority who gives the arresting officer a detention order for a juvenile arrestee). I told Sergeant Kenerson that I already made the call but was told that no one was available at this time to roll out. Kenerson got upset and went on and on about the subject's age. I emphasized that this little fuck just shot another kid in the face and no Intercept Officer would ever question such a detention. I asked him if he wanted me to release the little monster to his parents. He got pissed off and finally gave me booking approval for attempted murder.

While I was writing the arrest petition, I got a call from the Newton officers that Miguel was still in surgery and hanging in there. I knew that if he expired, the CRASH detectives would take the baton. Just then Arlene, Diablo's mother, walked into the CRASH office with a visitor pass pasted on the bare cleavage of her voluminous breasts. She was beautiful and built like a playboy centerfold. Eddie, her thirty-one-year-old, heavily tattooed, ex-con boyfriend was with her. John asked them for ID and sat them in separate interview rooms—I took Eddie, and John took Arlene.

It wasn't but a couple of minutes when I heard screeching coming from the room John was in. I told Eddie to stay in the room and walked out to see Arlene motherfucking John and threatening to sue the world. John and I told her if she didn't calm down, we were either going to arrest her or throw her out of the station. We told her where Diablo was going to be detained and that she could go there to see her son. The authorities there would answer all her questions. There was no need at this juncture to question her about the stolen 9 mm. She'd just tell us to go fuck ourselves! Our CRASH detectives would handle that end.

Meanwhile, Eddie was going back to the joint for possession of stolen property (the gun Diablo used in the shooting) and for violating his parole. When John told Arlene that Eddie was going back to the joint for the stolen gun, she smiled at John and handed him her telephone number as if to say "I'm all yours." As tempting as Arlene was, we knew that she was the purest form of evil, and she made our skin crawl. John threw the number in the round file.

Neither John nor I ever received any subpoenas on this case. I suspect Arlene got a high-dollar lawyer through illicit means and that Diablo never saw a day of jail time for the shooting after he was released from juvenile hall. Diablo would go on to be lionized by his gang and hurt as many human beings he could before he was either jailed for life or murdered by another gangster. There is no end to this madness.

—

We weren't done for the night. All the units shifted to Rampart Division for the rest of the night watch. The Westside 18th Street gang was fighting a gang war on two fronts, one with Harpys and the other with Echo Park. There was a total of nineteen shootings in twelve days among that lot.

On the other front, Harpys was shooting at anything and everything that resembled an 18th Street gangster. We were all monitoring the Net (radio) in between stopping every gangster we could legally stop in hopes of preempting more slaughter. Then an ambulance-shooting call came out at one of the dilapidated apartment buildings in the Pico Union area. Most of the tenants in the apartment were illegal aliens from South and Central America, mostly from El Salvador. It was the late 1970s, when El Salvador, Honduras, Guatemala, and just about every other banana republic were at war with their corrupt governments.

When we arrived, there were several Rampart patrol units there cordoning off the entire apartment building. The Rampart blue-suiters told us to go to the fourth floor where four gunshot victims were piled up. We took the stairs, since none of us ever trusted those old fucked-up elevators. When we got to the fourth floor, we saw four gunshot victims stacked on top of each other in the center of the narrow hallway. They had all been shot in the head several times with a .45 caliber semi-auto.

It was impossible to examine the bodies without drenching our shoes and slacks in the sea of blood around them. There were no obvious witnesses since the entire apartment building was on a self-imposed lockdown in fear of being killed. I noticed a single door creep open at the very end of the hallway. I could see the terror in the tenant's eyes when she peeped her head out the door, and there were two young children kneeling below their mom peeping out as well.

A couple of city paramedics walked up to examine and pink-tag (pronounce dead) the bodies. After they left, I started to head back down when I heard someone yell, "Corky!" Shit, it was Rick Beach, my old Huntington Park High School best buddy. Without even thinking, I brushed up against the wall and stepped over the dead to go say hi to Rick. Just as I reached out to shake Rick's hand, it struck me that there were four dead human beings behind me. I recalled a scene from the 1971 movie, *The French Connection,* in which Gene Hackman portrayed a New York detective, Popeye Doyle. He and three other detectives are driving in a car and spot a horrific traffic accident. They pull over to see if they can help when Popeye and another detective get into a heated argument over an ongoing investigation and become completely oblivious to the mangled bodies at their feet. My God, had I lost all my humanity as well?

When I shook Rick's hand, he noticed that I went dark for a moment and asked if I was okay. I nodded and forced a weak smile.

Rick, too had managed to master the survival skill of psychological dissociation as he did when he was with Bravo Company, First Battalion, Ninth Marine Regiment in the first battle for Khe Sanh in 1967, one of the bloodiest battles the Marines fought in the war. He received two of his three Purple Hearts in that hand-to-hand engagement.

The Rampart coppers were not CRASH officers, but they were nonetheless experts in the gang wars of their division. They knew this was no doubt a Harpys hit on 18th Street. Rick and I decided to question the woman who had opened the door as a possible witness. My heart dropped when I saw the look of horror on her face and the faces of her two little girls, maybe six and eight years old. She spoke broken English and I spoke enough Spanish so we could understand one another. Her name was Martha and she was from El Salvador. I assured her that I wasn't the immigration police; I just wanted to know if she saw who the shooters were. I sensed she had some information, but she was afraid to tell us anything. I promised her I wouldn't list her as a witness or tell anyone that she cooperated with the police.

She said she had just returned from buying some groceries and was walking into her apartment with her children when she noticed the four victims standing in the hallway talking to each other. One of them lived on the same floor at the end of the hall. He was a gang member but he was always nice and respectful to her and the kids. She said he was also from El Salvador like most of the other tenants in the building.

When I asked her if she had seen the shooters, she cringed, and I knew she had seen something. She said that when she entered her apartment and closed the door, she heard a loud argument in the hallway and someone kept screaming, *"De donde eres, perras?"* ("Where you from, dogs?") Then she heard multiple ear-piercing gunshots.

While the shots were going off, she tucked her little girls under her arms and curled up in the empty bathtub, hoping that would protect her and her girls from a stray bullet. None of us would dare implicate these helpless souls as witnesses; it would mean certain death for all. But how the hell was I going to convince our supervisors it was gang-related without jeopardizing the lives of these innocents?

Shit, of all the supervisors to roll up, it was Sergeant Kenerson; he had his head up the Lieutenant's ass and was his in-house snitch. I told him what we had without telling him how I knew. It was gang related! But he knew the Lieutenant was obsessed with doing everything in his power to underreport the true gang-related stats in Central Bureau. Kenerson ordered us to pawn the shooting off to the Rampart patrol officers just like numerous times before. They, like the other four division patrol officers, were furious with CRASH's bullshit. This type of maleficence became the rule rather than the exception year after year. Upper management in the Glass House, the City Council, and the mayor's office conveniently played dumb. But we all knew exactly what the fuck was going on.

Fast forward ten years later, to February 19, 1988. The city's criminal cover-up would surface at a Los Angeles County Board of Supervisors meeting when Sheriff Sherman Block courageously disclosed the cover-up and told the five county supervisors the truth about the suppressed gang-related statistics. Block told the board that several law enforcement officials said political pressure had resulted in some crimes not being listed as gang related with the intent of reducing the potential fear level of people coming into the community.

I apologized to Rick and my brother Rampart patrol officers at the murder scene. However, my role in eventually bringing the underreporting policy to light would, in time, have life-threatening consequences for me.

—

A couple weeks later, John transferred out of the unit and got a sweet spot in badass METRO. The word was out that he was going to be replaced by a female officer. What the fuck? Most of us felt this was the last place for a female officer. There were much too many altercations with inebriated and doped-up gangsters; how in the hell was she going to carry her load?

Her name was Lynn Cummings. She was in her mid-twenties, tall, nice looking, and fit as hell. However, her voice sounded like a high-pitched siren blaring down the street, and it drove me crazy. Of all the officers in the unit, she was partnered up with me on her first night out. After roll call, a couple of the guys told me to tone my shit down and not get into the shit as I normally did until I could sauce her out, to see if she could hang. I told them that I didn't care who came into the unit, male or female, as long as the person could carry his or her load like the rest of us.

On our first night out together, Lynn rode shotgun and grabbed the rover (radio): "1 CRASH 3, clear." What the fuck! She sounded like shit, and I told her I'll do all the talking on the mic for Christ's sake. We were working back in Rampart that night, and I spotted a couple of gangsters driving a brand-new beige two-door 1979 Fiat convertible. I pulled up behind them and Lynn ran the plate; it came back a Beverly Hills stolen vehicle. Before I lit them up, I requested a rolling backup in case the stop went sideways, but the suspects pulled over into a gas station before we got our backup.

As we pulled up behind them with our red lamp blaring atop our dashboard, I started to tell Lynn to get the shooter, but she beat me to the punch. She was on it, with the shooter in hand and barricading herself behind the passenger door. Again, she beat me to the punch and shrilled out on the P.A. system, "Motherfuckers, put your hands up and freeze!" as she chambered a round into the shotgun.

Shit, her scary-ass voice almost made me drop my gun. Her commands and tactics were textbook. Both suspects complied, exiting the stolen vehicle and assuming the position: facedown, arms and legs spread out, frozen in time.

I followed Lynn toward the suspects, slightly to her left rear since she had the shotgun, and I didn't want to get hit if she had to open up on them. She stopped at the feet of the suspects while I searched and cuffed them. After we secured them in the backseat of our car, Lynn searched the Fiat and recovered a fully loaded, six-inch .357 Magnum from under the passenger's seat. The two suspects were Rampart gangsters from Temple Street enroute to blow up some Varrio Alpine gang members.

Alpine is one of the oldest gangs in the city, formed about 1890 around Chinatown in Central Division. The founder of the gang must have been a Democrat—the original gang was the essence of diversity with Mexicans, Italians, Irish, and even a couple of Jews. However, the diversity faded by the 1970s, and now it was exclusively Mexicans. Our labors would ensure another day of life for some Alpine gangsters this night, and they wouldn't be any the wiser.

We booked them for the stolen vehicle and receiving stolen property, the .357 Mag. The gun was taken in a residential burglary in the city of Vernon. We celebrated Lynn's first CRASH arrests at Tommy's Burgers on Beverly and Rampart Boulevard, my treat.

After Code-7, we made a few more stops that night and got some good F.I.s from a couple groups of Westside 18th Street gangsters loitering around Pico Union. I was shocked at Lynn's command presence while we made all those contacts that night, and the gangsters were obviously perplexed when they were being jammed by a female CRASH officer.

It was toward the end of watch when we started heading back to our new headquarters. Damn, Lynn observed a couple of gang members beating the hell out of a citizen. At first, I didn't see a thing. Then I saw the attack at the very back of a parking lot. These fucks were beating and kicking the victim back into the Stone Age.

Lynn put out an assistance call and our location while I punched the accelerator and drove toward the suspects. There was no driveway in sight, so I crashed over a curb, sending us a bit airborne. The gangsters were so focused on their attack, they didn't even notice us coming at them in full flight. I stopped the car just feet away from the suspects, and Lynn was out of our car as fast as I was. Incredibly, the suspects never stopped their attack. We both drew our .38s and screamed at the suspects to stop and prone out.

They were too slow in complying, so Lynn drew her hickory (baton) and started beating them like a stepchild. Christ, it was a sight to behold! She was working them like a Tasmanian devil while I just stood back and learned a thing or two. I felt I was in the presence of a descendent of Boudica, Celtic Britain's famed warrior queen.

Within a minute, Lynn had beat the hell out of these two bad guys, handcuffed them, and was ready for more. The suspects were Westside 18th Street gang members, one out on parole for robbery and the other with numerous outstanding felony warrants. These homies were going back to their second home for the next five to ten years.

On the way back to the station, I stopped and bought a six-pack of beer for Lynn and me. There was no way I wasn't going to celebrate the christening of our CRASH Boudica without sharing a few cold beers with her after watch.

A couple of weeks later, Lynn was partnered up with one of the best CRASH officers in the unit, Dean Brinker. They made for a special team and put some serious gangsters in the big house. In addition to her natural street prowess, she was a real morale booster for the guys, and now we had someone to search our female gangsters on the street.

6
The Genesis of My Armageddon

WITH EXCEPTION, when the city's gangsters went out for their nights of murder, they were high on drugs. At that time, it was mostly PCP, one of the most popular drugs in the late 1970s to early 1980s. It was dirt cheap and made the user mad-dog crazy. At that time, our unit was making an inordinate amount of drug arrests for possession and under the influence of PCP. The Lieutenant was nonstop bitching about it.

One day, Lieutenant Lynch called me into the office after roll call. The conversation with him couldn't have gone worse, and I wasn't as diplomatic as a Police Officer II should have been. He started off with, "Why are you making so many dope arrests? CRASH is a gang suppression unit, not a narcotics unit!" Then he went on about how I was unnecessarily listing witnesses as victims on crime reports, thereby increasing the gang-related crime stats.

He brought up two recent crime reports that I took, both Northeast Division shootings. The first was when three gang members from Cypress Park were shot at by Avenues gangsters, and only one was hit, but I listed all three as victims. The second was between the same gangs, but in reverse—Avenues shot at four Cypress Park gangsters, two were hit, but I listed all four as attempted-murder victims. I told him that in both cases, the victims were all standing within close proximity of one another talking when the suspects drove by and fired over fifteen rounds at the group. They were all obviously intended targets, and the law mandates that I list all of them as victims of attempted murder.

He replied that it was CRASH policy to only list the subjects who were hit as victims. I fired back: If the same scenario happened in Brentwood or Westwood, they all sure as hell would be listed as victims! I had no choice but to follow the law. I could see that Lynch was about to burst with fire and brimstone, but he was well aware that I was right.

I was committed at this point to saying what everyone in the Bureau wanted to say to Lynch regardless of his retribution and from those in higher places. I brought up his obsession with mandating high-arrest numbers to justify the existence of the unit with piss-ant arrests like "drinking in public," a worthless infraction with no more teeth than getting a traffic ticket. Our units would sweep through parks or neighborhoods and arrest countless groups of gang members and anyone who resembled a gang member for drinking in public.

In fact, once or twice a year, a platoon of METRO officers would come to assist the CRASH officers to see who could bring in the most arrests in a single p.m. watch. This was a shameful waste of time, money, and manpower that could have been spent on tracking down the real hard-core gang members.

Several of the unit's sergeants had pressed the Lieutenant for years on doing away with this worthless obsession of his "high arrest numbers." Their approach was to concentrate our unit's efforts on hard-core gang members and their leaders, to dismantle their leadership to demoralize them into nonexistence. I suggested that if the department was really serious about forever stopping the gang murders in L.A.'s neighborhoods, the unit should be increased to divisional strength.

I was all in at this point, and there was no turning back. I told Lynch he had it all wrong about our unit making all those dope arrests. The penalty for personal possession or possession for sales of drugs was exponentially more punitive than that bullshit arrest for drinking in public. Drug arrests would put these gangsters in prison for years and make the streets much safer for the public.

At this point, Lynch was about to explode but knew that I was right again. He let me finish but told me that from now on, I had to call a supervisor out to every shooting scene I was handling and get permission to list who and who was not a victim on the crime report.

Then he told me to get the fuck out of his office.

I knew I was on the Lieutenant's menu, but I was on the side of right, and all of my commendations justified my confidence.

My latest rating report read:

> *Officer Moreno has distinguished himself as one of the more aggressive O.C.B. CRASH field officers on the night watch. He has the ability to immediately recognize those gang members who are prone to gang violence and his experience and field knowledge enable him to concentrate his efforts effectively in the most active gang areas. His tactics in routine and stress situations are exceptional and he utilizes other CRASH units in a team effort in order to maintain complete control. Moreno's overall duty performance contributes toward the attainment of CRASH goals in lowering gang crime, and his work stamina sets an example for other less productive officers to follow.*
>
> *Moreno is alert to respond to possible gang-related radio calls and assume investigative responsibility if it is within CRASH criteria. He continues his quality arrest or investigation with thorough reports that reflect his hard work and contain the necessary elements for successful prosecution. Regardless of how hectic the situation may be, Moreno never compromises completeness for speed.*
>
> *Officer Moreno displays particular skill when handling armed suspects, as he recovers more weapons in the field than any other CRASH officer yet has avoided involvement in an Officer Involved Shooting.*
>
> *—Sergeants Noetzel, Wynn, Kenerson, Detective III States, Lieutenant Lynch, and the new Central Bureau Commander G. A. Morrison, September 2, 1979*

In retrospect, I couldn't have been more wrong about my future in the unit. It was an immature, myopic view of the big picture. I pissed off management, and the Lieutenant was well connected and supported by powerful forces in the department's hierarchy. It was just a matter of time before he got his pound of flesh for my unbridled temerity in calling him out.

It was a career death sentence, and I never saw it coming.

—

Meanwhile, Westside 18th Street was still immersed in their two-front war against Harpys and Echo Park, and again, innocent nongang members like twenty-year-old Michael Mitchell from Montana paid the ultimate price. Michael was mistaken for a Harpys gang member and gunned down in cold blood by Rocky Glover, founder and leader of Westside 18th Street.

Entire neighborhoods went into virtual lockdown in fear of being the next Michael. Mothers would not let their children go outside and play after school in fear of their taking a bullet from the daily drive-by shootings. Mothers and young girls were looking over their shoulders when they walked to the corner store in fear of being robbed, kidnapped, or raped. Tens of thousands of innocent Angelinos were living this nightmare 24/7, and God help you if you ever stood up to the marauding vermin on the streets.

A May 3, 1979 *Los Angeles Times* article, "She Stood Up to Gangs, but Lost: Diminutive Landlady Evicted One of the Homeboys," by Jerry Belcher, brought this bête noire into prospective.[1]

> *To the gang that ran the neighborhood, Ramona Sanchez was "doing rata:" talking to the wrong people, snitching to the cops, causing trouble for the homeboys. And the gang could not let her get away with it. After all, she was just a lone woman, five feet tall and one hundred pounds, divorced, in her early thirties with no one to protect her. How would people in the Los Angeles barrio that the gang controlled react if this woman were allowed to defy them? So, they decided to make her pay a price for standing up to gang power, and at last, for standing up in a court of law and testifying against the gang's homeboys. It was a heavy price paid in installments over fourteen months.*
>
> *Twice, gang members beat her up for beginning eviction proceedings against one of their leaders who had decided he should live rent-free in one of the three small rental units ad-*

---

joining the modest barrio home Ramona owned. Once, the evicted gang leader's wife stabbed Ramona five times in the back and chest.

During the same attack, a male gang member stomped her, shattering her left ankle and right knee. The house and the rental units were vandalized again and again, sprayed with the gang's graffiti signature, riddled with pistol shots, pocked with shotgun blasts, hacked with hatchets.

The two people she loved most, her thirteen-year-old daughter and her crippled ninety-five-year-old grandfather, were repeatedly threatened and terrorized. One day, the old man, paralyzed and living out his last days, was wheeled out onto the front porch for a breath of air. He was "used for target practice" by gang members who fired all around the helpless old man, barely missing him.

Ramona Sanchez hung on. Walking with the aid of a cane, she went to court and testified against gang members involved in the terrorism—testimony that eventually would be instrumental in sending at least three of them to jail or California Youth Authority camps.

During one court session while Ramona was on the witness stand, a woman gang member sitting in the spectator's gallery said: "Bitch, I'm gonna kick your ass." Municipal Judge George W. Trammell III heard the threat, had the spectator arrested on the spot, found her guilty of contempt of court, and sentenced her to five days in jail.

Shortly after one of her court appearances, two shots were fired at Ramona, narrowly missing her. The next day she received a series of phone calls at her house. The message was the same: "We are gonna kill you!"

She told Detective Gary Derenia, one of the veterans of the Los Angeles Police Department's CRASH unit, about the latest attack and threat. She was scared and Derenia agreed that she had reason to be. "It was my belief," said Derenia, "that they probably would retaliate, so that afternoon I put

Jim McCann, my partner, and another officer, John Petievich, into her house for protection." An undercover police van with two other officers in it was parked nearby. That night, two pistol-packing teenage gang members launched the attack. There followed a running gun battle in which one suspect was wounded in the neck and the second spattered with shotgun pellets at long range.

No one in the Sanchez house was hurt. Detective McCann and Petievich, subsequently decorated with the police star for valor for their actions, also escaped injury. McCann was unstinting in his praise for Ramona Sanchez's cool courage during the shootout.

McCann said that when he took off in pursuit of the gunman, Ramona grabbed the portable radio transmitter he'd left behind and calmly used it to direct some police helicopters and other police to the scene of action. She also went to court again to give testimony against the two sixteen-year-old gunmen. They wound up in CYA (California Youth Authority) camp.

But even after the dramatic demonstration that the police would protect her, threats resumed against the gritty little woman. And at last, apparently, it was too much even for her—she told Derenia and McCann she wanted their help in getting out of the neighborhood. On August 3, 1979, on the basis of a petition in which Derenia detailed her trial by terror, a superior court judge ordered the county of Los Angeles to pay $600 to relocate Ms. Sanchez, her daughter, and grandfather to another part of the city.

Today, the woman referred to in this story as Ramona Sanchez—it is not her true name—lives with her daughter in a neighborhood miles from the old one. She uses another name. McCann and Derenia said the ordeal of Ramona Sanchez was extraordinary even in the tough neighborhood where she lived. "The amount of violence," said Derenia, "was extreme, atypical."

And, they also agreed, the woman was extraordinary as well. "She stood up," said Derenia. "Why? She just had more guts than most people." The detectives have not seen the Sanchez family since they relocated. They heard that the old man died of natural causes a few months after the move.

They also heard that Ramona Sanchez eventually was forced to sell the little house she had so doughtily defended, and at a loss. The house was razed some time ago. Today, nothing remains except the weed-grown foundation. Even the gang graffiti is gone.

The shameful truth is these true stories of Michael Mitchell and Ramona Sanchez are not the exception to the rule. I personally experienced the same type of intimidation and murder in my neighborhood as a child and young adult in the 1950s and 1960s growing up in the Florence and Watts communities of Los Angeles. It was daily terror for all the families in the barrio.

Any civilized society must have zero tolerance for such inhuman behavior. Yes, I grew up in a shithole with an abusive, alcoholic, ex-con father, with eleven brothers and sisters, and we were extremely poor. I was a pathetic D and F student all through grade and high school because of an undiagnosed case of dyslexia, and if that wasn't enough, I was crippled for four years. I got in trouble with the law as a young man. So, don't anyone dare try to feed me the bullshit and perennial excuses that those raised in the barrio and hood haven't got a chance to make it in America.

If ever Commander Vernon's roll-call dictum was applicable then, it is now sorely overdue. Is grabbing or pushing a gang member under exigent circumstances "improper tactics" or "excessive force"? Is using tactical language when dealing with a violent, armed gang member inappropriate? Michael Mitchell and Ramona Sanchez's families, friends, and neighbors can answer that question. Can you?

—

Our unit received a tip that some suspects from Varrio Alpine wanted for the rat-pack murder of Raul Sierra (aka Caveman) were going to be at one of their Rampart hangouts on Custer Street, a cul-de-sac south of Sunset Boulevard cradled between the 101 and 110 Freeways. I was working with Dean Brinker that night. Poppin' Fresh and Rudy De La Fuente had our six. When we drove into the cul-de-sac, we saw three gangsters standing on the sidewalk on the northeast corner. As we approached the three, we could see two of them fumbling with a handful of tinfoil packets of PCP.

We ordered them to place their hands behind their heads and assume the position to pat them down for weapons. There was a bright street lamp directly overhead, and we could clearly see their faces. Shit, they were mad-dog "dusted" (under the influence of PCP). Their eyes were bloodshot with that characteristic crazy gaze, and we could smell the overwhelming odor of ether. We all knew this wasn't going to end well.

We continued to order them to place their hands behind their heads, but they refused to comply. We drew our batons in a demonstration of force to cow them into compliance—no luck. The two suspects holding the tinfoil bundles moved their hands to their backs and dropped the bundles, as if we couldn't see what they did—that's how stoned they were. At this point, the four of us closed on them to force them into compliance. The fight was on: baton strikes, punches, and kicks flew in all directions. All that cool shit they teach you in the Academy about compliance goes out the window in the real world of street combat.

All three suspects were dusted to the max, and this street brawl wasn't going to end any time soon. Fortunately, a couple Rampart patrol units rolled up and got into the fur ball with us, and at one point I lost my baton. Good thing, because half of the baton blows were friendly fire—we were beating the hell out of each other from the deflecting and misguided strikes. In the midst of the brawl, I felt an excruciating pain in my right hand and instantly knew something really, really bad was up. A couple more Rampart patrol units came screaming in a few moments later and finally cuffed these fucks. Poppin' Fresh walked up to me and asked what was wrong. Damn, he and all the rest of the guys were a mess, their uniforms were torn and splattered in blood—and he was asking me what was wrong; Lord, talk about a brotherhood!

When I finally brought my right hand up for a look, oh God—the right ring finger was crushed all to hell and fixed at a ninety-degree angle straight downward. Poppin' Fresh threw me in his car and rolled Code-3 to White Memorial Hospital in Hollenbeck. By the time we arrived, both my hands were badly swollen. The staff ordered x-rays. The right ring finger was broken in three places at the joint of the metacarpal. The left hand had two separate hairline fractures on the small bones of the palm. The pain became unmanageable at this point, but I was told that I had to wait for the on-call orthopedic surgeon before they could give me any pain medication.

It was almost two hours before he arrived, and by then I was about ready to eat my gun. The surgeon examined the x-rays and told me he needed to manipulate the break into the correct anatomical position. My right hand would need a plaster cast halfway up my forearm. My left hand also needed to be placed into a plaster cast, what the fuck! How was I going to do anything? Worst of all, I was going to be placed on the "Geek Squad" for God knows how long.

Poppin' Fresh stepped up and upholstered his .38, unchambered a bullet, then stuck it in my mouth. "Go doc, he'll be okay," he said. I bit down on the bullet and mumbled for the doctor to do his thing. The doc and nurse looked at us like we were crazy. The doctor went about pulling and twisting, then pulling and twisting some more. I never screamed, but I felt like I was going to pass out a couple of times. When he was done, I had just about chewed through that bullet. Poppin' Fresh and the other CRASH officers all had looks of revulsion—I thought they were about to hit the deck. When it was over, my shirt was drenched in sweat, and I felt like I had given birth to a twenty-pound baby. Both hands were in casts halfway up my forearms.

Back at the station, we booked the suspects on numerous charges including Felony Assault on a Police Officer, Possession of Phencyclidine (PCP) for Sale, and Possession of a Deadly Weapon. One of them had a "dirk" (Scottish dagger) in his waistband but fortunately never got a chance to use it on any of us.

We all got off on time for once and headed for our private watering hole under the First Street bridge. This dark, gritty, dissolute space of nothingness become our favorite open-air bar for the next few years. Although many of us had court the following morning, that didn't dissuade the lot of us from having one too many beers after watch. The nightly ritual of "choir practice" was an exorcism of sorts to purge our thoughts of the beastly behavior that we dealt with on a daily basis.

I have no idea what life was really like for the married men in the unit, but I damn sure know it wasn't good because hubby or Daddy was never home. He left for work in the early afternoon and didn't return until well after midnight. He hung out with his CRASH brothers after watch for a few beers, only to return home for a couple hours of sleep before heading off to court in the early morning. God bless their families!

My car Lady Aston was a stick shift, so the guys offered to drive me home; no thanks, Bros. Driving my beautiful lady was a bit tricky at first, but I learned to improvise and managed well enough.

I had a preliminary hearing in Division 35 the following day, and I wasn't going to miss this one for all the tea in China, although I could have been excused. Most street cops have an intrinsic loathing for defense attorneys and vice versa, and in this case, it was no different. The case involved six black gang members from Newton Division's Eastside Blood Stone Villains. The victim was forty-two-year-old Pablo Roldan, married with three little girls. It all started when he was walking to his second job on Main Street at Fifty-Fourth Street when he was stopped by a rat-pack of gangsters who surrounded him and demanded money. Pablo only had three dollars, but in fear for his life he reached for his wallet, at which time one of the thugs cold-cocked him, knocking him to the sidewalk. They all went into a frenzy of punches and kicks until Pablo looked like he had gone through a meat grinder. Moments later, steely-eyed Officer Frankie Flores, one of the smaller men in the unit but one not to piss off, and his partner, "Big Red" Mike McDonough, who looked like he was on leave from the Los Angeles Raiders' training camp, were hailed down by a citizen and told there was a dead man up the road. They stuffed the witness in the backseat of their car and alerted the other CRASH units working Newton about the attack.

When they arrived at the crime scene, they saw Pablo trying to get back on his feet; he was near death. Remarkably, Pablo was able to give Frankie and Big Red a detailed description of the six thugs. The hunt was on and the guys were pissed. They found all six fucks on Fifty-Second Street and recovered the blood-soaked three dollars crumbled up in one of the suspects back pants pockets.

Your generic street gangsters aren't rocket scientists—that's why our jails are overflowing with that pond of human excrement.

When we got to the preliminary hearing, the D.A. looked like shit. He was overwhelmed with an unmanageable case load like the rest of the city prosecutors and staff. On the flip side, the criminal defense attorneys were dressed like pimps, Rolex watches and all. The D.A. and the CRASH officers knew this wasn't going to go well for Lady Justice.

We all had our fingers crossed. But on cross-examination, it turned into a judicial gang attack by the suspects' six defense attorneys. Pablo couldn't even remember his first name by the time they were done with him. The suspect who had the three dollars in his back pants pocket said that he found the money. Everyone in the courtroom, including the judge, knew that was a lie of biblical proportions.

At the end of the hearing, the judge was unable to mask his contempt as he dismissed the case. All six defendants let out a primal scream in celebration, at which time the judge stood up off his chair, and about split his desk in two with his gavel. "There will be order in this court! If I hear so much as a breath of air come out of your mouths, I will hold all of you in contempt of court and have the bailiff take you all into custody!"

All of us felt like we needed a shower. The six gangsters walked out of the courtroom while all the CRASH officers circled around Pablo in a vivid demonstration of support and to convince the thugs that if they had any notion of retribution, we'd all be up their asses. Poppin' Fresh assured Pablo that he and the other CRASH officers would make it a point to drive by his residence every time we worked Newton and ask the Newton patrol officers to do the same. It was unbearable watching Pablo slowly walk away, knowing that he knew there was a strong chance the gangsters would seek revenge on him and his family. This had all the earmarks of another Ramona Sanchez tragedy.

The gangsters were still celebrating their victory at the end of the hallway. A Will Rogers quote came to mind: "I don't think you can make a lawyer honest by an act of legislature. You've got to work on his conscience. And his lack of conscience is what makes him a lawyer."

After that day I was on I.O.D. (injured on duty) status, and I was not required to attend court until I was released by the doctors to return to work.

It was Christmastime 1979, and for the first time in five years, I would have the holidays off. Many of the single guys on the job volunteered to work the holidays so the married guys could be with their wives and children. It was just the right thing to do.

The sixty-three days that I was on I.O.D. status were both restorative and plagued by a sense of emptiness and guilt. My R & R buttressed my faith in the human condition in the tranquil setting of Hermosa Beach. But I'd often catch myself thinking just how far removed these folks were from life in the barrio and hoods.

I hadn't seen or spoken to Susan in months. The last time we spoke, she told me she had completed her certification to work in the O.R. and she loved it. She also mentioned that she was seeing a doctor she met in the O.R.

Our relationship was indeed unique. I know she felt someday we would come to our senses, get married, and have a family. But we were so immersed in our careers that we lost sight of what life was really all about.

My stewardess neighbor Brandy invited me to her twin sister Laura's Christmas party in Manhattan Beach. Laura also flew for United and was married to Harry, a wealthy insurance broker for Lloyd's of London who was surprisingly unpretentious for being so wealthy. They owned a beautiful beachfront property on the Strand between Second and Third Street. The Christmas party guests were comprised of Harry's fellow brokers, attorneys, physicians, and the like. I had little in common with this cerebral lot, but I could hold my own with them in subjects other than their professional disciplines.

Unfortunately, Laura at one point mentioned that I was a police officer. And, as always, here came the ignorant questions about some bullshit ticket they got. Isn't it true that the police have ticket quotas? There were questions about police brutality and cops shooting down innocent citizens on the street. This is precisely why cops keep an insular circle of friends; America doesn't have a clue! Your run-of-the-mill citizens aren't cop haters, they just live in what I call "different conditions" when it comes to comprehending what their Keepers of the Gate experience on a daily basis.

I quickly learned how to stop the ignorant questions in their tracks. I would tell them I worked the gang wars in Los Angeles and hadn't written a ticket in years. Then I would go on to tell them a story or two of one of the more graphic gang killings that I could think of. That would upset their sensibilities so much that they immediately changed the subject. It worked every time. Brandy knew exactly what I was doing and would always get a kick out of the listener's response—pure horror and revulsion. Brandy and I spent many lovely evenings with Laura and Harry at their beachfront home that winter.

New Year's is my favorite of all the holidays. I suspect because it is a time of renewal and hope for a better future for mankind. Brandy was working that New Year's, so I "flew" with TWA, Cherry, a close friend and lover. Cherry was a bit crazy; she loved making love in the most unique places—and I mean anywhere. The response from the shocked voyeur was priceless. She was also a screamer, which pushed even my limits, but Cherry was a bombshell, and a man's gotta do what a man's gotta do.

The time off from the job also gave me an opportunity to see more of Mom and the kids.

So much had changed at 7932 Lou Dillon Avenue. The lovely trees that once graced the neighborhood sidewalks were long gone. The iceman who delivered the blocks of ice for our ice-box (before refrigerators) was gone. The fish man who delivered the wonderful, fresh catch-of-the-day from the nearby San Pedro and Los Angeles waters—he was gone, too. The Helm's doughnut truck no longer thrilled the children with its assortment of magical pastries.

However, there was one thing that never changed in the barrio—the mindless butchery of one another.

There were only four kids remaining in the Moreno household. Robert was working for a car parts company in Vernon. Alfie had a good job with the Edison Company. Ricky went from job to job, looking for his place in the sun. And Cristina was a freshman at Saint Matthias Catholic all-girls school in Huntington Park.

Seeing Mom was always such a deep joy for me. She was still struggling with the loss of Dad and her father, exacerbated by the death of her favorite neighbor and protector of the Moreno family, Spanky, from across the street. But Mom was still strikingly beautiful.

At times, I wondered if she had a "Dorian Gray" portrait of herself hidden in some attic. She was ageless. She still turned heads at almost fifty-eight.

—

One night after some drinks at the Short Stop, I was low on gas and needed to find a service station before I hopped on the freeway for Hermosa Beach. I couldn't find an open one anywhere, so I headed for Alameda Street. Enroute, I caught a red light southbound on Alameda at Sixth Street. All was calm at this precise moment in the City of the Angels. I had a mild buzz, and there was a sweet tranquil rain coming down while I listened to one of the most beautiful songs I've ever heard, "Yesterday When I was Young," by Roy Clark, where he sings *"The taste of life was sweet as rain upon my tongue..."*

After the sweet melody's ebb and flow, I reached down to change the station.

When I looked back up, all had turned to hell! A Hispanic man ran into the intersection, chased by four knife-wielding Hispanic suspects. The attack was really strange—once the victim reached the intersection, he started running in circles, trailed by all four suspects, one behind the other in single file. The lead suspect was armed with a foot-long kitchen knife and the others had smaller blades.

The victim was dressed in a white long-sleeve shirt covered in blood, most of it on his back. Each time the lead suspect got close enough, he plunged the knife into the victim's back. Miraculously, the victim didn't go down. Then I understood why the victim was running in circles. He had spotted my car and hoped I would help him.

A million thoughts raced through my head. I knew that if I didn't come to his aid, he was a dead man. However, there were four suspects, and my gun hand was in a cast. I also considered the crazed mind-set of these knife-wielding murderers. Unlike a suspect who shoots his victim, stabbing someone to death requires a greater commitment of evil. When you shoot someone, you're standing back and letting the bullet do the killing. When you knife someone, it's close and personal.

The killer has to force the steel into the victim's body and can feel the action of the thrust and sees the victim's agony at close range.

How was I going to hold my off-duty, piss-ant, two-inch, five-shot .38 revolver without dropping it from the recoil? I was acutely aware of the worthlessness of the knockdown power of the .38. Each round would have to be a perfect headshot to take these crazed fucks down, all four of them! It was also raining—what if I slipped and fell? I'd be butchered to death.

I thought of John 15:13: "What greater love hath no man than this, that a man lay down his life for his friends." I didn't know this man, but he was a human being. I reached down to my ankle holster and took my piece out, then route-stepped toward the four suspects with my Marine Corps war face.

By now, they had surrounded the victim in the center of the intersection. I could see the blood dripping from their knives. When I looked into their crazed faces, it was like trying to stare down Satan himself. When I got within their striking range, I let out a scream that raised the hair on the back of my neck. "*Deja la puta cuchillo!*" (Drop the fucking knife!) Oh, hell yes, I used tactical language!

It was a stand-off as I traversed the barrel of my .38 from face to face. Just then, the victim collapsed from loss of blood and the four suspects bolted away.

At that very moment, I saw a lone black-and-white drive into the intersection. It was a Central Division morning watch sergeant. I flashed my badge at him and he pulled up. I suspect he thought that I shot the victim lying in the street, but realized what had happened when I reached into his car and put out a crime broadcast on his radio. A horde of motivated Central morning watch coppers flooded the area and found and arrested three of the four suspects.

When I told the sergeant and a couple of the coppers standing next to him what went down, they all looked at each other with a "what the fuck!" The two Central coppers told me that the supervisor asked for a copy of the report and said he's talking about putting me up for the Medal of Valor for this crazy shit.

This was the second time I was told something to that effect—first by Sergeant Terry Cunningham at Hollywood Division when I shot Eric Vincent Bell through the legs instead of killing him. I never heard anything after either of these two incidents from the department, but truly, I couldn't care less. I've never been into that hero bullshit anyhow. I knew that these incidents put a smile on our Creator's face, and that was good enough for me. When I reflect on those life-or-death incidents where I didn't use lethal force, it gives me an indescribable sense of serenity.

—

After sixty-three painful days, the doctors removed my casts and gave me the okay to return to the streets with my CRASH brothers.

The whole time I was on I.O.D. status, Poppin' Fresh kept me in the 411 of what was going down in the unit. The city's Praetorians were kicking serious gangster ass, not to mention the historic law enforcement arrests made by Detectives Gerry Derenia and his bookend Jim McCann. They nailed Rocky Glover, the leader of 18th Street, for the Michael Mitchell murder. Glover, was good for at least half a dozen other 187s (murders), but this one nailed him for good.

Derenia and McCann were without equal when it came to solving gang-related cases. Their union as partners was nothing short of mythical. After their out-of-the-box investigation that nailed Glover for the Mitchell murder, they went into a blitzkrieg that decimated the leadership of both Varrio Alpine and Westside Varrio Diamond Streets, two of L.A.'s oldest gangs. They arrested fourteen Alpine gangsters for the killing of twenty-two-year-old Raul Sierra, who was rat-packed to death with fists, kicks, and a nineteen-inch Japanese ceremonial sword.

Derenia and McCann went on to do their own "rat-pack" of sorts when they arrested eighteen Westside Varrio Diamond Street gang members, eight adults and ten juveniles, for the brutal armed robbery and assault of four unarmed Bank of America security guards. As many as forty-three gangsters were involved in this attack, but the security guards were only able to identify eighteen. These two separate mass arrests, one for murder and the other for armed robbery, were without precedent in California criminal jurisprudence.

My first night back, half the unit was assigned to Newton Division, and I was partnered up with Poppin' Fresh. When we worked together, we always carried two Ithaca shotguns, and if ever that proved to be a sound tactical move, it was this night.

Right out of roll call, an ambulance shooting came out at Seventh and Broadway, one of many known gathering places for the Westside 18th Street gang. When we arrived, both the victim and shooters were gone. However, there was a crowd of shoppers at the location, and they pointed to a thick trail of blood alongside the curb in front of a taco stand. The blood ended just before the intersection on Seventh Street. As usual, "no one saw anything."

Poppin' Fresh contacted CRASH-90 (the CRASH desk officer) to phone the local hospitals in the area to see if they had any gunshot victims. There were none. Shockingly, this was not unusual. Gangsters would do anything to avoid law enforcement's participation. They preferred to make things right on their own. If they thought their wounds were not life threatening, they either had one of their homies treat the wounds or found someone in the gang with connections to someone who worked in the medical field. This was seen as badass by their peers and raised their standing in the gang.

This was a Central Division caper, and we were assigned to work Newton this night. There was no way to confirm this crime was gang related, so we let Central Patrol pick it up from here.

Seconds later, another ambulance shooting call came out, this time in Newton. The shooting was on Ascot Avenue, a couple blocks west of the Pueblo Del Rio government housing projects.

Straightaway, Poppin' Fresh recognized it was a retaliation hit from a previous shooting he handled while I was I.O.D. It was between the 52nd Eastside Pueblo Bishop Bloods (EPBB) and the Southside Blood Stone Villains, both black gangs. Sweet-Ricky, an EPBB gang member, had shot an eleven-year-old girl, the sister to one of the Southside Blood Stone Villains, a couple weeks ago. Poppin' Fresh knew Sweet-Ricky lived on Ascot with his parents.

Sure enough, Poppin' Fresh was right. Sweet-Ricky was being treated by an R.A. unit crew on the street in front of his parents' house for a shotgun blast to his abdomen. The single blast was not meant to kill him straightaway. It was strategically placed so he would die a slow and agonizing death.

While the paramedics were scraping Sweet-Ricky off the street and placing him into the ambulance, a citizen screamed from the south corner of Fifty-Second street, advising us that there were two men with shotguns shooting some people at the projects. Poppin' Fresh figured that it was the Blood Stones taking care of more unfinished business. But for some reason, we had an unsettling feeling about this citizen that called us over—was it a setup for another cop ambush?

We slowly cruised about the project with one hand on our shotguns at our sides. The projects run from Fifty-First to Fifty-Fifth Street, all along Long Beach Boulevard. We spotted a huge group of pissed-off gangsters in front of the last building on the corner of Long Beach and Fifty-Fifth Street. If ever there were a time to demonstrate command presence, it was now. We radioed in for some backup and a couple of Newton patrol units flew in. Poppin' Fresh and I exited our car, each of us holding our shotguns at a high port. As we closed toward the group, we chambered a round and the gangsters instantly made a hole to an apartment entrance. We cautiously walked in with the four Newton coppers at our six.

There must have been at least thirty gangsters in the small apartment. Poppin' Fresh recognized a couple of them in the crowd. They were 92nd (Nine Deuce) Bishop Pueblo gangsters, and they all had murder in their eyes.

The first victim was nineteen years old, sitting on a soiled white sofa, his hands cradling his intestines. Like Sweet-Ricky, he had taken a single shotgun blast to the stomach. The second victim was an older man in his mid-thirties, covered with prison tattoos, grossly obese, with no shirt or shoes on. He was lying on the cement kitchen floor rolling from one end of the kitchen to the other. He, too was shot in the gut at close range and had voided all twenty-two feet of his small intestines. The hideous sight was amplified by portions of his entrails sticking to the cement floor at each end of the kitchen, still anchored to his abdomen.

Poppin' Fresh and I had seen enough horror by now to last a lifetime, but this one was a sight that would stay with us the rest of our lives. And there was more—just outside the apartment's rear door was a third victim, a black female in her middle teens missing her right leg below the knee. The killers spared her life but they wanted to leave a message. One of the witnesses walked up to me holding the severed body part, and I told him to stuff it in the freezer, thinking the doctors might be able to reattach it.

One didn't have to be a CRASH officer to know this was gang related. Then Sergeant Kenerson pulled up and asked me what we had. I told him the circumstances of both shootings. He told us to give it to Newton patrol because it was a dope-related shooting. He knew this would please the Lieutenant. This was bullshit of the first order! I got into an argument with him on the spot, but he left with strict instructions not to take either shooting report. The Newton coppers were used to it by now, so was the rest of the Bureau, Hollenbeck, Northeast, Central and Rampart. The Captain IIIs of all five divisions were livid because their patrol officers were forced to handle obvious gang-related crimes, thereby tying up calls for service in their respective divisions.

How Lieutenant Lynch got away with this for so many years always puzzled me, until I looked at the big picture. Subordinates, even captains, have to keep their mouths shut if they want to be promoted. I didn't have any aspirations for promotion other than becoming a P-III. I intended to play out the rest of my time on the mean streets of L.A. And I didn't keep my mouth shut.

Poppin' Fresh and I felt like shit pawning off both shootings to our Newton brothers. When we got into our car, he looked over at me and said, "Honey, just another day at the office." His dark humor soothed my spirit.

—

The following day after roll call, the Lieutenant was still in the CRASH office. It was obvious that Sergeant Kenerson told him about our argument the night before. He gave me a look of pure contempt before I walked out to my car. Poppin' Fresh had a couple days off, so I was working with one of the new guys, Officer Al Gonzalez. We were assigned to work Rampart that night, where 18th Street and Westside White Fence were blowing the hell out of each other and the innocents that were in the wrong place at the wrong time.

We were trolling the back streets of Baxter Avenue and Cerro Gordo on the north of Rampart Division. It was quiet there, but all that changed when we got a call for assistance on a multiple shooting from some of the other CRASH units at the very southern tip of Rampart. We took Alvarado southbound because it was the most direct route. As we approached Seventh Street, we saw a northbound vehicle swerve into the southbound number-one lane. Christ, he was going to kill someone unless we stopped him. However, we knew that we would catch hell for getting tied up on a DUI arrest while our CRASH brothers were desperately in need of assistance.

We made the stop anyway. The driver was polluted. I drove his vehicle into an abandoned lot while my partner placed the arrestee in the backseat of our car. I radioed Communications for a C.T.D. (Central Traffic Division) unit and she gave us a five-minute E.T.A. The five minutes turned into ten minutes, and the CRASH units down south were asking us where we were. We told them that we were stuck in traffic and would get there as soon as possible! By now, it was well over fifteen minutes, and there was just no way we could wait any longer. The suspect lived about a half mile away from our location, so we decided to lock his keys in his vehicle and drive him home, then drive like hell to the shooting scene.

Just as we started to drive off with the suspect, the C.T.D. unit pulled up alongside of us. I knew that the exchange of information, including dealing with the suspect's vehicle, was going to burn another ten minutes, and there was no way in hell we could wait that much longer.

I shouted out my window that we were unable to wait any longer and were driving the suspect to his residence to release him. When we drove off, I could see the C.T.D. officers didn't understand and they looked pissed! After dropping off the suspect, we headed for the shooting scene but were advised it was a Code-4 (all is secure).

Evidently, the C.T.D. officers complained to their supervisor, and their supervisor called the CRASH office to bitch about the incident. Of all the supervisors to take the call, it was Sergeant Kenerson. He fast-tracked it to Lieutenant Lynch, who ordered a 1.81 (personnel complaint) for Neglect of Duty. We were hammered with a five-day suspension without pay. I knew that if it had been any other CRASH sergeant, he would have understood.

Christ, I was still blind as a bat. The writing was on the wall, and I should have transferred out of the unit after the suspension, but I loved my job in CRASH and I was crushing it. A lot of the original guys in the unit had transferred out by now because of all the Lieutenant's bullshit. I should have followed their exodus.

Most of the original CRASH officers were in METRO Division now. That was exactly what I intended to do, but I needed to get promoted to P-III before I could apply. I was confident I'd nail the test when it came around, and my outstanding rating reports (along with fifty 1.27s) would lock me in for the spot. After three or four years in METRO, I planned to apply for "D" platoon SWAT, where I planned to spend the rest of my career.

A couple days into my suspension, I got a call from Officer **Brinker**. He was a big-time water skier and had his own beautiful white-and-powder-blue, eighteen-and-a-half-foot ski-boat. He told me that Danny Torrey, a patrol officer friend of his from Hollenbeck Division, was selling his ski boat for almost nothing. It was a Southwind, with an eighteen-and-a-half-foot racing hull, a 450-cubic-inch inboard engine, and Berkeley jet drive. It was painted in a brilliant red-and-yellow scheme. I'm a natural athlete, but I sucked at water skiing. Be that as it may, I was off to the credit union, and they came through for me once again. I got the boat for a steal at $5,000. I asked Mom if I could store the boat in her garage on Lou Dillon, and all was good.

—

When I returned to work from the suspension, I didn't sour up like some of the guys do after taking a big hit. I took the punishment and went back to the job I was born to do.

My first night back, I worked with ex-Secret Service Agent turned L.A.P.D., Officer Bill Menzel. He was one of the few remaining original CRASH officers and a joy to work with. Bill, Poppin' Fresh, and Dave Cantley were a perfect fit for me, and I recovered more guns in the field when I worked with this Praetorian triad. Bill owned a pit bull named Rocky, and there was nothing he didn't know and share with me about the breed. It was Rocky this and Rocky that all night, but he made it interesting.

We were back in Rampart that night working the 18th Street and White Fence war in the Silver Lake area. Since 18th Street had slowed its engagements with Echo Park and Harpys, they were moving to decimate Westside White Fence once and for all.

Bill was going on and on about Rocky when he suddenly screamed, "Gun!" I'll be damned, there were a couple of gangsters ten feet away from us on the corner, one handing the other this big-ass six-inch revolver. I figured the gangster with the gun was going to start firing at us, so I crouched down on my seat and reached for my gun, waiting for the barrage of bullets.

But hell, if I were going to die, at least it would be in a blazing gun battle face-to-face, and not cowering in the passenger seat of the car. I opened the door and bolted out, gun in hand. To my surprise, the armed suspect was running away.

The chase was like something you would see in a Hollywood movie. A suspect with a gun, and a cop running after him dodging traffic and narrowly being struck by skidding pissed-off motorists all honking their horns at the both of us. In full flight, the armed gangster looked back at me. I was within just two feet of him. Then he turned with the gun and made his move, raising the gun toward my face.

Instead of putting a bullet in his fucking head, I struck him over the top of the head with my gun. We both went down, and fortunately he lost the gun when he hit the deck. Bill came screeching in with our car and shielded us from being run over. He jumped out and pounded the suspect for a minute, then cuffed him. "What the hell, Al!" Bill yelled. "He narrowly killed you; why didn't you shoot?"

By now I could have been in three or four dozen justifiable Officer Involved Shootings, but I had this unique gift of walking the razor's edge and feeling bulletproof. I'm not saying that I wouldn't have put an asshole down if necessary. I fully understood that my actions in the field didn't stop with me alone—if I got it wrong, that could mean the death of my partner or perhaps an innocent bystander. There's absolutely no way in hell I would ever encourage any brother or sister officer to do what I've gotten away with so many times.

We took the suspect to the station to get booking approval for Attempted Murder of a Police Officer and Possession of the stolen gun. Sergeant Wynn didn't look any too pleased with my story of the incident. Then he loosened up and said, "Moreno, I've never met anyone else like you who would rather kick someone's ass instead of shooting them." We both started laughing, and he shook his head and walked away.

7

In Over My Head

IT WAS SPRING 1980, and I was crushing it with the assistance of my triad of badasses, Poppin' Fresh, Menzel, and Cantley. I received five commendations in April alone—three were for arresting armed gang members without capping a round in their ass—and God knows, they would have put me and my partner down if they had the chance! The other two were for arresting an escapee from the California Youth Authority who was doing time for multiple armed robberies, and the other arrest was for capturing a hard-core gang member wanted for an attempted murder. By the end of 1980, I received another ten commendations. However, that hard work and stellar performance didn't endear me to the Lieutenant, because I continued to take crime reports, if, in my expert opinion, they were gang related. This infuriated him.

I didn't have a lot of time off as I was working heaps of overtime, going to court, and working off-duty security jobs to pay for my apartment, Lady Aston, and my new badass ski boat. But when I could take two or three days off in a row, it was off to the Colorado River for water skiing with friends. Susan was still dating her doctor, Brandy was now dating a second officer for United, but Cherry couldn't wait to go water skiing with her lawman. She knew everything about pulling a boat, docking, launching, fueling, driving the boat, and pulling a skier. Oorah!

On the day of our trip, I got out of work early and picked up Cherry and Pamela, her partner in crime and a fellow TWA stewardess. We needed three people to go water skiing: driver, skier, and a flagman to watch the skier. Pamela and Cherry could have been sisters—both were in their midtwenties, blond, with blue eyes and great figures. The girls were flight attendants, so naturally they were prompt and prepared with everything we needed for the trip, including some eye-popping sexy outfits for the crazy pubs along the riverbank on the Arizona side of the lake. Cherry knew exactly where the best pubs were on the waterfront.

I borrowed my Uncle Inez's pickup truck to tow the boat. The river was a little under three hundred miles and more than eight hours away from Mom's. We had a couple of vodkas with orange juice on the way, and plenty of intellectual stimulation. Both Cherry and Pamela were very bright and had some college. Looks are the hook, but intellect is the cement to a successful long-term relationship.

Pamela suggested we all take a turn talking about our favorite subjects, starting with me. That was easy—my favorite subject is history, namely the Victorian Era, 1837 to 1901. I struggled to keep it short, not wanting to hog the time with my love of British history.

Pamela interrupted, "Wasn't Churchill one of Queen Victoria's prime ministers?" I advised that cerebral beauty that he was one of Britain's prime ministers, but not during Victoria's reign. Churchill served as PM twice, first in 1940 through the end of WW II, then once again from 1951 to 1955.

I mitigated my time on the stump to one or two facts about Victoria's four prime ministers, starting with Sir Robert Peel. Peel was responsible for the Metropolitan Police Act, encouraged by Wellington, and passed in 1829. Although it only encompassed the London police at the time, it laid the foundation for the modern-day New Scotland Yard.

I kept glancing at the girls while I was going on and on to see if I was boring them with what is perceived to be ancient and inconsequential history to most Americans. But they loved it. After tutoring my beauties about Queen Victoria's four favorite prime ministers—Lord Melbourne, Sir Robert Peel, William Gladstone, and Benjamin Disraeli—I closed with Winston Churchill, not one of Victoria's prime ministers, but my favorite prime minister and savior of the English people.

It was almost 9 a.m. when we finally arrived to a brilliant sunrise, and it was heavenly. Black Meadows Landing was located in a valley of sorts, surrounded by low desert hills, towering palm trees, and pristine sandy beaches. The river was like blue glass. The marina was low dollar, and the green two-story motel and café didn't look much better. But Mother Nature was at her best in this little patch of earth. I never imagined the desert could look so grand.

Cherry's family had been coming to the river since she was in her early teens, so she knew everything about this treasured place. Before we launched the boat, we went to our motel room and took a quick shower, then went down to the no-frills café for a bite. After some greasy ham and eggs and a cup of coffee that made Poppin' Fresh's CRASH brew taste like java roast gourmet, we headed out to my Southwind.

Cherry told me to ride shotgun while she backed the trailer into the water to launch the boat. Pam had water-skied for years as well. I parked the truck and trailer while Cherry and Pam anchored the boat a short distance from the beach. We loaded up the boat with the skiing equipment, an ice chest full of beer and goodies to eat, three beach chairs, large beach towels, and sunscreen.

Cherry took the helm for the first part of the day, showing me the ropes on driving, gassing up at the marina, pulling a skier, and a plethora of safety issues. It was late May, and there weren't a lot of people out on the lake as of yet. I watched Cherry's every move as she skillfully parked the boat next to the fueling dock and filled up.

Pam was first off on her single ski. She got up on the first try as Cherry drove toward Crazy Horse in Havasu, some fifteen miles upriver. It was spectacular watching Pam cut back and forth across the wakes at twenty-five miles per hour, leaving a giant rooster trail behind her.

A few miles before we got to Crazy Horse, Cherry drove into a large cove on the California side of the river to set up a day camp. We were the only skiers in the cove at this time, and it was magnificent. There we were, sitting on the beach in our lounge chairs while Cherry was fixing some screwdrivers. It didn't matter that the sun was roasting hot and we were sleep deprived—we had the world by its reproductive organs.

We were listening to the Rolling Stones' greatest hits. "Flight 505" came on, and Cherry and Pam started singing along at the top of their lungs, belting out "...*happy being on my own, living the life I lead...*"

Their ear-piercing sing-along echoed throughout the cove. Cherry called me out, "Corky, you're up." She loved my nickname. But I needed a little more time to visualize the technique, so I said, "Ladies first; you're next, Cherry." Pam took the helm and I rode shotgun. Lord, Cherry crushed it, and she looked hot as hell in her tiny bikini top.

After endless broad circles and hard turns, she dropped the ski line. Shit, it was my turn. I jumped into the warm calm water with the single ski, and Pam handed me the towline. Pam punched it, and the towline tore from my grip. I could see the care in Cherry's eyes as she handed me back the rope. "Corky, you have the ski much too straight up. Lower the front of the ski and tuck it into your chest and lean a bit forward right before the takeoff. You'll pop right up."

Unbelievably, it worked. I popped up but went down when I got cocky trying to jump the wake. I was hooked! Skiing would be a part of my life from here on out. Within a few runs, I managed to jump the wake and parallel the boat on the hard turns, but took some epic falls. We took turns for the next few hours and weren't a bit tired.

Cherry suggested to break camp and cruise upriver to Crazy Horse. She wanted to show me the whole river scene. This time I was at the helm driving my new beautiful Southwind inboard for the first time. I couldn't help putting the pedal to the metal to see what she could do. When the water calmed, it was like driving on glass. It got serenely quiet but for the thunderous sound of the 450 doing its thing. I looked at Cherry, then glanced back and smiled at Pam in the backseat. Their youthful, hard bodies were at the apex of their lives.

Being with Cherry and Pam made me think of my Ensenada trip with Claudette and her sister Lulu, my Southern Bell topless dancers. I met and dated Claudette weeks before I shipped out to Vietnam. We had the time of our lives at Hussong's Cantina. And now, I was with two new beauties. God is good!

When we arrived at Crazy Horse, we anchored the Southwind off the beach and set up a mini-base camp. After sunbathing for a while, having a few drinks, and absorbing the island's ambiance, we took a walk across the historic London Bridge. The bridge was built in the early 1800s across the River Thames. In 1971, it was dismantled brick by brick and numbered for reassembly, then transported to Lake Havasu City where it stands today, connecting Havasu City over the canal to the small island.

We stocked up on some more vodka and orange juice, Cherry's favorite drink. Pam is a health nut and grabbed some luscious plums, nectarines, and grapes, wonderful fresh meats and cheese from the market deli, tomatoes, lettuce, avocados, and fresh-baked baguettes. I bought a bottle of Gusano Rojo Mezcal, the same brand of Mexican hooch Claudette, Lulu, and I had in Ensenada eleven years earlier. And I planned on sharing that wild and crazy Ensenada story with the girls; I knew they'd love it.

It was starting to get dark by now, and we were exhausted. We headed back to Black Meadows, anchored the boat, and made for our rooms for a catnap. When we woke, it was still quite warm, and there was a brilliant full moon out.

Cherry suggested we head out for a cove not far off. I was a bit apprehensive about taking the Southwind out at night, but Cherry knew these waters like the back of her hand. The night boat ride was magical. Once in the cove, the girls stripped butt naked, and I followed suit for some river skinny-dipping. I've never been much of a swimmer—I narrowly drowned more than once back in my surfer days—so, after a short while, I got back in the boat. Cherry fixed us some drinks while Pam made some Dagwood sandwiches. The girls loved the mezcal, grub and all.

We never bothered to get dressed the whole time we were in the cove. A couple other boats anchored not far from us. The nearest one had four people in it, two guys and their girlfriends. They kept looking over at us and snickering at our unmasked bodies. Ten minutes later, one of the girls stood up and stripped, followed by the other three. Pam shouted out for them all to paddle their boats next to ours for a drink of mezcal. Within five minutes, all three boats were tethered together, sharing drinks and casual conversation. It was a short party; we needed to get back to our hotel and get some sleep.

The next morning. I felt and looked like shit. But when we went out again, I got up on the first try, on a single ski. But again, I got in over my head as usual, and paid dearly for my hubris with some spectacular hard falls.

Cherry wanted to show me Copper Canyon Cove, which got its name from the beautiful bronze steep cliffs. It is the Mecca for walking on the wild side, with a little too much drinking, crazy cliff climbing, and jumping off the near one-hundred-foot walls in the nude. The cove was saturated with boats by now. We all agreed it was getting a bit too unhinged, with too many kids drunk out of their minds, and headed for Crazy Horse instead.

It's difficult to describe just how wonderful all this was—the people, the weather, the river, the food and drink—only in America!

Throughout the day, Cherry kept talking about the "Strip," a chain of riverfront bars and restaurants a short distance south of Parker Dam on the Arizona side of the river. She told us that besides the great food, beverages, and rocking music, there were pool tables and video games to play. Around 6 p.m., we headed out for the chain of bars. Our first stop was Sundance, and it was everything Cherry said it would be. It was filled with vacationers and locals out for a night of fun and debauchery. The girls looked radiant with their golden tans, blond hair, and sexy spring dresses. We had no problem making new friends.

Next, we were off for Fox's, then to the Roadrunner, the best place, where we spent the rest of our night meeting skiers from both Arizona and California. Pam met Fredrick, a second officer for Pan American and a former Navy Grumman A-6 Intruder pilot in Vietnam. Pam nicknamed him the Red Baron, after Manfred von Richthofen, the dreaded German fighter pilot of World War I.

The Baron looked straight out of central casting—tall, blond, with piercing green eyes. We partnered up for some pool, Cherry and I versus the Baron and Pam. It developed into a kind of Marines versus Navy thing. To be completely honest, the Marines took heavy casualties that night. The Baron could run the table with one eye closed. The next day, the four of us were off for a day of unabashed skiing.

It was getting late, and it struck me that I would never make it back to work on time for 3 p.m. roll call on Friday. I needed to call the CRASH office for a special (day off). Sergeant Kenerson answered the phone; I immediately hung up. There was no way in hell that Witchetty Grub would give me a special. I called back a half hour later and kept my fingers crossed. Eureka! Sergeant Raul Vega answered the phone.

Vega—like the "Righteous Brothers," Sergeants Mike Wynn and Ray Noetzel—was a no-nonsense supervisor with a famed badass past, but he, too would do anything for his men. I told him straight out what I was doing, no excuses. He said things were really heating up on the street, but he would give me a *by-your-leave* just this once. "But Al, get your ass back here by Saturday, or it will be my ass with the Lieutenant!"

Meeting the Red Baron was great. Now Pam had someone to be with. We closed out the bar, returned to the Landing, and for the first time, got a little over four hours sleep. Best of all, Cherry didn't snore that night. A little after 7 a.m., there was a thunderous search-warrant-type knock on the door. It was Pam and her Manfred von Richthofen. We all headed down to the café for breakfast and played it safe, again ordering pancakes like the day before.

We set up camp in no time and took turns skiing. The girls knocked it out, the Baron went supersonic. Throughout the day, I never got it and took some epic falls. I was done for the day and stopped before I broke my neck. At noon, I helped Pam prepare the Dagwoods, and we all chilled for the rest of the day on our little beachhead. We were heading back home in a few hours, so we kept the Kamikaze drinking down to a few rounds. The conversations were mostly about the Baron's and stewardesses' experiences with passengers on their flights, and it was nonstop laughing at some of the craziest stories. The Baron and I didn't get into our Vietnam experiences because it wasn't the right time or mood for death and destruction stories.

We planned to leave for home at about midnight, which would get us home by about 8 a.m. We mostly talked the rest of the day and headed back to Black Meadows around 5 p.m. We went back to Sundance that evening, boat in tow, for dinner and a couple drinks. After saying good-bye to Pam's new flame, we were off for L.A. a little after 11 p.m. The drive wasn't bad, and we got to Mom's a little after 9 p.m. Cherry and Pam helped wash the boat. We said good-bye to Mom and returned the pickup to Uncle Inez. We got back to the Gallery a little after 1 a.m., and after a catnap, it was back to protecting the widows and orphans.

Before that summer was over, we got back to the Colorado River three more times. The Baron met Cherry, Pam, and me at Black

Meadows twice, and he brought his beautiful nineteen-foot-deep lime pickle-fork with a monstrous blown racing engine. He had it tricked out with Bassett headers and a V-drive.

Meanwhile, things were heating up in the City of the Seraphs. While I was off, the unit handled the largest single gang-related shooting in California history. Nine Westside 18th Street gang members were gunned down at 1700 South Burlington Avenue, just south of Pico Union in Rampart Division. The victims were partying when three Harpys gangsters snuck up and opened fire with two shotguns and a rifle.

This shooting was different from the usual drive-by shooting. The three Harpys shooters used what can only be described as military tactics—after they shot the victims, they stayed and methodically checked each victim for signs of life. If the victims showed any singes of life, they fired a coup de grace to the head. After executing the first three and moving on to the fourth victim, they heard a siren screaming and bolted.

In an attempt to expedite the investigation into this ruthless slaughter, the bureau commander assigned a special nine-man task force to exclusively work the Rampart murders. The special team of homicide investigators was spearheaded by our detectives, Gary Derenia and Jim McCann. Within a week of the murders, Derenia and McCann had the three shooters in custody, including full confessions from all three. Yes, these were mythical homicide detectives!

A week later, the exhausted detectives stumbled into an unrelated carjacking-shooting in progress. Three Capone Gang members had just murdered two innocent men who had hesitated to surrender their vehicle in a carjacking. They then set the car ablaze to destroy any evidence. After the murders, the suspects attempted a second unsuccessful carjacking. This was when they saw Derenia and McCann in their plainclothes police vehicle. They all opened fire on the two detectives, striking their vehicle over twenty-five times.

Derenia and McCann returned fire but quickly ran out of ammo with their worthless six-shooters, leaving them at the mercy of the suspects' superior weapons and firepower. They slumped down in their seats to reload, then bolted from the safety of their vehicle to reengage the suspects.

If ever there were divine intervention, it was this night. Gary, Jim, and their murder suspect crowded in the backseat were not hit. The lone female in the second carjacking also escaped uninjured.

Minutes after the shooting, it seemed that every black-and-white in the department had responded to the Officer Needs Help call broadcasted by McCann. Everyone gasped at the condition of the police vehicle. It looked like it had been hit by a Dillon Aero Gatling gun. What was equally astonishing was Lieutenant Lynch's on-scene response to Gary and Jim. After asking them if they were okay, he quickly proceeded to admonish them for having their ties loosened.

Commander Mark Kroeker, the new Central Bureau commander, was within earshot when Lynch was getting into Gary and Jim's shit about their ties. He went sideways and got into Lynch's ass in front of all the troops. Good thing, because the street cops were fixing to stick their size-twelves up the Lieutenant's ass.

We all learned later that the only reason Lynch responded to the shooting scene was because Commander Kroeker ordered him to do so. Our CRASH office was now headquartered in the sprawling Central Division building, and our new office was next to the Bureau Commander's office. When the Officer Needs Help call came out and identified as CRASH officers screaming for help, Kroeker flew out of his office and saw Lieutenant Lynch through the open door just sitting in the office, ignoring the call. Lynch was still pissed off at Gary and Jim because they were temporarily assigned to Rampart.

⁓

Summer turned to autumn, and then it was Christmas season once again, with no mercy on the gang-infested streets of Los Angeles. By now, only a few of the original CRASH officers were still in the unit.

As much as I loved my job in CRASH, it was time to get the hell out and join my former CRASH brothers in METRO before the Lieutenant got another shot at my ass.

Cherry had left the Gallery apartments and moved out of state for some new assignment with TWA. Brandy and I continued to date, but it was never really going anywhere. I dated some of the other girls at the Gallery, but it was just reciprocal fun stuff. Then that December, I got a call from Susan.

I was really excited because we hadn't seen each other for some time. She asked me to meet her at Fat Face Fenner's Falloon, the restaurant where we first met years ago. I couldn't wait and thought this might be the right time to close the deal. We truly were perfectly suited for one another. I lost Danique to the department, and I wasn't about to lose Susan for anything in the world. I mean, how many chances does a man get in his lifetime for the perfect match?

I'll never forget our meeting. It was a Thursday, and she looked as radiant as the first time we met. Her hair was much longer now, and she still had a trace of summer on her lovely face. She was dressed in tight jeans and a dark-green, long-sleeved blouse. Then my heart sank to the deck—she had an engagement ring on her finger big enough to choke a horse. She saw the shock on my face and gave me a hug, saying, "I needed to tell you in person, Al."

We took a table and ordered a double-shooter of the best tequila in the house. Her eyes watered up when she saw the overpowering lament in my face. She reached out for my hand. "Al, I'm sorry. I always thought you were the one."

As we exchanged sweet stories of our past, I was struck with an overwhelming epiphany. I would never marry and have a family. My beloved Los Angeles Police Department was to be my bride—not Danique, not Susan, not anyone.

I needed to know something about the man she was going to marry. She told me his name was Aaron, he was a year younger than she was, originally from Dallas, and owned a home in Malibu. His parents were in the oil business and so was he. When I looked at that rock on her finger, I knew this guy must have been very wealthy.

She told me her girlfriend Diana introduced her to Aaron. Diana was now married to Rob, a Pan Am second officer. Both Rob and

Aaron owned an A.T-6 Trainer and shared the same hanger in Compton Airport. I asked Susan if she had a picture of Aaron. When she showed it to me, I was amazed. He looked like he could be the Red Baron's younger brother; he was super good-looking. Aaron was also into sailboat racing; he owned and raced a Schock 35'. Susan had fallen into the lifestyle of the rich and famous. Frankly, I wasn't surprised. She was born for that lifestyle. She would end up with a beachfront home in Malibu, while I got the blood-soaked streets of L.A.

After a couple hours, we went our separate ways in life, and I never saw or heard from her again, just like with Danique.

—

For the first time in my life, I backed off the dating scene and completely immersed myself in work. I closed out the last deployment period in 1980 on fire with arresting more armed suspects than anyone in the unit. Even Lieutenant Lynch couldn't ignore that fact when he stated, "Moreno has an uncanny ability to find and arrest armed suspects."

Even Sergeant Kenerson couldn't ignore my prowess for gun arrests. He wrote this 1.27: "On 12-19-80, Officers Moreno and McCorkle recovered two handguns on two separate incidents...both officers are to be commended for their attention to duty, initiative, and their thorough investigation, possibly preventing acts of gang violence."

This was the thirteenth consecutive day in a row that I arrested a gang member with a gun without shooting him. The day after the hot streak, I was called in out of the field by the "Righteous Brothers," Mike and Ray. They told my partner to wait outside the office. I had no idea of what was up. Did I screw up, or what? Mike and Ray told me that I was "too hot," and they feared "Murphy's Law" was lurking at the door. They worried that some gangster was going to luck out and put a bullet in my head.

They asked me if I would consider working the desk for a couple days to chill out. "Al, you can call one of your girlfriends to hang out with you in the office and take all the time you want for Code-7," they told me. I will never forget that incredible gesture of concern. I thanked them and returned to the "Gladiators Arena."

Four weeks later, Lieutenant Lynch called me into his office after roll call. He told me I would be assigned to desk duty that coming weekend. Evidently, a local news agency was going on a ride-along to do a story on L.A.'s gangs. I told him desk duty is considered by all as a punishment. He refused to give me an explanation and ordered me out of his office.

I was furious and made no effort to conceal my objections. The Lieutenant feared I was going to tell the reporter about him "cooking the books" in an effort to conceal the true number of gang-related crimes in the city.

The citizens of Los Angeles would have to wait another seven years before the department's dirty little secret was exposed by Sherman Block, Sheriff of Los Angeles County, on February 19, 1988. He confessed to the five-member Board of Los Angeles County Supervisors that Los Angeles police agencies were underreporting the gang crime stats.

Gang Crimes Understated[2]

Several law enforcement officials who attended a summit meeting on gang violence last week admitted that political pressure in their communities has led to an under-reporting of gang-related crime, Los Angeles County Sheriff Sherman Block said.

In a report to the Board of Supervisors, Block called the meeting a success and said that the participants recognized that the number of gang-related crimes in the county is increasing. But Block told the board that the actual number could be much higher because several law enforcement officials said "political pressure" resulted in some crimes not being listed as gang related.

Afterwards, Block declined to identify the law enforcement officials or their communities but explained, "What they ad-

---

[2] Copyright © 1988 *Los Angeles Times*. Used by permission.

mitted was that in some communities, statistical profiles were set up so they could report the crimes but it would not come across as gang related.

"The obvious intent was to reduce the potential beer level of people coming into the community," he said. Block added that he and other law enforcement officials will press for "more accurate, objective reporting" of gang-related statistics.

Three days later, on January 20, 1981, Lieutenant Lynch called me back into his office. He told me that I was "Administratively Transferred" to Northeast Division patrol. I fell into a state of shock and disbelief. I so dearly loved my job in CRASH, but there was nothing I could do about it.

The following day, I was back to working the armpits of the department patrol. I got on well with the coppers and supervisors at Northeast and partnered up with Officer Bill Wong. Of all the special human beings I met on Mother Earth, Bill become my best friend, ever. This fateful friendship would end in an unthinkable tragedy a couple years later.

Bill did not fit the perceived stereotype of a Chinese American man. At about 185 pounds, he was built like a world-class light heavyweight boxer. He was a martial arts expert and on occasion brought a set of *nunchakus* to work for a flawless demonstration of blazing moves. Bill went to Fremont High School in South Central Los Angeles, and he sounded more like a soul brother when he spoke than a second-generation Chinese American. In short, Bill was one badass natural street cop. We became inseparable and my family loved him.

Bill's parents, Henry and Helen, were from Guangzhou (Canton) in southern China and spoke little English. When they left Canton, they moved to Montebello, California, where Bill was born. I used to relish the times when he invited me to his home for dinner. He had moved back home with his parents after a contentious divorce. His mom and pop were very traditional, which meant visitors removed their shoes before entering their home. His mom was a gourmet cook, and she set a beautiful traditional dinner table with white linens, the finest porcelain, and home-cooked Cantonese cuisine. Everyone at the table used chopsticks.

Dinner with Bill at Mom's was nowhere near as formal, but he absolutely loved Mom's Mexican dishes. In the coming spring and summer, Bill became my new skiing partner. We also made a couple of crazy fun trips to Acapulco and Mazatlán, Mexico.

Bill made working patrol palatable and fun at times. Northeast was somewhat like Venice Division in that it wasn't crazy with calls for service, which gave us time for preemptive policing to excise the cancer before it metastasized on the innocent public. I shared my gang expertise with him and my Northeast patrol brothers and supervisors. Northeast Division was infected with the same disease as the rest of Central Bureau. Some of the more problematic Hispanic gangs were Toonerville on the northeast end of the division, Frogtown on the southeast, Cypress Park on the south and southwest, and, the most murderous of all, the Avenues.

Between the radio calls, I instinctively went into my CRASH mode. Bill, like my Hollywood patrol partner John Gamble, was a perfect match for me, and we were on a continuous hot streak with high-quality gangster arrests. We recovered heaps of guns.

On March 7, 1981, I spotted Ralf Castillo, a violent Avenues gang member who I had arrested before while working CRASH. He was standing in front of a busy supermarket showing another gang member his gun. It was just getting dark and the two hadn't seen us yet. Bill put out an "Officer Needs Assistance, Man with a Gun" call. Then we rolled up hard on them and barricaded ourselves behind our car doors. We ordered Castillo to drop the gun. He bolted inside the market, and the other suspect fled down the street.

Our backup units hadn't arrived as of yet, and we feared that Castillo would end up taking hostages, possibly resulting in innocents being murdered. Bill looked dead into my eyes and said, "Fuck it, partner, let's go."

As we entered the market, people were running out in groups, some yelling and screaming, holding their children. I took the right side of the market and Bill went left. We cleared one aisle at a time, then Bill pointed to the suspect cowed behind a double-food display rack. Instead of lighting that asshole up (shooting him), he rushed him and martialed arts his ass like a buzz-saw.

Castillo was armed with a .45 semi-automatic that had been taken in a Bakersfield burglary. Lieutenant II, Jim Troutman, commanding officer of Detectives, and Captain III, Smithson, commanding officer of Northeast Division, wrote us up for the Obs arrest.

A week after that, Bill was off and I was working an L-car (one-man unit) when I arrested another gang member with a gun. It, too was stolen in a burglary. Then on May 16, Bill and I arrested a gang member with a gun. After this arrest, I received a 15.02 (long-form commendation) from the new commanding officer of the Bureau, John Konstanturos, for a series of similar arrests.

A few days later, I was called into Sergeant John Mack's office after roll call. He informed me that there was a serial rapist wreaking havoc in the division, and the local P.T.A. and members of the school district had requested a meeting with a police officer. I told Sergeant Mack that wasn't my forte. I knew that Northeast, like all the other divisions in the department, had a community relations officer who worked that sort of thing. I told him I was a street cop and would be more efficient on the street hunting for that monster.

But Sergeant Mack thought for some reason that I would be best suited for the job, and that was that. When I walked out of his office, I thought to myself, what the fuck, I've gone from being a CRASH officer to having coffee with sweet schoolmarms?

When I met with the ladies and saw the fear on their faces, though, it pissed me off on their behalf. I was all in and gave them a detailed overview of what to watch for, how to go about their daily lives and make themselves a harder target, and how to seamlessly work with the department so we could all get this animal off the street.

Days later, one of the ladies in the P.T.A. recognized a suspect displaying the M.O. I had warned about. She called the police and the serial rapist was arrested. Of the seventy-plus commendations I received, this was one of my very favorites. The president of the P.T.A. and principal of the Monte Vista Street Elementary School wrote this heartfelt letter to Captain Smithson:

> *Dear Captain Smithson,*
>
> *On behalf of the parents and community members of Monte Vista Street School, I would like to take this opportunity to commend Officer Moreno. Officer Moreno conducted a most informative presentation on the topic of a serious crime problem which has been occurring in our school community area.*

Several women have been raped by an individual utilizing a similar method of operation.

Officer Moreno very effectively conveyed the concerns of the Northeast Division regarding these acts of violence. He enlisted the cooperation of our community to assist Northeast police officers in the apprehension (and) subsequent arrest of the individual suspect in these crimes. His presentation was clear, concise, and extremely instructive.

In addition to conducting an outstanding discussion, Officer Moreno demonstrated a friendliness, concern, and willingness to actively involve himself by the conveyance of information regarding this topic of urgent concern to our community.

By presenting this topic to our P.T.A., Officer Moreno enthusiastically displayed his commitment to the importance of open communication between the Los Angeles Police Department and community groups. The P.T.A. and the administration of Monte Vista Street School feels that positive experience such as this presentation will help to encourage cooperation and will, in addition, foster improved attitudes between the Los Angeles Police Department and members of this community.

Again, I wish to command Officer Moreno for his presentation and extend a personal "thank you" from our community.

Sincerely,

R.P. Enriquez, Principal
Andrea J. Allen, Title Coordinator

Captain Smithson penned a note at the bottom of the lovely missive:

I am proud of your positive attitude and professional demeanor in this situation.

Thank you.
Capt. R. Smithson

My mojo is back! In the midst of all this, Bill told me that he had spoken to a friend of his who worked in the Los Angeles Police Protective Union. His friend told Bill that the Administrative Transfer from CRASH to Northeast could have grave consequences for any promotion opportunities and permanently stain my record. He went on to say that there is a formal grievance procedure for such a thing, and that the chances of my winning were assured because it violated department rules.

I contacted the Protective League on March 6, 1981, and they filed a formal grievance. I was told it could take a few months. My plan was once I won the grievance, I would return to CRASH for a short time until I passed the P-III test, then transfer to METRO and join the original CRASH officers I learned so much from and admired. I suggested to Bill that he also apply for the unit so we could partner-up again in CRASH. That suggestion would come to haunt me for the rest of my life.

I won the grievance and returned to CRASH on Saturday, May 16, 1981. I cleared my good name and would shortly transfer to METRO. Oorah! After roll call, I was summoned to the Lieutenant's office by Sergeant Kenerson. It was a short, ominous conversation. "Welcome back, Officer Moreno," he said. "You have just made the biggest mistake of your life; now get out of my office."

When I walked out, I knew I was the first and only police officer to have the balls to expose his pattern of corruption, and come hell or high water, he was going to realize his revenge. I had to watch my back.

That night, I worked with Officer Dave Cantley, CRASH's gang expert of experts. Dave was older than most of the guys and had been in the unit from the jump. Once in the car, he told me that the unit had been working Northeast a lot because of several shootings between Barrio Highland Park and the Avenues. Of course, I was well aware of the war and the main players.

Dave told me that the unit was looking for Crazy Cisco, a murder suspect form Barrio Highland Park. He lived on a corner house on Range View and Nolden. We set up a Code-5 (surveillance) about one hundred yards north of the suspect's home, completely undetected. It was rather dark and cloudy that night, so we were good to go. About an hour later, Dave spotted Crazy Cisco and four other gang members coming out of the home. "He's got a gun, Al." I got on the rover and coordinated two other CRASH units to park on either corner of Range View. Once the time was tactically right, we would roll in on their gangster asses like a CRASH tsunami.

The two other CRASH units got into place, and we waited for the right moment. A short time later, the gangsters all walked out of the front yard onto the sidewalk, drinking their beer and smoking dope. We made our move, sweeping in like a heat-seeking missile. The gangsters had nowhere to run and froze in place. Crazy Cisco still had the gun at his side. It was obvious he was thinking about his options. *Should I blast my way into gangster mythology and maybe hit one or two cops before they light me up? Or drop the gun and spend the rest of my life in the joint for the murder?* All five of them were looking down the barrels of three Ithaca shotguns and three piss-ant .38s. We knew they were all tanked up and expected a gun battle of the first order.

It looked like Cisco was leaning toward gangster mythology, and we had no idea of how many more of the other gangsters were armed. I swear, right in the middle of this shit, I thought of the Gunfight at the O.K. Corral. But Crazy Cisco threw the revolver over the fence into his front yard, then all five went down on their faces. We cuffed the lot, and Dave recovered the fully loaded .357 revolver.

When I think about the lethal variables and possibilities of that night and how all my brother CRASH officers held their fire, walking that razor's edge between life and death, it makes my heart soar with pride to have worked with such extraordinary men.

A few days later, Bill Wong transferred into our unit. Oorah! Unfortunately, we couldn't partner-up since I was on loan to the homicide unit. My plan to leave the unit was getting closer with the P-III test just around the corner. However, every time I saw the Lieutenant, it sent chills up my back. He was well connected with upper management and would stop at nothing to get back at me for filing and winning the grievance. I needed to secure some type of security while I was still under his command. Then it occurred to me to go to the top and talk to the new Commander of the Bureau, Mark Kroeker.

I told the Lieutenant that I was going to see his boss. He looked like he was about to give birth to a twenty-pound baby. He told me that there was no need for me to see the Commander because it would only create great difficulties for the unit. When I mentioned his threats toward me, he told me to leave his office. It was just before roll call, and I knew the Commander would be in his office next door.

When I walked into Kroeker's office, I told his secretary I was "requesting mast," and she gave me a blank stare. I advised her that "requesting mast" is a military term used by a subordinate to talk to a unit's top commanding officer. She told me to have a seat, then walked into the Commander's office. Minutes later, she came out and told me he would see me.

Commander Kroeker had a unique reputation for caring for his troops, unlike most of the other staff officers in the department, and I experienced it firsthand in our two-hour meeting. I told him about my time in OCB CRASH. He rarely interrupted me while I enumerated the unit's grievances. I could see he was totally aware of them, but no one had dared to risk his future in the department by stepping forward.

Everyone in CRASH knew that the five captains of the bureaus had complained for years about CRASH officers pushing off gang-related crimes to patrol officers, thereby taking them away from their primary responsibility for calls for service.

I told the Commander how the Lieutenant went sideways when the CRASH officers made dope arrests; how METRO came in once or twice a year for a contest to see who could make the most arrests in a single p.m. watch; and how the majority of arrests were for drinking in public and other low-grade infractions, giving the Lieutenant high-arrest numbers to justify his leadership. We were also fiercely encouraged to underreport the true number of victims in shootings by listing intended victims as witnesses even when they came within inches of being hit with the gunfire.

The Commander stopped me and asked if anyone in the unit would support and confirm my disclosures. My blood ran cold. I told him that both Sergeants Wynn and Noetzel were working tonight and that they were men of impeccable character and honor. If anyone would ever step up to the plate, it was the Righteous Brothers. He laughed when I called Ray and Mike the "Righteous Brothers" and asked me to return to the CRASH office and summon them.

Neither sergeant had a clue on what was going on, and when I told them what I had done, their complexions turned ash gray. From the time the unit came into existence, these two old warriors were at loggerheads with the Lieutenant's incompetent and corrupt management, and now was their chance to finally correct the unit's ills. To be perfectly honest, I wasn't sure if they were willing to put their careers on the chopping block.

The Righteous Brothers walked into the Commander's office and were seen separately while I waited in the CRASH office for their return. I'll never forget the glowing looks on their faces when they returned—they did it, they confirmed my disclosures! This matter would no doubt go directly to Chief Daryl Gates.

But the legal statute that protects whistleblowers was years away, and I would eventually pay the ultimate price for being an honest cop.

8

Moonshine Melee

THIS SUMMER WAS SHAPING UP to be an even better water-skiing season than the last. I missed Cherry and her crew, but there were plenty of other athletic beauties at the Gallery. It was the first week in July, and I had already made a couple of trips to the Colorado River with Bill Wong and another badass CRASH officer, Dean Bunker.

We planned a three-day trip to the river at Havasu City for July 13 to 15. They were weekdays, so it was much easier getting three days off in a row. Unfortunately, Bill Wong had family commitments and wasn't able to join us.

The previous week, I was at my second home, the Los Angeles Criminal Courts building, testifying in a preliminary hearing on an attempted-murder case. While I was having lunch in the courthouse cafeteria, I bumped into Mike Casey who I knew from Hollywood Division when we both worked there.

Mike was a P-III and would have been a catch for any special-ized unit in the department. However, some years back, he took a six-month suspension for having an inappropriate relationship with a seventeen-year-old. Because of that suspension, Mike would work a black-and-white for the rest of his twenty years on the job. However, this punishment did not diminish his love for service to the public.

I told Mike about our upcoming water-skiing trip and he agreed to join us. Dean and I brought our boats to work on July 12 so we could leave right after p.m. watch. Dean invited three other friends to join us: Dolores Holt, a nurse he was dating from White Memorial

Hospital; Scott Gills, a neighbor and street cop with Pomona City Police Department; and Scott's wife, Jackie.

We all got off on time and caravanned to Black Meadows landing on the California side of the Colorado River. It was a little after 8 a.m. when we arrived. We immediately anchored the two boats off the beach. Everyone camped out on the beach for the trip, but not me; I got a room in the skank green hotel.

When I hit the sack, I went out like a light, but within an hour there was a knock on the door. It was an attractive girl in her early twenties with shoulder-length auburn hair. I thought she had the wrong motel room until she called me Al and introduced herself as Patty Falls, Mike's probationary trainee.

I told her I would join them downstairs at the cafe after I showered. Everyone was at the cafe when I arrived, anxious to go waterskiing after breakfast. I introduced Mike and Patty to the group and everyone got on sterling. Patty was in the last stage of completing her year-long probationary period, and Mike was her training officer—damn, not good! Mike was a superior cop but had a crippling character disease when it came to lovely young women.

After breakfast, Mike and Patty jumped in my boat. Dolores, Scott, and Jackie rode with Dean in his boat. After gassing up, we decided to head for Crazy Horse and use that as our day camp. It was a typical scorching mid-July day, but glorious just the same. As the day went on, our L.A.P.D. group only got closer. Everyone took turns skiing and Dean was top dog.

After a full day of skiing, eating, and drinking, we returned to Black Meadow around 6 p.m. Everyone used my shower. We barbecued some steaks with fresh corn on the cob, fixed a delicious salad, sourdough baguettes, and of course, plenty of beer and spirits. I made sure to bring a couple bottles of mezcal to liberate the storytelling. The meal was great and the conversations brought nonstop laughs.

After dinner, it was a beautiful starlit night, and we decided to take a night cruise to one of the nearby coves to knock down a few more beers and finish the bottle of mezcal. Scott had a flare for telling great jokes, and Dolores had some sick-ass E.R. stories. Throughout that gorgeous star-filled evening, I couldn't stop thinking of how magical it would be if I had Danique or Susan sitting there next to me. But those two cerebral beauties were gone forever.

The next day, Tuesday, July 14, 1981, was the day that would forever change my life. We all got up at 7 a.m. to ensure we would get a good camping spot in one of the larger coves upriver. We got a prime spot where Cherry and I used to camp out. I had the best day ever on a single ski, but nowhere near as good as Dean's. We planned to go bar hopping on the Arizona side of the river that night. So, we headed back to Black Meadows around five to get ready for a night of brilliant fun.

We arrived at Fox's R.V. Resort at about 7 p.m. for drinks and dinner. It was high-skiing season and Fox's was jam-packed with partygoers. After dinner, we walked out to the floating dock to enjoy the sights and watch the beautiful people.

One of the partygoers on the dock looked familiar. Lord, it was Mark Woody form South Gate High School. I hadn't seen him since 1964, and he hadn't changed a bit. He still had that long blond hair and year-round Southern California suntan. I walked over to him and he jumped in delight. Woody was with a river local and friend, Fred Steffey. He didn't look any too enthusiastic about our reunion. I introduced Woody to my friends and he bought everyone a round of drinks.

A short while later, Woody invited my crew to join him for some bar hopping downriver on his twenty-three-foot ski boat docked just feet away. We all thought it would be a blast and joined him and his friend. Our next stop was the Roadrunner. We docked the boat and went on partying. By now, Woody's friend Fred was off talking to other locals that he knew. No one paid much attention to him, including Woody. We all were having too much fun.

A short while later, Woody suggested we go to another bar farther downriver, the Moonshine Saloon. I'd never heard of that bar; Cherry had never even mentioned it. We all piled back into Woody's boat, anticipating even more fun.

Nightfall had set in, and maneuvering the boat in the fast and shifting current was substantially harder than it was upriver north of Parker Dam. But Woody evidently knew these waters like the back of his hand. He skillfully maneuvered his twenty-three-footer into the narrow floating dock slip without a hitch.

The Moonshine layout was much like Fox's and Sundance's, with a floating dock at the river's edge and an attached wooden walkway leading to the main entrance on the north side of the bar next to an unpaved parking lot. While I was walking toward the entrance, I noticed a low-rent, two-story apartment building approximately thirty yards directly to the rear of the bar. The property continued eastward for about another one hundred yards, leading to a highway.

Once inside, I immediately noticed that this was no Fox's or Sundance! There were about twenty grumpy patrons seated around a large circular bar, with widows all along the west wall, and a few more windows wrapped around the northwest and southwest walls ending at the front door about ten feet down. A few feet from the front door, the bar's north wall extended another five feet outward at the front door. There were pool tables and video games, with another fifteen to twenty much older patrons standing in that area.

None of them looked any too happy to be sharing their bar with our L.A.P.D. group.

One of the patrons standing at the southeast end of the bar having a drink looked about as big and ugly as Jabba the Hutt in *Star Wars*. He was in his midthirties, about six feet, four inches tall and 250 pounds, with medium-length blond hair. He wasn't wearing a shirt, no doubt to show off his numerous battle scars and prison tattoos. He had one large tattoo on his upper back depicting a Viking with a sword, and a spider web tattoo on his left elbow, signifying that he had murdered a person of color.

My gang expertise convinced me he was definitely an ex-con and an obvious member of the Aryan Brotherhood.

He gazed at us with pure disdain as we filed by. Evidently, he was a local, and I noticed that he visually acknowledged Woody and Fred as they walked by him. Our group ordered some drinks, then walked over to the pool table and video games and started playing pool. After losing a couple games, I found a vacant seat at the center of the bar and took a seat. When I sat down, I noticed a prominent tattoo on one of the barmaids—"All Aryan Woman."

What the fuck?! This was a white supremacist hangout; what was Woody thinking when he brought us here?

A short while later, a seat to my left become available, and Patty walked over and sat down with her back to the bar, slightly leaning forward and away from the shirtless monster seated next to her on her right. His name was Gerry Hallam, aka Crazy Gerry. Hallam's friend Ron Wood was also heavily tattooed and no doubt an ex-con. I heard Hallam start to chat Patty up. He asked her questions in rapid succession: "Are you a cop? Are you with anyone?" Then he pointed to one of the many scars on his shirtless body. "This one is from a shotgun blast. My wife shot me, and I cut her fingers off with an ax for cheating on me."

Normally, anyone would have immediately bolted from this ogre, but Patty was a cop. He repeated his barrage of crudities, at which point Patty pointed to Mike and said, "I'm with him," hoping to back Crazy Gerry off. He replied, "You're with that fucking wetback?"

Patty stood up and walked over to Mike, standing between an old stove-pipe heater and the pool table. Hallam looked directly at Patty and yelled out, "I'd like to fuck that cop in the ass." Then he boasted, "I'm going to kill a cop—I'm in Arizona and no one will do anything about it."

In rapid succession, Mike and Dean immediately started to shepherd our group out the north entrance, girls first. I made sure to walk out last to cover our rear. Just as I started out for the front door, I felt a massive-like vice-grip clamp down on my shoulder. It was Hallam holding onto me and cocking his other hand with a closed fist to take my head off. In fear for my life, I went into his ghoulish face like a buzz-saw, but my God, I didn't put him down. At this point, the bar turned into a gaggle of fists, kicks, flying pool cues, screams, and complete pandemonium.

At one point in the fight, I managed to wheel around Hallam and jump up to place him in an armlock around his tree-trunk-like neck from behind. It worked. He fell backward onto me, cushioning his fall. The impact forced all the air out of my lungs, and it was impossible to breathe under his struggling massive body. But I knew that if I released my grip from around his neck, I was a dead man.

It was impossible to see what was happening around me. I felt multiple kicks and someone digging their fingernails into the arm around Hallam's neck. Lord, I was losing it! He wasn't going out from the chokehold. And the lactic acid building up in my arms was overwhelming my grip. My arm gave out, and Hallam rolled over and away from me.

When he stood up, he no doubt was feeling the effects of the chokehold and slowly walked off toward the front door. Everyone in our group was scrambling every which way at this point, but I'm sure they were all mindful to head for Woody's boat.

When I got outside, I looked around for anyone in my group, then headed for the boat. I saw Dean and Jackie running ahead of me for the boat. Just then, I heard several people hysterically screaming, "He's got a gun, he's got a gun!" Christ! I was unarmed, and I knew Hallam had murder in his malevolent heart.

Seconds later, I saw Hallam rapidly coming around the northwest corner of the bar screaming, "I'm going to kill you motherfuckers!" My heart sank to my stomach. Had he already killed members of my group? My mind was going completely crazy with horrific thoughts. Had any of my friends jumped into the river and drowned in an effort to get away from that crazed monster with a sawed-off shotgun?

When I turned back, Dean and Jackie were gone. Hallam was within firing range and started to level the shotgun at me, but I managed to jump into the dark swirling water before he got his shot off. My endurance was fading as I struggled to keep my head above water. Miraculously, I made my way to shore a bit downriver. I rolled onto my back to catch my breath and wits. I needed to locate my friends!

Just then, Dolores ran up to me in complete hysteria. "He's got Patty!"

Evidently at the end of the fight, both Dolores and Patty ran to the rear of the bar and squeezed in between a large metal trash dumpster up against the rear wall of the bar. That's when they saw Hallam remove a sawed-off shotgun from his pickup truck. After getting his shotgun, he headed for the dock and spotted Patty and Dolores behind the dumpster. The girls ran for their lives. Patty left Dolores and ran back into the bar for shelter. Dolores continued southbound along the river and spotted me. That's when she told me Crazy Gerry had Patty.

It was dark, but I was able to see a trailer park off in the distance—the Jolly Roger Mobile Home Park. I ran up to the trailers and started fiercely knocking on front doors. I needed to use a phone and call for help. Finally, one of the residents, Don Cantu, opened the door, and I pleaded with him to let me in to use the phone. He looked at me in shock and shouted to someone in the bedroom that someone claiming to be a Los Angeles policeman wanted to use the phone.

They let me in. I identified myself as a Los Angeles police officer and told him that a female in my party was taken hostage at the Moonshine and that I needed to use their phone to call for help. The other resident, Don Yard Sr., pointed to the phone, and I spoke to an operator who connected me to the Yuma County Sheriff's Department. I explained the emergency. She told me they were already responding due to numerous calls about a "man with a gun and shots fired." I made sure to fill in some details so she could relay it to the responding units.

A cold chill surged through my body. I envisioned a mosaic of the hundreds of dead I've seen throughout my life, with Patty's lifeless body among them, torn to ribbons from shotgun blasts. We were in a desert, and I had no idea how long it would be before the police arrived. I sensed it would probably be too late by now, but I needed to return to the Moonshine and help my sister officer. I knew I would never be able to live with myself unless I went back.

I asked Mr. Yard if he had any firearms in the house. He said yes, walked into the bedroom, and returned with a .30-30 lever-action rifle with metal butt-plate, then handed me six rounds. I could see he was concerned about getting his rifle back. He asked me to give him my police identification card as security; under the circumstances, I complied.

I knew exactly what I was heading back to—a mob of Adolf Hitler worshipers and their hero, Crazy Gerry.

I loaded the rifle and started back to the Moonshine along the riverbank and spotted Mike on the way. I told him I was going back for Patty. He joined me, and I recall him continually saying, "Make it a good shooting, make it a good shooting." Somehow, I found that statement odd.

When we got to the Moonshine, we looked inside the southwest windows. The bar was almost empty. We cautiously walked to the southeast corner of the Moonshine and spotted both Hallam and

Wood. They were standing next to the large dumpster at the rear wall of the bar with their backs to us.

I was unable to determine if Hallam still had the sawed-off shotgun. I screamed at them at the top of my lungs with threatening tactical street language to scare them into submission, like I've done a hundred times before when disarming and arresting armed suspects. Hallam went straight down on his face, like he had done numerous times before. But Wood hesitated, forcing Mike to kick him in the upper body like we were taught in the Academy. Wood then complied.

Mike and I knew we only needed to keep them on ice until law enforcement arrived, which would be at any moment, hopefully. Hallam moved his hand toward his waistband. I gave him a firm compliance tap on the shoulder with the butt of my rifle and told him if he did that again I would blow his fucking head off. He complied and moved his massive arm back away from his body.

Seconds later, numerous black-and-whites came screaming in. There were three law enforcement agencies that responded: Yuma County Sheriff's, Arizona Department of Public Safety, and San Bernardino County Sheriff's Department. This was not unusual; many smaller police departments throughout the United States have a mutual assistance agreement. As they pulled in, I placed the rifle down until the officers could sort out who was who. The whole time Mike was prominently waving his L.A.P.D. badge to the responding units.

The lead officer walking toward us was Deputy Gail Lee, a Yuma County Sheriff Deputy. When she got within a few feet of us, she yelled out to the other officers, "It's Crazy Gerry!" Clearly, she had dealt with him before.

She handed me two sets of handcuffs, one for Hallam and the other for Wood. Just as I was about to cuff Hallam, she pushed me aside, took a knee, and firmly struck Hallam in the groin with the butt of her shotgun when he again started to move his hand toward his underbelly.

In the midst of this horror, I kept thinking about the possibility of Lieutenant Lynch and the department somehow scrambling this event to their advantage. They could make me the fall guy to get rid of me and stop Commander Kroeker's investigation of the CRASH unit's malfeasance.

After I cuffed both Hallam and Wood, I told Deputy Lee what happened while Mike went to look for Patty. Lee asked Hallam where the shotgun was and he denied ever having the shooter. While Deputy Lee watched over the suspects, I joined some of the officers looking for the stashed shotgun and asked numerous uncooperative pissed-off locals, kids and adults, which vehicle was Hallam's. One of the kids pointed to a pickup truck. I searched the unlocked truck and camper, with no results.

After an unproductive search for the shotgun, Hallam started complaining to the police that I beat him over the head with the rifle butt before they arrived. Charles Rourke, a Moonshine regular, and Scott Engel, one of the kids I asked about which vehicle belonged to Hallam, supported Hallam's story. I could see Deputy Lee and the other experienced officer weren't buying a damn word, but Hallam knew he could go back to prison for attempted murder and was trying anything to get out of it.

However, there was one irrevocable hole in his complaint of being hit on the head with the rifle butt. The rifle had a metal butt plate, and if he had been struck on the vascular soft tissue of the skull, he would have been a bloody mess! I saw Deputy Lee closely examine that monster's skull, and there wasn't a scratch.

Deputy Lee was obviously a solid and experienced street cop. She asked Officer Dave Artis, an Arizona Highway patrolman, to examine the rifle stock for trace evidence, blood, hair, and tissue. The rifle was clean.

Because of the numerous emergency calls made about a man with a gun and shots fired, an R.A. unit from Buckskin Fire Department also responded to the scene. Mike Ward, the paramedic, examined Hallam for injuries. His examination revealed minor cuts and abrasions on Hallam's face and back from the bar fight, but no skull injuries consistent with being beaten with a metal rifle butt. Wood also feared going back to the joint and cleverly complained of chest pain as a divergence and was transported to Parker Community Hospital. There was nothing wrong with his heart; he was then transported to the Yuma County substation for further investigation.

At this point, Deputy Lee and I were looking for Mike and Patty. Some witnesses said that Patty returned to the bar after the fight, then escaped through a restroom window. But where was Mike? He left the scene shortly after he told Deputy Lee that he was going to look for Patty. What in the fuck was Mike thinking? Then it came to me. He lost it; he knew this incident was going to get back to the department, and, given his previous six-month suspension, he logically surmised he could be fired for another inappropriate relationship with his female trainee, Patty.

We were almost killed, but when Mike left the scene like that, it muddied the waters of what would have been a straightforward opportunity to put Hallam in prison for the rest of his life.

Deputy Lee had no alternative but to take me into custody along with Hallam to sort this thing out at the police station. Deputy Ken Schwab transported me to the Sheriff substation, but gave me the dignity of not handcuffing me. When we arrived at the station, I was placed in the coffee room while Deputy Lee spoke to the watch commander. He advised her to phone the on-call D.A. for advice. She spoke to Deputy District Attorney Mike Donovan, who advised her to release me, Hallam, and Wood until she could interview all the L.A.P.D. officers and their friends, then proceed from there.

One of the deputies drove me back to Fox's, where I had left my car, then I drove back to our campsite in Black Meadows. Everyone was there, including Mike and Patty. The first thing I did was confront Mike. Why the hell did he leave like a thief in the night? Then I asked Patty how she managed to escape with her life.

Mike reiterated that old wives tail I've heard over the years about how the Colorado River law enforcement agencies hate the L.A.P.D. because we've caused them problems in the past. Mike said he felt he wouldn't get a fair deal from the cops at the scene.

I thought that was one sorry-ass excuse but left it at that for the time being. When I spoke to Patty, I could see she was still in shock, so didn't hit her with endless questions. She said that when they walked out the front door of the bar, she heard what sounded like a fight and started to walk back in to help her brother officers but was stopped by Dolores. Within a short time, the noise stopped and Hallam walked by them. That's when someone yelled he was getting a gun. In a panic, she and Dolores ran to the rear of the bar and hid behind a larger trash bin. They saw Hallam walk to a pickup truck and remove a sawed-off shotgun.

For some reason, Patty stood up, and Dolores pulled her back down, causing her to fall back and hit the rear wall of the bar. Hallam heard the noise and walked toward them with the shotgun. He saw them both and pointed the shotgun at them. Patty screamed, "Please don't kill us!" and both she and Dolores ran southbound in different directions. Patty thought some of us were still inside the bar and ran in to join us, but no one in our group was there. One of the barmaids cautioned her to take cover in the women's restroom. There was a single female with a small child in the restroom hiding under the sink. She told Patty she would walk out and see if all was clear.

Patty didn't trust her, so she escaped through a small window and ran downriver where she was spotted by Woody, who picked her up in his boat. At one point, everyone was in the boat but Dolores, Mike, and me. Woody continued to circle the area and finally spotted and picked up Dolores, then sometime later Woody spotted Mike and picked him up. Patty said that Mike told everyone in the boat that I was okay, and that's when Woody drove them back to Fox's. This was a foul lie, but I didn't confront Patty with it, since she was an emotional wreck.

Deputy Lee wanted us to return to the substation in the morning to give her a formal written statement. Everyone agreed and we called it a night. The following morning, we all met for coffee at the restaurant, but Mike and Patty were gone. They left in the middle of the night without telling any of us.

We were all furious, but what could we do? When we arrived at the Yuma County substation, I told Deputy Lee about Mike and Patty, and she got mad-dog pissed off.

I knew this would all but destroy any strong chance for the D.A. to file any charges against Hallam. After we completed our written statements, Lee calmed down, and I could only apologize for the lost opportunity to put that ex-con in jail for the rest of his life. Before we left, I asked her to please send me a copy of her investigation so I could attach it to my 15.7 (mandatory incident report). She gracefully agreed, and we left for L.A.

When I returned to work, I was still on loan to the CRASH homicide unit and told my partner John Petievich about the night of horror at the river. But I wasn't about to tell anyone else until I got Deputy Lee's report. My 15.7 would be bulletproof with her unbiased investigation. I knew Lieutenant Lynch would be chomping at the bit to twist this attempted murder to his advantage and get back at me for filing the grievance and reporting his criminal behavior and malfeasance to his boss, Commander Kroeker.

Meanwhile, John and I had our hands full working several gang-related homicides in the Bureau. The daily overtime was crushing, but at least the detectives had weekends off to catch their breath. However, each homicide team worked two on-call alternating watches: Monday through Friday night, and a single weekend out of the month. Nine times out of ten, the weekend team was called up.

On July 27, 1981, thirteen days after the Colorado River night of horror, I got Deputy Lee's report. It started with her receiving the emergency call at 2137 hours from the Moonshine Saloon. Her radio call actually mentions Hallam by name—"Crazy Gerry is chasing people with a shotgun," she said. Her report included the additional units responding Code-3.

She wrote that when she arrived, she saw Mike and me standing over Hallam and Wood. Mike was identifying us by waving his L.A.P.D. identification at the responding officers. In paragraph 6, she wrote, "I handed my cuffs to Moreno and asked him to cuff him (Hallam). Moreno placed one cuff on Hallam's left wrist, then brought his hand down to his back. Hallam started to roll to his left side and brought his right hand toward his body as if he was going to reach underneath himself. I dropped to my knees and with the butt of my shotgun, I gave him a quick tap between the legs in the groin area and ordered him to put his hand back. At this time, Moreno took ahold of his wrist and brought it behind him and cuffed him."

Lee used the same tactical maneuver I used moments before they arrived, when Hallam started to move his hand beneath his waist. But instead of his upper back, she smacked him in the balls.

Lee's report was extremely detailed and unbiased. Her report was critical so as not to give Lieutenant Lynch any wiggle room to screw me. On page 2, she went on to describe Hallam's injuries: "Hallam had a considerable amount of blood about his face, he had a split lip and a small abrasion next to his eye. Hallam refused any treatment." Her report confirmed there were no injuries to Hallam's skull.

On page 3 of her report, she stated that Mike Ward, the paramedic from Buckskin Fire & Rescue, heard Officer Moreno make disparaging remarks to Hallam while he was on the ground. Maybe Mike Casazza was right about the Colorado River authorities not liking L.A. cops?

In addition to obtaining the detailed statements from the L.A.P.D. group, Deputy Lee incorporated both written and verbal statements from the Moonshine employees and white supremacist regulars.

"Eyewitness statements by Shelly Sprague and Patricia Senecal were in stark contrast to Hallam's friends. They made no mention of Officer Moreno beating Hallam with the metal butt end of the rifle."

Sprague's statement read: "I looked out of the upstairs window (the apartment directly behind the bar) and saw Gerry carrying a double-barrel shotgun. Gerry carried it behind the motel, and I thought he threw it over the fence. I saw Gerry and Ron Wood fall to the ground on command from L.A.P.D., and I saw an L.A.P.D. officer hit Ron Wood and kick him in the side."

Senecal's statement read. "Coming out of my trailer is the night officer. I saw Gerry walking between the houses and room fifteen, going behind room fifteen carrying a gun."

Cynthia Norris stated she was in the bar when the fight broke out between "two of the men I knew" (Hallam and Wood). She said the fight was over a woman. After the fight, the participants left the bar, then a few minutes later, she observed two men returning with a rifle (Moreno and Casey). Carla (Carla Troutman, owner of the Moonshine bar) was outside talking to Hallam and Wood. Then she heard someone yell to hit the ground, "which Gerry and Ron did. I ran back in and called Parker P.D. and the sheriffs. Later, a man came in with another rifle (Don Yard Sr.) and identified himself as a local. He said he lent a man a rifle who identified himself as an L.A.P.D cop because a bartender was being held hostage, which was not true."

What Norris failed to tell Deputy Lee was that she was in the bar after the fight and had an unobstructed view of the floating dock where Hallam was chasing the L.A.P.D. group with the shotgun.

Dawn Albany, another local, stated that Officer Moreno walked up to Hallam and struck him in the face, then took him down and started choking him. She went on to say that Ron Wood was hit over the head with a pool cue.

However, like Norris, she made no mention to Deputy Lee about Hallam chasing the L.A.P.D. group with the shotgun, or about Officer Falls coming back in the bar in complete hysteria, or Hallam returning to the bar armed with the shotgun looking to murder anyone in the L.A.P.D. group.

On page 1, paragraph 3 of Deputy Lee's report, she mentioned Charles Rourke and Scott Engels's verbal statements: "Rourke and Engel stated that Moreno kicked the subjects (Hallam and Wood) laying on the ground in the head."

Lee also attached the evidence report, listing Yards' .30-30 Winchester rifle, serial no. 3789432. The rifle was stolen in a burglary in Santa Ana, California.

Deputy Lee closed her report by stating that all the L.A.P.D. group with the exception of Officers Casey and Falls returned to the substation the following day to submit written statements.

On July 16, Deputy Lee called the L.A.P.D. Hollywood Station and spoke to the Watch Commander, Sergeant Houchin. He asked Deputy Lee if she wanted Officers Casey and Falls to return to Arizona to submit written statements in person. Deputy Lee said mailing their statements would do.

I never stressed about waiting for thirteen days to submit my 15.7 of the Colorado River incident. I knew Officers Casey and Falls had already notified the department in a six-page-typed 15.7 report, thereby fulfilling the department's notification requirement. But just the same, I was going to write a 15.7 and give it to Lieutenant Lynch.

A couple days later, on July 29, 1981, I had just gotten home from day watch and was about to head down to the Jacuzzi with a glass of wine. John Petievich and I were on call that night, and yes, I got a call from Poppin' Fresh who was the desk officer. He told me a drive-by murder had just occurred in Northeast Division and gave me the address. I washed up, dressed, and drove to the murder scene in my department take-home car.

The homicide was at 5233 Buchanan Street. I arrived within an hour at 2000 hours. John hadn't arrived as of yet, but the Northeast patrol officers were doing a great job with the crime scene. One of the officers approached me with the murder log. It contained everything that transpired from the time the first unit arrived at the crime scene.

The deceased was sixteen-year-old Kenny Joe Mosqueda. His body was lying on the front porch covered in a white sheet. R.A. 55 had already left and pronounced death. Unlike in the majority of gang murders in our city, there was an eyewitness willing to talk. But before I interviewed him, I cautiously walked up to examine the deceased like I've done a hundred times before, keeping in mind not to compromise or destroy any evidence with a misplaced step.

I knelt next to Kenny Joe and slowly pulled the blood-soaked white sheet away from his face and torso. One eyelid was closed, and the other was exaggeratedly wide open with a look of horror. No doubt this kid knew he was going to die.

I lifted his T-shirt and observed multiple tearing entrance wounds from his umbilicus up to his abdomen, rib cage, sternum, neck, and ending at his lower jaw. There was a great deal of bleeding, which indicated he did not die quickly, and judging from the amount of entrance wounds, he was shot more than once.

I could hear crying from inside the residence. As I walked toward the single witness, I noticed one of our unit's new guys, Detective II Bernie Skyys, approaching me. He had recently transferred into our unit from Hollywood. He told me they were unable to get ahold of John, so he was going to take his place and work the homicide with me. Then came a barrage of questions, but he chilled once he saw how I was orchestrating the crime scene.

By now, I had confirmed and advised CRASH-90 of the murder, and Danny made the standard notification to Detective Headquarters Division. Scientific Investigative Division (S.I.D.) rolled out to take crime scene photographs and assist in collecting evidence. The busy coroner was enroute as well, but it could be hours before he arrived. There were other dead in the city to pick up ahead of this dead kid.

The eyewitness was Ramon Sanchez. He stated that he went to school with Kenny Joe and they were good friends. Kenny Joe had come over to his home for a visit. While they were seated on the street curb in front of his home, they noticed a yellow Chevy Nova slowly driving toward them.

The vehicle continued westbound on the narrow street and stopped directly in front of them. Sanchez recognized the three occupants as hardcore Avenues gang members: Arnold Aguirre, aka Little Harpo; his brother Richard Alex; and Mark Kuklinski. A short verbal altercation ensued, at which time Little Harpo raised and leveled a sawed-off 12-gage shotgun at Kenny Joe and fired both barrels into his torso and face. The force of the blast blew Kenny Joe out of his right shoe and catapulted him several feet back on the front lawn.

Sanchez was struck with a single shotgun pellet to his left shoe but was miraculously uninjured. He turned and ran for cover while Kuklinski fired several rounds from a .357 Magnum at Kenny Joe while he was stumbling toward the front porch. After they emptied their weapons, they drove off westbound at a high rate of speed. When Ramon mentioned Arnold and Richard Alex Aguirre, I knew exactly who they were from previous field interviews and their numerous arrests for violent gang-related crimes.

Years later, the Avenues gang would earn all of America's ire with the vicious murder of three-year-old Stephanie Kuhen in 1995, and again in 2008, with the murder of off-duty L.A. Deputy Sheriff Juan Abel Escalante.

On September 17, 1995, at approximately 0145 a.m., Stephanie's family got lost while looking for a shortcut home in the family car. Unbeknown to them, they had driven dead into the heart of the Avenues gang turf. Baby Stephanie paid for it with her life when she was shot to death. Twenty-eight-year-old Anthony Gabriel Rodriguez, twenty-two-year-old Manuel Rosales, eighteen-year-old Hugo David Gomez, and seventeen-year-old Augustin Lizama were arrested for the murder. Rodriguez, Rosales, and Gomez were sentenced to fifty-four years to life, while Lizama, a juvenile, pleaded to assault. The American Civil Liberties Union stated that the only reason the case got national attention was because Stephanie was white.

In Deputy Juan Escalante's drive-by murder on August 2, 2008, he was off duty visiting his mom and dad in Cypress Park. When he left, he reached back to adjust the baby's seat when Avenues gang members Carlos Velasquez, Jose Renteria, Armando Albarran, and Roberto Salazar drove by and shot him in the back of the head. If that wasn't enough, they continued firing into his vehicle, striking him several more times.

—

I spent several more hours at the crime scene taking endless measurements, directing the S.I.D. photographer, and again canvassing the neighborhood for additional witnesses. Then the coroner finally arrived to move Kenny Joe's body to the morgue. The coroner was working alone that day, so I needed to assist him in wrapping the body in a thick, clear plastic sheet and placing it on the gurney.

After we put the body in the van and were about to close the folding doors, two kids in their late teens ran up to me screaming and crying hysterically. They were Kenny Joe's brother and sister. Evidently, they just got word of their brother's murder. To this day, I can still picture the horror and unearthly lament in their sweet young faces.

They begged me to let them see their brother one last time before the coroner drove off with his body, and I had conflicting thoughts about that. I didn't want them to see Kenny Joe's death face, and he was a bloody mess. But they were in such a state, tearing at my clothing, that I couldn't help but give them one last look at their little brother. When I told the coroner to unlock the doors, I could see that he was hesitant as well. I warned the kids about Kenny Joe's condition, but that did not dissuade them.

I partially rolled the gurney out and made sure to only expose his face. Thank God his death eye was closed. I stepped back, and the kids both started kissing and fondling his face, blood and all. After about a minute, I couldn't tolerate this anymore, so I asked two Northeast patrol officers to help me move the kids away.

The coroner drove off, and I met Detective Skyys back at the CRASH office to start the reports. Skyys worked on the search warrants for the Aguirre brothers. They only lived five minutes away from the residence where the murder occurred. I worked on the murder and death reports and criminal background information. At sixteen years old, Little Harpo had already been arrested eleven times, mostly for violent crimes and dope. We were going to follow up on Kuklinski after the Aguirre arrests.

At approximately 0315 hours, we secured the arrest and search warrants for two of the three murderers, Arnold and Richard Alex. I contacted the Northeast morning watch commander to have him roll a couple uniformed patrol units to meet us a couple blocks from the suspects' home. At 0430 hours, we made entry into the Aguirre home. Like all search warrants of this nature when the suspects are armed murderers, the entry must be loud, disorienting, and thunderous! This shock tactic is employed to psychologically defeat or preempt any notion of the suspects to resist.

Shockingly, all the commotion didn't wake Arnold. He was sleeping like a baby. Christ, this fuck just murdered a human being hours earlier! I kicked the side of his bed and he woke up, staring down the barrel of my shotgun. We closely watched him as he removed the bed sheets from around his body, anticipating that he may have a handgun at his side.

Once he was dressed, we asked him and his parents where Richard Alex was. They all gave us the "go fuck yourself" look. We searched the home for the murder weapons but came up dry, then transported Little Harpo to the CRASH office to complete the arrest reports, booking, and interrogation. This murderous soul may have only been sixteen years old, but he was as hardcore and sophisticated as a thirty-year-old ex-con, and I knew we weren't going to get anything from him in the interrogation. If he ratted out his accomplices, he would be a dead man within days.

It was about 0730 now, and the CRASH homicide boss, Detective III Ron Quagliana, had just walked into the office. After we gave him a detailed report on what we had, Skyys and I proceeded to interrogate Little Harpo. Skyys told me he wanted me to be the main interrogator and to start with letting Aguirre tell his story. I knew Skyys was an experienced homicide detective from Hollywood Division, but he had only been in CRASH for a couple of months and obviously didn't understand the mind-set and mentality of hardcore gang members.

However, I was only a P-II, and he was a D-II, so I didn't try to tell him he had his head up his ass with this one. Besides, unlike most of the gang murders, we had a solid eyewitness and we didn't need a cop out. As I sat a couple feet away from this little murderous monster and looked into his lifeless black eyes, I swear the hair on the back up my neck stood up.

He was still in a state of ecstasy from pulling the trigger and enjoying the sick antisocial climax of the murder he just committed hours earlier. I've seen that sick look before. After thirty minutes or so, we weren't getting anywhere; I motioned to Skyys to walk outside the room with me.

Once outside the interview room, I told Skyys this was all a waste of time. We had Harpo by the balls with our witness. Skyys insisted on continuing and employing the "good cop, bad cop" routine. Again, I told him I knew this little fuck, and we were wasting our time, but he outranked me, so we went back in.

Just as we started round two of the interrogation, Skyys reached over and turned off the tape recorder. I thought that was odd, but I went on with the interrogation. This time, I started with pounding and kicking the table, but Aguirre just smirked. Then I stood up and grabbed Aguirre by the lapel of his shirt and shoved him back up against the wall like I was about to kick his ass, but he wasn't a bit afraid and looked dead into my eyes with resolute fury! I wheeled him half around and shoved him toward his seat. He pretended to slip and fall against his chair and fell to the floor, and I stormed out of the room.

This is when I thought Skyys was going to tell Aguirre, "You really pissed my partner off, you better cooperate." Instead, a couple minutes later, Skyys came out of the room and said, "You physically assaulted that arrestee under color of authority and I'm going to the old man [Lieutenant Lynch] with it."

I was so stunned I didn't utter a word. I simply sat there dumbfounded. It wasn't like I beat that little bastard; I just grabbed and shoved him.

Then the "lights" came on. Skyys knew the Lieutenant wanted my ass, and Detective III Quagliana was shortly transferring out of the unit, leaving a vacancy for a new head of the CRASH detectives.

After we booked Aguirre for murder, one of our CRASH units transported him to Eastlake Juvenile Hall. Then Skyys made a beeline to report me to the Lieutenant. I told Ron (Quagliana) that I needed to get back to day watch—I sure as hell wasn't going to work anywhere around Skyys. I was partnered up with Bill Wong, and all was good, although I knew the Lieutenant was going to throw the book at me for grabbing and shoving that murderous fuck. I had no prior beef for "improper tactics"—in fact, my record of dealing with arrestees was pristine, and my biannual ratings reports and unprecedented seventy-plus commendations proved it.

A few days later, I was informed that both the Colorado River incident and grabbing and shoving the murderer of Kenny Joe Mosqueda were combined. Internal Affairs Division was going to investigate the complaints.

9
Fruit of the Poisonous Tree

"FRUIT OF THE POISONOUS TREE" is a legal metaphor in criminal law used to describe tainted or illegal evidence. The logic of the term is if the source (the tree) is tainted, then the evidence (its fruit) is tainted and inadmissible as well.

Internal Affairs Division (I.A.D.) was assigned to investigate the Colorado River complaint, and CRASH Sergeant Ray Noetzel was to investigate the Avenues gang member complaint. Both complaints were later combined and adjudicated by a Board of Rights.

A few days after I received a copy of the charges against me, Maria Hernandez, our CRASH secretary, approached me in the hallway and told me she has a close friend who worked in I.A.D. as a secretary. At the start of the I.A.D. investigation, her friend overheard Sergeants Sewell and Lamb, the two investigators assigned to the Colorado River complaint, proclaim, "We're going to fry Moreno's ass." Maria feared that if I revealed this information, her friend would be fired. Accordingly, Maria only identified her friend's first name as Erlinda.

Maria stuck her neck out by telling me this and feared she, too, could lose her job if I disclosed this bombshell to anyone in the department, so what was I to do? I graciously thanked her and assured her I would not violate her trust.

The following week, I received a call from Sergeant Dave Gossman, one of my training officers from Venice Division. Dave was a Sergeant II now working in I.A.D.. He heard about my beef and told me to watch my back because the department was going to have my job. I asked him why he felt that way. He told me he overheard Sergeant

Herb Zinman, the I.A.D. advocate (department prosecutor) who was assigned to my case, state, "Moreno is going to be fired regardless of the evidence."

Predicated on the statements made by I.A.D.'s Sergeants Sewell, Lamb, and Herb Zinman, any and all alleged prosecutorial evidence amassed by I.A.D. should have been construed within the doctrine of "Fruit of the Poisonous Tree" as tainted evidence.

By now, it was abundantly clear that the department was furious at me for filing the grievance against Lieutenant Lynch and then blowing the whistle to the Bureau Commander about Lieutenant's Lynch's malfeasance in running the CRASH unit. However, Commander Kroeker was an honorable and decent man, and once he completed his investigation, I believed upper-management heads were going to roll.

—

On July 30, 1981, Sergeants Sewell and Lamb were in Parker, Arizona scouring the area around the Moonshine Saloon looking for witnesses in what would be an unprecedented seven-month-long investigation to crucify me. Ultimately, they would include thirty witnesses for their report, most of whom were friends of Crazy Gerry and shared his Aryan Brotherhood philosophy. Of all the thirty interviews Sewell and Lamb conducted during their investigation, Crazy Gerry's interview on August 12 at his mother's residence in Ontario, California, stood out and took my breath away.

On page 63 (paragraph 2, lines 14 to 17) Sewell and Lamb quoted Hallam: "Hallam made numerous threats to Moreno's life. He explained that he knew Moreno worked juvenile problems, and friends of his from 'La EmE' (Mexican Mafia) would locate him. When Moreno was located, he was going to kill him."

In the same page (paragraph 2, lines 20 to 22) I.A.D. stated: "He indicated that he would kill Moreno, if given the chance, even if it meant going back to prison."

After listening to Hallam's death threat, Sewell and Lamb were lawfully and dutifully bound to arrest Hallam on the spot for attempted murder—not for the attempted murder in Arizona on July 14, 1981—that crime was out of California's jurisdiction—but for the threats and actions Hallam confessed to I.A.D. on August 12 in Ontario, California.

Hallam completed the qualifications for committing a crime on that date when he confessed to obtaining information about where I worked in preparation for my murder, thereby consummating the statute for attempted murder. The elements of the statute read: One, that you took at least one direct but ineffective step toward killing another person; and two, that you intended to kill that person.

If it weren't for the recorded statements in I.A.D.'s report No. 81-677, any rational person would be justified in thinking that I was bat-shit nuts in concluding that the department purposefully ignored the death threat. In my opinion, the Los Angeles Police Department became a coconspirator to Hallam's planned murder when they refused to take him into custody and refused to provide a security detail for me and my family.

The department had well-established protocols for dealing with credible death threats to their officers. In this case, once Crazy Gerry told Sewell and Lamb about his planned murder, they notified their immediate supervisor, Lieutenant J. I. Davis, of the death threat. Lieutenant Davis fast-tracked the information to his boss, Captain A. M. Fried, Commanding Officer of Internal Affairs Division. Captain Fried notified the Commander of Central Bureau, and then it no doubt was discussed in the Chief's office.

But at some point, the department ignored the established security protocol. Robbery Homicide Division (R.H.D.), METRO Division, and Special Investigations Section (S.I.S.) were not employed to render their services to protect me and my family against the imminent death threat of the Aryan Brotherhood.

Within a day, R.H.D. would have normally initiated a joint task force with the Yuma County Sheriff's Department in Arizona. Both Los Angeles and Yuma County authorities would secure a court-ordered wiretap for Hallam's residences in both California and Arizona. Once the wiretap confirms the murder threat, R.H.D. or Yuma County authorities would take Hallam into custody for attempted murder; that is, if S.I.S. didn't get that monster first. And throughout this period, METRO Division would have placed a security unit at both my and my mother's homes.

Reprehensibly, none of these long-standing security protective measures were undertaken by the Los Angeles Police Department. In fact, I was not notified of the death threats until August 18, six days after Sewell and Lamb interviewed Hallam.

Two days after the I.A.D. interview, I received a telephone call from Yuma County detectives that their department had received credible intel that Hallam was about to consummate his murder plan. I asked them if they had contacted the Chief's Office, and they assured me they did, but wanted to personally notify me as well. The department still sat on their hands and did not initiate the protective protocol for me and my family.

———

In mid-December 1981, Sergeants Sewell and Lamb completed their seven-month investigation and came up with eight charges of misconduct against me for the Colorado River incident. They then combined this with the Arnold Aguirre murder suspect complaint, for a total of ten charges of misconduct.

> *Count 1: On July 14, 1981, at approximately 2000 hours, you, while off duty, in the Moonshine Saloon in Parker, Arizona, unnecessarily struck Gary Hallam in the face with your fist and applied a carotid hold on him.*

> *Count 2: On July 14, 1981, you, while off duty, in Parker, Arizona, misrepresented the circumstances of a "Man with a Gun" incident in order to gain temporary possession of Donald Yard Senior's firearm.*

> *Count 3: On July 14, 1981, you, while off duty, in Parker, Arizona, improperly surrendered your department identification card in order to gain possession of Donald Yard Senior's firearm.*

> *Count 4: On July 14, 1981, you, while off duty, in Parker, Arizona, without provocation, kicked Gary Hallam in the*

body and struck Hallam about the head and back with the butt of the rifle.

Count 5: On July 14, 1981, you, while off duty, in Parker, Arizona, without permission or authority, searched private vehicles.

Count 6: On July 14, 1981, you, while off duty, in Parker, Arizona, made improper remarks to Gary Hallam ("Where's the fucking shotgun?").

Count 7: On July 14, 1981, you, while off duty, in Parker, Arizona, improperly tried to influence (witness) Scott Engle to change his statements regarding his observations of your actions.

Count 8: After being arrested in Parker, Arizona, on July 14, 1981, you failed to promptly notify the Department with a 15.7.

Count 9: On July 30, 1981, at approximately 0745 hours, you, while in the interview room at Central Station, unnecessarily grabbed Arnold Aguirre by his throat and pushed him backward, causing him to fall to the floor.

Count 10: On July 30, 1981, you, while in the interview room at Central Station, unnecessarily held Arnold Aguirre by the back of his neck and pushed him toward a chair.

The department had even bifurcated a single charge for the same act into two separate charges (9 and 10), further revealing their unbridled zealousness for finding me guilty for as many counts of misconduct as possible!

I was ordered to a Board of Rights (BOR) hearing to adjudicate both complaints.

Officer Dean Bunker was charged with two counts of misconduct:

Count 1: The department alleged Officer Bunker, during a barroom altercation in Parker, Arizona, without cause struck Ronald Wood on the head with a pool cue.

Count 2: The department alleged Officer Bunker made false statements to another police agency (Yuma County Sheriffs), which was investigating the altercation.

224 L.A.'s Last Street Cop

Officer Mike Casey was charged with four counts of misconduct:

Count 1: You maintained an improper relationship with your probationer, Officer Patty Falls.

Count 2: You, while off duty in Parker, Arizona, after becoming aware that Officer Falls was not being held hostage by Gerry Hallam, failed to advise Police Officer Moreno, who was armed with a rifle and confronted Gerry Hallam.

Count 3: You, while off duty in Parker, Arizona, failed to cooperate with Yuma, Arizona Sheriffs' deputies by leaving the scene of a criminal investigation.

Count 4: You, while off duty in Parker, Arizona, failed to cooperate with Yuma, Arizona, Sheriffs' Deputies when you did not respond to the Sheriff's Station after being requested to do so.

Probationary Officer Patty Falls was summarily terminated on probation. To this day, I agonize about Patty's termination. She did not do a damn thing wrong and richly deserves to be vindicated!

Hollywood Division's Watch Commander, Sergeant II Houchin, Lieutenant Pilot, and Captain Bushey determined the L.A.P.D. group were victims of an attempted murder and absent of any misconduct.

Officer Scott Gills was not charged with misconduct by his department, Pomona Police Department.

However, L.A.P.D.'s staff management—Lieutenant J. I. Davis, Captain K. E. Fried, and the Chief's Office—embraced the voracity and character of Gerry Hallam, Ron Wood, and his white supremacist supporters over that of their own officers, their civilian friends, and their wives.

I needed to get the best defense representative in the department. Officer Bunker told me he got Sergeant Hank Hernandez to represent him. Hernandez was a patrol sergeant working Hollenbeck Division and had nearly completed law school. I met with him days later at Hollenbeck Station, and he agreed to represent me in my BOR. I knew Sergeant Hernandez's defense investigation was going to require nothing short of a Herculean effort. That meant going to the Moonshine Saloon in Arizona and interviewing every hostile white supremacist witness on Deputy Lee's report, including Crazy Gerry and Ron

Wood. Additionally, he needed to obtain diagrams of the Moonshine, the boat dock, the parking lot, and the sleazy hotel and trailer park, and take photographs of the surrounding properties.

As for the murderer of Kenny Joe Mosqueda, I admit to grabbing and shoving his killer Arnold Aguirre, a hardcore Avenues gang member. I was fully prepared to take that hit. However, I vehemently deny the charge of "excessive force." It was an act of "improper tactics." This claim would be irrefutably proven later from the department's own records.

On Thursday, December 24, 1981, I was called into Lieutenant Lynch's office where he reiterated that I was ordered to a BOR set for December 28, 1981, and I was to be relieved of duty without pay pending my BOR. At that time, I would have to surrender my badge, weapon, and police identification.

In effect, I was no longer a police officer. Lynch made no effort to mask his delight.

A short time later, I went to Glass House with my defense rep, Sergeant Hernandez, to select the three captains who would serve on my Board of Rights. I selected Captains Jerold M. Bova, Jess Rodriguez, and Dian Harber.

Captain Bova was the officer who killed twenty-five-year-old Leonard Deadwyler in 1966, just ten months after the infamous August 1965 Watts Riots. The killing of Mr. Deadwyler came within a breath of igniting a second riot in South Central Los Angeles. Mr. Deadwyler was frantically driving his pregnant wife to the hospital when Bova stopped him for speeding. Bova approached Mr. Deadwyler's vehicle and stuck his revolver in the open window, then fired a single shot, killing Mr. Deadwyler. Bova's excuse was the vehicle lurched forward, causing him to fall back and accidentally discharge his weapon.

I calculated that that unspeakable tragedy would give Bova a special insight into my police record of unparalleled restraint in all the guns I took off suspects without using deadly force.

My second choice was Captain Dian Harber. Being a female, I reasoned she would appreciate my response in going to the aid of Officer Falls, a sister female police officer.

My final pick was Captain Jess Rodriguez. He was of Hispanic descent, and I hoped that he came from a similar background as me and would appreciate my character of overcoming endless obstacles to become an "outstanding" Los Angeles police officer.

I was still convinced that the Board members would recognize the department's two alleged victims, Hallam and Aguirre, as the loathsome criminals they were.

As to the department's prosecutorial witnesses, they were Moonshine Saloon regulars and white supremacists. Many of them had seen Hallam on numerous occasions enter the bar with his sawed-off shotgun and enjoyed listening to him speak about his brutal stories of inflicting pain and misery on innocent people. I was confident that the Board members would see that lot for what they were.

On Monday, December 28, 1981, I reported for work and was ordered to surrender my police identification card, badge, and weapon. I left in disgrace.

I drove to Mom's. I had not yet told her about the Colorado River incident or the Aguirre complaint. Her plate was overflowing with the family's own survival issues. But I had no choice at this point but to tell her what was going on.

When I told her about the Aryan Brotherhood death threat, her face turned ash-gray with shock. Then I had to tell her that the department refused to provide a protective security detail for me and the family.

"Is that why you visited so often in the past six months, was it to protect me and the kids?" she asked.

"Yes, Mom."

Then my modern-day Queen Boudica gathered her composure and looked dead into my soul.

"Fight them, Corky—and leave me one of your guns."

10
Et Tu, Brute?

I WAS IN DESPERATE STRAITS. My Board of Rights wasn't scheduled until February 1, 1982—five weeks hence. My apartment rent was due in a few days, and then there were my monthly payments for my Aston Martin and Southwind ski boat—not to mention living expenses. Additionally, I could no longer take lucrative, armed off-duty security jobs, since I had lost my license to carry a concealed weapon.

The department appointed Sergeant Herb Zinman as their advocate (prosecutor), the same sergeant who had said, "Moreno is going to be fired regardless of the evidence."

On February 1, 1982, at 0933 hours, I went before the Board of Rights. The chairman was Captain Bova. He asked both parties if they were ready to proceed. Zinman and Hernandez stated yes. Captain Bova read the ten charges against me, then asked, "How do you plead?"

I answered, "Not guilty."

Zinman presented an overview on how the department intended to prosecute their case. Then Zinman had the temerity to request that nineteen of the Moonshine and law-enforcement-officer witnesses be questioned by telephone.

Sergeant Hernandez vehemently objected and emphasized that the defense has the constitutional right to cross-examine all witnesses in person! Zinman rebutted that it would be cost prohibitive for the department to fly in all the Arizona witnesses to California, put them up in hotels, pay for meals, arrange transportation to and from Parker Center, and then fly them back to Arizona.

228 L.A.'s Last Street Cop

Bova sustained Hernandez's objection. Zinman asked for a short recess to consult with his I.A.D. bosses.

At 1045 hours, Bova stated, "For the record, the Board is back in session." Zinman advised the Board that the department was going to proceed with only six Arizona witnesses, one of whom was a police officer.

Bova advised Zinman that the BOR would allow hearsay evidence from the other Arizona witnesses who did not attend the BOR.

Then Zinman requested a continuance to February 16, 1982, at which time the department would fly their six Arizona witnesses to Los Angeles.

Sergeant Hernandez objected. He advised the Board that the department had five weeks to prepare their witnesses and that I had already suffered a great financial burden from being without a paycheck for that long. There was also the matter of the death threat from the Aryan Brotherhood. This needed to be resolved quickly. The department had still refused to provide security for me.

Instead of gasping in disbelief, Captains Bova, Rodriguez, and Harber did absolutely nothing. That was when I realized that this BOR was nothing more than a preplanned charade. I was doomed.

The department did not subpoena their two victims, Gerry Hallam and Arnold Aguirre, because they knew the mere optics of those two monsters would have destroyed their case against me.

Then came the coup de grâce. During the recess, Zinman conferred with Hank Hernandez. When the Board reconvened, Zinman stated that the department spoke with the defense representative during the break who indicated he needed no witnesses from Arizona; therefore, he said, the department will only call the prosecution witnesses. Bova allowed them to proceed.

Sergeant Hernandez had thrown me under the bus. Instead of seizing the defense's legal right and obligation to confront every witness Internal Affairs interviewed, he handed the department my head on a silver platter. Later that day, I learned Hernandez did absolutely nothing in preparation for my defense in the six months leading up to my trial.

The only interview he conducted was with Officer Dean Bunker, and that was only because they worked in the same division, Hollenbeck. Hernandez not only failed to interview any witnesses, he also failed to drive to the Moonshine Saloon and secure critical line-of-sight diagrams of the bar, which would have been of enormous value for the defense.

The Board asked Zinman if there were any witnesses who could testify today. Zinman said that under the circumstances, he was going to "mishmash" the prosecution: First, he was going to call Officers Scott Gills and Dean Bunker for the Crazy Gerry complaint. Then, he would switch midstream to the Avenues gang member complaint and call OCB CRASH Detective II Berny Skyys and Detective III Ron Quagliana.

Then, when the Board reconvened on February 16, Zinman said he would call Officer Artis, who assisted Deputy Lee at the crime scene; Don Cantu and Don Yard Sr., who gave Officer Moreno the (stolen) .30-30 rifle; Fred Steffey, Woody's friend; Scott Engel, the juvenile who stated he saw Officer Moreno beat Crazy Gerry with the rifle; and Betty Culp, another eyewitness who saw Officer Moreno beat Crazy Gerry with the rifle.

Patty Falls would not get her chance to testify.

Officer Scott Gills was the first witness. He stated he was a San Bernardino County Deputy Sheriff for two years prior to joining Pomona Police Department. While in the Sheriff's Department, he had one law enforcement encounter with Crazy Gerry. Officer Gills stated that Hallam was wreaking hell in San Bernardino, California, as in Yuma County, Arizona.

Scottie brought a copy of Crazy Gerry's rap sheet, at which time Zinman objected, stating the document was marked "Confidential." The prosecution and defense went back and forth on this issue, when Bova stipulated Hallam was a violent career criminal and member of the Aryan Brotherhood. The rap sheet was admitted into evidence.

On cross-examination, Officer Gills reiterated the circumstances that led to the fight and how he escaped and returned to the L.A.P.D.'s campsite at Black Meadows Landing.

Officer Bunker was called next. On direct examination, Dean's testimony reflected the same facts he told I.A.D., with no exceptions. He started with how the L.A.P.D. group met Woody at Foxes, and how they ended up at the Moonshine Saloon. He stated he was playing pool with his girlfriend, Dolores, when Jackie, Scott's wife, came up to them and said Scott knew Hallam to be a violent criminal and they should leave at the time. Hallam started with his vulgarities and threats, saying, "I'd like to screw that female cop (Patty). Then Patty walked toward Officer Casey, and Dean said Hallam said, "It wouldn't bother me to kill a Los Angeles police officer in Arizona."

Officer Bunker explained that was when the L.A.P.D. group started to leave the bar by going out the front door. Once the girls were out, he said, it was only he and Al left. Before they got out, Hallam grabbed Al by the shoulder with one hand and had a clenched fist with the other hand. Al punched Hallam, then several of the bar regulars went to Hallam's aid. There were several bodies on the floor going at Al, so Dean said he started to help him when he was struck from behind and fell.

Bunker described how after the short fight, every member of the L.A.P.D. scattered in different directions when Crazy Gerry went at them with the sawed-off shotgun. He told the Board he, Jackie, and Al were forced to jump into the river when Hallam pointed the shotgun at them just before they reached Woody's boat.

Dean's testimony was exactly like Scottie's. Zinman had nothing to work with here.

On cross, Hernandez again emphasized how the L.A.P.D. group did the prudent thing in attempting to avoid any trouble by leaving the bar after Hallam started with the threats, only to be attacked in the end by that shotgun-wielding madman. There was the standard "redirect and cross" by Zinman and Hernandez, but it came to no aid for the prosecution. Dean was excused.

After a short recess, the department interrupted their prosecution for the Colorado River complaint and called CRASH Detectives Berny Skyys and Ron Quagliana. This was nothing more than a procedural necessity. I was guilty of grabbing and shoving Aguirre.

Under normal circumstances, this type of mistake, with no priors, would result in a stern verbal or written admonishment or a couple days' suspension. However, my logic was predicated on the Board of Rights and the department being judicially unbiased; they were not.

After the two detectives' testimonies, the BOR adjourned. Captain Bova ordered all parties to return on February 16 at 0930 hours. Hernandez and I said virtually nothing to one another after that first day.

As I exited room 500 in Parker Center, I was wearing a visitor pass for the first time in almost seven years. It's impossible to convey the feeling that overcame me that very moment. This was an incomprehensible nightmare and I hadn't woken up yet. The department I loved more than my own life was taking the side of a career criminal who represented everything repugnant to any civilized society.

I didn't want to go home and face Mom, and I couldn't help going over and over the possibility of getting fired. It was crystal clear at this point that the department was playing with a stacked deck against me. I thought about what Maria, our CRASH secretary, had told me about what the two I.A.D. investigators avowed at the beginning of their investigation, "We're going to fry Moreno's ass."

But how could the department possibly justify a single guilty verdict in the Colorado River complaint when the evidence did not support a single guilty count? I knew that of all the ten counts in both complaints, only Count 4—beating Hallam over the head with the metal butt plate of the rifle, a felony assault with a deadly weapon—would justify my termination. I thought about the exculpatory evidence of Deputy Lee, Officer Artis, and paramedic Mike Ward regarding Count 4. They are experienced police officers and expert medical personnel, and their reports found only cuts and abrasions on Hallam's face and not a trace of evidence on the butt plate of the rifle!

Later that night, thank God I got a call from Rick Beach. He and our friend John Mahli were well aware of what was going on with their old friend. Rick was still working Rampart Division and had three girls by now. John had left the department after ten years to become a successful commercial real estate broker. He also had a lovely family of his own.

They took me to the Short Stop for a couple of beers. As usual, the bar was full of coppers from Central and South Bureau. The camaraderie from Rick, John, and my Praetorian brothers was intoxicating. I tried to mask my angst all night. Rick and John made like they didn't notice it, but I could tell what they were thinking. I was a bit surprised about how many of the guys knew about both complaints, and they made no effort to mask their disgust for the department management and Detective Skyys.

I was crazy surprised when Maria Elena walked up to me. She was the beautiful Mexican foreign exchange student from Mexico I met when I was working Hollywood Division a few years back. She graduated from UCLA with a business degree and was attending UCLA's Anderson Business school part-time for her masters while working full-time in Century City for some Fortune 100 company. Her English was flawless now, and she had an air of sophistication about her.

I lost all awareness of Rick, John, and my other brothers, and they gave me a brotherly "by your leave" nod as Maria Elena and I took a corner table in the bar. We were oblivious to everything and everyone around us. Maria Elena was a godsend, and for the first time since that horrid night of July 14, 1981, I actually felt a sense of peace.

Maria Elena told me that I had walked right passed her when we entered the bar and made no effort to say hi. Just then, I fell back on my lament, and realized I would be pushing it if I needed to buy her a drink, since I was broke. The only cash I had was from selling my beautiful living room and bedroom furniture when I had to move out of the Gallery apartments in Hermosa Beach. I sold it for pennies on the dollar.

Just the same, I offered to buy her a drink, but she responded with, "It's my round." This lady wasn't only drop-dead beautiful and intelligent, she was also a gracious soul. She came back with a Mexican boilermaker (a shot of tequila and a beer chaser).

Time flew by, and it was about closing time when Rick and John came up and told me it was time for us to leave. Maria Elena interrupted and told them she'd drive me home. I wasn't about to contest that magic. I walked John and Rick outside and they were all smiles. They assured me they had my six.

When I walked back in, Maria Elena was ready to leave, and we walked out to her BMW. We were at Mom's within an hour. She had to be at work in a few hours, but I didn't want to let her go. We spoke for a few moments, and then she asked me what was wrong. Obviously, I did a poor job masking my troubles. I apologized and told her I would tell her the whole story the next time we got together. She said she needed to hear all about it when I came over for dinner Saturday as she handed me her address to her apartment on Lafayette Park Place. I knew the location; it was only blocks from Tommy's

Burgers on Beverly Boulevard in the nicest part of Rampart Division. She leaned over and kissed me on the cheek, and drove off.

It was about three in the morning when I walked into Mom's place. She had sweetly made a bed for me on the couch. Since I lost my apartment in Hermosa and moved back to the hood with Mom and the kids, I insisted on bunking in the living room. I wasn't about to displace anyone from their living quarters in the three small bedrooms.

It was impossible to get to sleep. I just stared at the empty cold ceiling, thinking about the 16th when the BOR would reconvene. When I finally drifted off, I had horrible nightmares about Crazy Gerry killing my family. I saw Hallam and his vile, tattooed gang walk into my living room with knives and sawed-off shotguns, and no matter how hard I tried, I couldn't move. Then, the horrid screams and cries for mercy as the Aryan Brotherhood gang members slaughtered my little brothers, my sisters, and my mom.

The following Saturday, Maria Elena kept our date, but it ended up being in Mom's parked car where I had taken to sitting with a six-pack of my treasured Miller High Life, listening to the radio. Maria Elena and I shared beer and sandwiches as I told her everything. She was a welcome distraction. We never got into the heavy kissing and fondling, as she was an old-world Catholic. She went on about her parents and their successful textile business, then bragged a little about her two older brothers, Peter Jr. and Alfonso. I started to interrupt to tell her that Alfonso was also my full name, but I held back. I promised her I would fly to Mexico with her in the spring to meet her family. We kissed, and she left late that night, but not before I introduced her to Mom. These two old-world beauties hit it off speaking eloquent Spanish. Mom fell in love with her.

—

By the time the Board of Rights reconvened on Tuesday, February 16, I was a basket case.

Zinman called me to the stand first. On direct examination, he started with the Aguirre complaint first, then went on to the Colorado River complaint. I gave him nothing but the truth.

On cross-examination, I was shocked when Hernandez advised the Board that he had no questions, but he reserved the right to call me at a later time. It was the only good call he made throughout the BOR.

The Board had a short discussion off the record, then instructed Zinman to call the department's next witness, Dolores, Officer Bunker's girlfriend. Dolores's testimony was forthright and bullet-proof; she was the best witness for the defense. She went into the hair-raising account of how, after the fight, everyone scattered in all directions. She told the Board how she and Patty ran to the rear of the bar and hid behind a large trash bin, then saw Hallam unlock his pickup truck, obtain the shotgun, break it open, and load two rounds.

Dolores stated that it was at this point that Patty stood up and Dolores pulled her down, causing her to fall back against the rear wall of the Moonshine and make a loud noise, alerting Hallam to their location. That's when Hallam raised the shotgun at them and walked toward them saying, "I'm going to kill a fuckin' cop."

Dolores told the Board she ran for her life south along the shore-line without Patty, and to her horror, figured Hallam had taken Patty as a hostage because she was nowhere to be seen. Moments later, she saw Officer Moreno alone on the riverbank and told him, "He's got her!" She said that was the last she saw of Officer Moreno. She went on about how Woody finally picked everyone up in his boat except Al, and how Woody warned the L.A.P.D. group not to return to the Moonshine, and strongly suggested for all to drive back to Black Meadows so he could ascertain what happened to Al.

On cross, Hernandez sealed the fact that in my mind at the time of the incident, Patty was being held hostage by Crazy Gerry. Then came the predictable redirect and cross, but Dolores gave the department nothing for their shameful prosecution.

The Arizona witnesses had been flown in at taxpayers' expense. The department called eighteen-year-old Don Cantu and Mr. Don Yard Sr. up next.

Don Cantu stated that he, his mother, her boyfriend Donald Yard Sr., and Don Jr. were at the Moonshine Saloon earlier that day before the L.A.P.D. group arrived. He noticed Crazy Gerry exited the bar and returned with a sawed-off shotgun, and then said Crazy Gerry started bragging to the regulars about his life of crime. Sometime later, Cantu and his family left the bar.

Later that evening, Cantu said a man came to their trailer and asked to use the phone (Moreno). He alerted his mother's boyfriend, Don Yard Sr., in the next room. When Don came to the living room, he asked Officer Moreno for ID. Officer Moreno showed him his police ID and asked to use the phone. Officer Moreno told Don there was a barmaid being held hostage at the Moonshine and asked if he had any weapons in the house. Don gave Officer Moreno a .30-30 rifle but demanded Officer Moreno leave his police ID card as security. Officer Moreno then headed for the Moonshine. Cantu and Don Jr. followed him but waited behind a wall until they heard the police arrive.

Once the police arrived, they felt safe and walked over to see what was going on. At one point, Officer Moreno asked Cantu if he knew which car belonged to Crazy Gerry, and Cantu pointed to his pickup with a camper shell. Cantu saw him go inside, and it looked like he was searching the attached camper because a light went on inside the cab.

On cross-examination, Hernandez ascertained that Cantu and his family were good friends with Linda Fraser, one of the Moonshine barmaids and regular patrons of the bar. Hernandez asked Cantu if Linda had any Aryan Brotherhood tattoos.

Zinman objected but acknowledged, "I think we already know the type of characters we are dealing with." Cantu was excused.

Don Yard Sr. was called next. Zinman's first question was if Yard could identify Officer Moreno, and Yard pointed to me. Yard's testimony mirrored Cantu's. Zinman asked Mr. Yard if Moreno seemed to be intoxicated when he spoke on the phone.

Yard replied, "He seemed alright to me."

Yard said he followed Moreno back to the Moonshine, where he saw Ron Wood and Crazy Gerry sitting on the ground handcuffed, bleeding from the face. Yard asked Ron what happened, and he said, "That son-of-a-bitch [indicating Moreno] pistol-whipped me."

Zinman asked Yard if Hallam was a regular customer of the Moonshine. Yard said he was, and also admitted he and Wood had been friends for about five or six years, and that Wood used to work at the Moonshine as a bartender and was also a bouncer at the Windsor Circle.

Yard Sr., like Cantu, told the Board he and his family were in the Moonshine earlier that day before the L.A.P.D. group arrived. He stated Hallam was also in the bar telling the regulars about his life of crime. "He was mouthing off about all the time he spent in the joint and how he robbed a casino in Vegas and cut his old lady's fingers off with an ax," Yard said. "Then he left and came back with a chrome-plated sawed-off shotgun. Linda told him to get that goddamn gun out of here. He [Hallam] did and came back."

On cross-examination, Hernandez, asked if Yard Sr. ever got his rifle back. "No," he said, "they kept it because they said it was stolen in Santa Ana." Yard Sr. was a convicted felon.

Fred Steffey was called next. On direct examination, he said he worked as a contractor and part-time bartender. He had known Ron Wood for about three years and Crazy Gerry since that summer.

Zinman asked Steffey if any of the barmaids at the Moonshine had tattoos. He said yes; Cynthia Norris had one on her shoulder that said, "All American Aryan Woman." He said he was there when the fight broke out and saw Officer Moreno walk up to Gerry and punch him in the face.

On cross, Hernandez asked Steffey if he was a convicted felon; he stated yes. Then he was asked to describe Hallam. "He's about six feet, six inches and 300 pounds."

"So, you're saying that Officer Moreno, at five feet, nine inches and 170 pounds, walked up to Gerry and started the fight?" Hernandez asked. Steffey said yes.

"Did you hear Gerry make any derogatory remarks against cops?"

"He could have, I don't recall."

"Did you see Gerry with a gun?"

"Never did."

Jacqueline Gills, Scott's wife, was called next. Jackie's account of her night of horror described how she saw Crazy Gerry after the fight walk to his pickup truck and get a sawed-off shotgun. "He looked directly at me and pointed the gun at me." She said she was in fear for her life and jumped in the river. She stated she nearly drowned when her skirt got tangled around her legs. At one point, she managed to grab a piece of material at the south end of the floating dock that prevented her from being swept away downriver, but she was continually being struck in the head by a boat moored next to her.

"The whole time I feared Hallam would spot me and kill me," she recalled. "Eventually, some kids helped me out of the water. I saw Woody in his boat making circles in the area and was eventually picked up." She continually told the Board that she was in an uncontrollable state of hysteria.

Officer Mike Casey was called to the stand. Zinman pressed him for bringing his probationary officer, Patty Falls, to the river.

Why had he left the crime scene after he arrested Hallam and Wood? Why had he left the river during the night before giving Deputy Lee a formal written statement the following day? Why had he never told Officer Moreno that Patty had escaped and was okay?

Mike said his relationship with Patty Falls was purely platonic. He emphasized that they got a room with two beds at the hotel, and they planned to camp out on the beach with the rest of the L.A.P.D. group the following two days. He explained why he left the crime scene: He felt he and Officer Moreno weren't going to get a fair deal from the Yuma authorities when the owner of the Moonshine Saloon, Clara Troutman screamed, "I can get a dozen witnesses to say that you started the fight." Hallam's Moonshine friends had been extremely hostile to him and Officer Moreno during and after the arrival of the local authorities. That's why he and Officer Falls left that night. His plan was to write a comprehensive 15.7 of the incident for the department and mail a copy to Deputy Lee.

The advocate next called Internal Affairs investigator Sergeant Sewell. Sergeant Lamb was never called, nor did he ever appear before the Board. Sewell's testimony was nothing but a reiteration of his and Lamb's seven-month investigation. He and his partner lived up to their promise: "*We're going to fry Moreno's ass.*"

Sergeant Sewell gave perhaps the most stunning and chilling testimony of the entire Board of Rights trial regarding the death threats by the Aryan Brotherhood.

"Hallam's demeanor was—I'm trying to think of the best adjective—unkempt, surly, and yet talkative," Sewell recalled when asked to describe him. "His speech was interlaced with vulgarities and threats of violence to myself and to Officer Moreno. He was without a shirt. His upper torso was covered with scars and tattoos. He had a large scar on his shoulder. And he was a very large man. His right shoulder has a large scar. I asked him about it. He said that's when his wife shot him with a shotgun. He's very proud of his scars. And his violence-ridden past."

"During the interview, did he at one time say to you and your partner that he'd fight you and him there right now?"

"Yes, in the interview, he was telling me how brave and what a fearless warrior he is. He isn't afraid of anybody. In fact, he would fight me right here and right now."

"Would you say that based on the testimony you've heard, the description given of him of being very radical and very violent is a fairly good description of him?"

"Very accurate."

"Regarding the threats made by Gerry Hallam against Officer Moreno's life, specifically, what did he [Hallam] say?"

"Well, he—I remember on one occasion he said the only justice he wants is to get placed in a room with Moreno for five minutes and that's all that he wants. By the way, he referred to Moreno as 'Manchino,' and we did not correct him because we felt he was capable of carrying out the threats. We didn't want to give him any information regarding Officer Moreno that he didn't already have. He said he would kill him if—he said he was very accurate with a shotgun, and if he ever saw him again, he would kill him."

"Did he make any statements regarding some prison gang?"

"Yes. He said that he had some friends in EmE [Mexican prison gang]. He knows that Moreno works juvenile gang problems. And that he notified his friends in EmE to get Moreno."

"Did you do anything with that information?"

"I notified my captain who notified Operations—according to my captain, he notified Operations Central Bureau."

"And was that the only thing that was done with the information?

"Yes. Excuse me. I've also—I notified my lieutenant, who told me to notify Moreno's lieutenant, Lieutenant Lynch, and I did. I assumed that proper precautions would be made at this point."

At the conclusion of Sergeant Sewell's testimony, the Board of Rights adjourned for the day and advised all parties to return the following day, February 17, 1982, at 0945 hours.

On the 17th, the department produced its two "crown jewel" witnesses, Scott Engel and Betty Culp. Culp had not been interviewed before by either Deputy Lee at the crime scene on July 14 or Internal Affairs throughout their seven-month investigation. She volunteered to fly to California at the last minute to testify on behalf of Crazy Gerry.

On direct, Culp admitted she was a former manager of the Moonshine Saloon and a friend of Ron Wood. She testified she was with Charles Rourke's party the night of the fight.

Hernandez was only advised minutes before the Board reconvened on that day about their new star witness. He did not get an opportunity to interview Culp prior to her testimony, not that he would have anyway. I took copious notes on both Culp and Engel's testimonies in an effort to assist my worthless defense representative in his cross-examination.

Zinman methodically walked Culp through her testimony. After Zinman asked Culp about her background, including her previous employment as a Moonshine manager, she also admitted she was friends with Ron Wood.

Zinman asked her if she could identify the man she claimed started the fight with Crazy Gerry. She said, "That person is not here." Her response stunned Zinman and the three captains!

Zinman attempted to collect himself and pushed on. "Can you tell me how the fight started?"

"A man walked up to Big Gerry and punched him in the face, and they all fell to the ground. Big Gerry was on top of the man, and the man had him in a chokehold. I screamed, 'Someone help him!'"

"Did you see if Gerry did anything aggressive or hear him say anything before the fight?" "Not at that point. At one point, my son and Randy went over there, but Chuck [Rourke] got him back. Woody was able to free Gerry from [Moreno's] grip and everybody dispersed. Later, Gerry came back into the bar with a sawed-off shotgun through the rear door next to the dartboard. Chuck jumped up and grabbed ahold of Gerry and said, get rid of the gun. Gerry and Ron left by the bar back down to the parking lot. Ron has a trailer in the back by the Arches."

Culp pointed to addenda No. 2-A, a diagram depicting an overview of the property, and No. 2-B, depicting the parking area and saloon. The diagrams were drawn by Sewell and Lamb while they were in Parker, Arizona. Culp went on about when she first noticed the two men (Moreno and Casey) approaching the rear of the bar, one with a rifle, the other with a flashlight.

"Could you hear any conversation outside that bar?"

"None whatsoever; I was inside the building."

"What did you see Ron and Gerry do in that parking lot?"

"They got down on the ground face first, and I have no idea of the conversation. And then—"

"Was the person holding the rifle the same one who—"

"Who was choking Gerry."

"What was the light like?"

"It was after sundown and it was dark. But there's quite a bit of—there's light. And there's a little corner light on the building back there, a spotlight."

"The person with the gun, did you see anything he had done?"

"He struck Big Gerry on the head."

"With what?"

"With the butt of the gun, probably like in this manner. Two or three times."

"Did you see the person holding the gun do anything else?"

"Kicked him."

"Was Ron getting hit?"

"Ron was getting kicked; they both were getting kicked. But Ron was not getting hit with the rifle."

"Did you actually see the butt of the gun actually strike the body?"

"Yes."

On cross-examination, Culp admitted knowing Ron Wood for five years but denied ever knowing Crazy Gerry. Hernandez asked her if she recognized any of the patrons at the Moonshine that night.

"Probably over half of them were some of the people that I know."

"Then you saw someone approach Gerry from that group?"

"That's true."

"And this individual struck Gerry?"

Culp nodded. "And then everything started."

At this time, Hernandez challenged Culp's testimony under oath as to whether she actually was able to see Crazy Gerry and Ron Wood being beaten by Officers Moreno and Casey. Hernandez confronted Culp with I.A.D.'s Addenda No. 2-A. On the right corner of the diagram, there were three handwritten notations:

"A" noted the location of the parking lot area where Hallam and Wood were apprehended behind the Moonshine Saloon; "B" noted the location inside the bar where Culp and Rourke were seated and claimed to have seen the beating; and "C" pointed out the five-foot outcrop of the building on the north wall, *blocking* the view of Culp and Rourke.

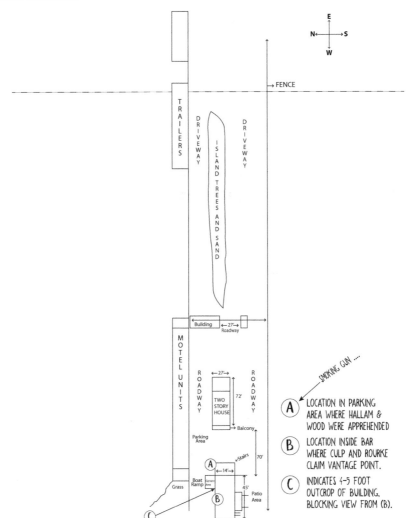

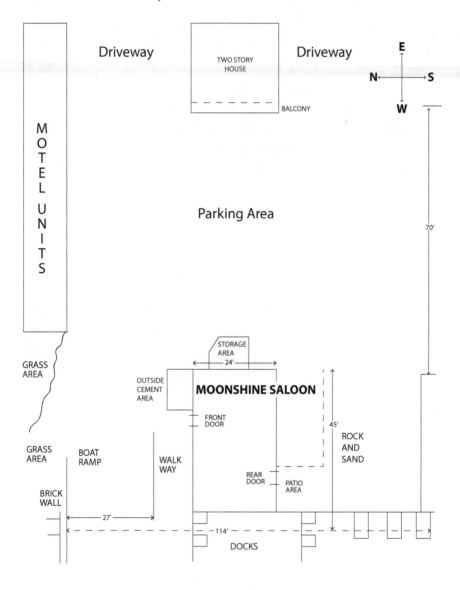

This was colossal! I immediately felt vindicated and waited for Hernandez to demand the removal of this perjurious witness. Ironically, it was Internal Affairs's own diagram of the Moonshine and surrounding property that irrefutably proved it was structurally impossible for Culp and Rourke to see the alleged beating of Crazy Gerry and Ron Wood.

Zinman, Bova, Harber, and Rodriguez all looked shocked. Then Zinman came up with a disgraceful rebuttal. He argued that I.A.D.'s diagram was not drawn to scale. There was an overwhelming sigh of relief from Captains Bova, Harber, and Rodriguez. They embraced that shameful argument and instructed Zinman to continue.

It was at this precise moment that I recalled what Sergeant Dave Gossman told me at the outset of the Colorado River complaint, when he overheard Sergeant Zinman proclaim, "Moreno is going to be fired regardless of the evidence."

After the Board's reprehensible decision in accepting Zinman's objection that the I.A.D.'s diagram was not made to scale, Hernandez continued his ill-prepared defense and continually challenged Culp's proclamation that she and Rourke had an unobstructed view of the beating. But it fell on deaf ears.

Before Culp left the stand, Captain Harbor asked her why she paid so much attention to the L.A.P.D. group sitting across the bar as opposed to the seven members of her party.

"I have bar eyes and ears, and it's just natural to me," she said.

I thought, yet she stated she did not hear Hallam making any of the vulgar comments and death threats that everyone else in the bar heard?

Throughout her testimony, Culp denied seeing Hallam chase any member of the L.A.P.D. group with the shotgun. One could measure this woman's odious character and veracity by a single fact: She volunteered to fly from one state to another to testify on behalf of Crazy Gerry, an ex-con and member of the Aryan Brotherhood. Shockingly, she further denied seeing Hallam come back into the bar after the fight with his sawed-off shotgun looking to murder anyone in the L.A.P.D. group.

Culp was dismissed. The department's second star witness was next—fourteen-year-old Scott Engel.

Engel was previously interviewed by Sergeant Lamb by telephone on August 4, 1981. In this interview, he stated he saw me beat Hallam with the butt of a rifle, and like Betty Culp, denied knowing Crazy Gerry. This gave Engel the critical stature of an independent witness.

On direct examination, Zinman asked Engel to tell the Board what he was doing on the evening of July 14, 1981. Engel stated that he was fishing next door to the Moonshine Saloon at the Cottonwood dock property north of the bar when he heard someone yell, "Freeze!" He ran toward the yelling, climbed up a brick fence, and saw two men, "spread-eagle."

"Did you know who the two men on the ground were at that time?"

"I knew one of them."

"And who was that?"

"Ron Wood."

"Did you know who the other person was at that time?"

"Un–unh, no."

"What was the man with the rifle asking the men on the ground?"

"He was asking him, where's the gun? And then he kicked the man in the face [Hallam]. And then he hit him on the back of the head with the butt of the gun twice."

"How far away were you?"

"Under twenty feet."

"What was the next thing you observed happen?"

"The Yuma County Sheriff came down the driveway."

"Did you leave your position and go down to the parking lot?"

"Yes, then the ambulance arrived and worked on Ron because he was all cut up and I tried to talk to Gerry. And after that I walked to the man that hit Gerry."

"Did you know Gerry prior to this?"

"Yeah, I mean, I've seen him. And my mom knows him."

"Do you know how your mom knows him?"

"Well, yeah, I think so, 'cause she's a bartender."

As I listened to the testimony, I knew at this precise moment Engel lost all his credibility. Zinman and the three captains were unable to mask their disappointment as well. Engel lied on three separate occasions about not knowing Crazy Gerry. First, on August 4, 1981, when he lied to I.A.D. Sergeant Lamb in his telephone interview, and again in his sworn testimony this day when he previously denied knowing Crazy Gerry twice.

The whole time Engel was on the stand he was profusely perspiring and squirming. Evidently, the setting and atmosphere was a bit too much for the fourteen-year-old budding white supremacist. He had known Hallam the whole time and no doubt wanted to endear himself to Crazy Gerry and the Moonshine adults.

Zinman continued asking questions. "When you walked over to the man who hit him [Hallam], did he tell you, 'Wouldn't you rather see me catch them and put them in jail instead of them killing me?'"

Hernandez objected to Zinman leading the witness.

Zinman asked Engel if he remembered talking to the sergeant from the police department, and he said yes. Zinman was attempting to prove that I had tried to dissuade Engel from telling the Yuma Sheriff that I beat Hallam with a rifle. He asked if Engel had made any statement like that to the Sheriff, but Engel said he did not.

On cross, Hernandez started by asking Engel where he was and what attracted his attention to the incident. Engel repeated essentially what he told Zinman on direct—that he ran to where he heard someone yelling.

"Prior to hearing the yelling in the parking lot, did anything unusual happen?"

"I remember some people coming out of the dock really fast and leaving; that was unusual."

"Did you see anybody jump in the water?"

"Un–unh, no, I didn't."

"Prior to the incident in the parking lot, did you see anybody carrying a gun?"

"No, I did not."

"Did you see anybody around the Moonshine with a gun?"

"No."

"I'm not trying to confuse you, but in your telephonic statement to Internal Affairs, you said you observed several individuals get into a boat prior to the lady jumping into the river. Do you remember making that statement?"

"No."

"You also stated in your phone interview, the boat drove away from the Moonshine and circled several times and picked up people. And after the ski boat left, you saw someone walk to the corner of the Moonshine on the front-door side with a large gun in his hands. Do you remember making that statement?"

"No, I did not make that statement."

"Scott, isn't it a fact that when you were fishing there, you saw Crazy Gerry coming around this building chasing a whole bunch of people with a shotgun?"

"No."

At this time, the Board held a discussion off the record. Then they instructed Sergeant Sewell to leave the hearing room and listen to Engel's tapped telephonic interview from August 4, 1981.

At this point, Hernandez attempted once again to clarify what I had said to Engel before the authorities arrived. This time Engel answered affirmatively. Hernandez then asked Engel if he told Sergeant Lamb on the phone that he did not know Crazy Gerry, and he said he didn't remember.

Hernandez repeatedly asked the same question, and Engel kept stating, "I don't remember." Then Engel relented and stated, "I could have said that, yeah."

"Do you have a river nickname?"

"Skunk."

"Did you know Gerry as Crazy Gerry before the day of the incident?"

"I knew him as Gerry, but not Crazy Gerry."

"Can you describe the two men you saw standing over Gerry and Ron?"

"No."

"The man with the rifle, what did he look like?"

"I don't remember."

"I want you to look around the room and tell me whether or not you recognize any of those two individuals who you saw with Gerry and Ron that day?"

"No."

"Have you talked to Gerry before the incident?"

"Yeah, we met in the bar."

"You go to the bar?"

"Well, yeah, my mom goes to the bar [Moonshine Saloon]."

"Captain Bova, I want to point out that in the telephonic interview, he [Engel] observed the suspect [Moreno] kick Gerry in the head."

Bova asked, "Can you describe the force of the rifle strike?

"They meant to hurt him," Engel answered.

Hernandez asked, "Do you remember where the other man [Officer Casey] was?"

"No."

The Board took a short break, and Engel was taken into the I.A.D. office to listen to the taped interview from August 4, 1981. Zinman then asked Engel if he still didn't remember making the statement about Officer Moreno trying to change his story. Remarkably, he said he did not remember. Engel was excused.

Finally, Officer Davis Carl Artis was called. Zinman asked Artis who he worked for and at what point he received the assistance call.

"I am an Arizona Highway patrol officer," Artis replied. "I got a call to assist the Sheriff's office regarding a bar fight and possible shots fired. I and other highway patrol units responded."

"When you arrived, what did you see?"

"There were subjects lying on the ground. And a man was standing next to her [Deputy Lee] and another man [Officer Casey], but I didn't remember what he looked like. The men on the ground were bloody and beat up. And she [Deputy Lee] had the men on the ground handcuffed."

"Did you talk to Officer Moreno?"

"Yes, and he was leaning over and talking to the man on the ground [Hallam]. Then this lady who was the manager of the bar [Clara Troutman] walked over to me and said, 'Come here; this officer [Moreno] is telling that guy that he is going to kill him.' I walked over to the guy and asked him [Hallam] if he was being threatened. He said yeah."

"Was the man [Hallam] intoxicated?"

"His breath and eyes looked like he had been drinking."

"Did you determine if Officer Moreno was intoxicated?"

"Yes."

"Did you know the men on the ground?"

"No. Several minutes later a bartender told me—I don't remember the exact words—that Officer Moreno was trying to talk the kid out of something. Who would you rather see go to jail, something to that effect. So, I walked over to Officer Moreno and told him to stop and stay away from the people."

Artis continued. "Later a man came up to me and told me he gave a .30-30 rifle to Officer Moreno and that he had his ID. I told him it [the rifle] was involved in a crime and he would have to ask the Sheriff for it. He got mad and walked away. I walked over to Deputy Lee and told her about what the barmaid said, about the man asking me for his rifle back and that man had officer Moreno's ID. And that's as far as I went."

"Did you talk to the paramedic [Mike Ward]?"

"Yes, he said that that guy [Officer Moreno] was threatening this man [Hallam]."

"Did you walk into the Moonshine Saloon and interview anyone?"

"Yes, and it was kind of like walking into a den of lions, because most of the people were intoxicated."

"Do you remember interviewing Charles Rourke?"

"Yes, he was sitting with Betty Culp. They told me about the fight inside the bar, where he [Moreno] struck [Hallam] for no apparent reason, and how he was beating him [Hallam] up in the parking lot with the gun."

Hernandez, on cross-examination, asked Artis if the owner of the bar told him about a shotgun being thrown into the bushes.

"No, Gail Lee did."

"When you were interviewed by Sergeant Lamb, do you remember telling him the owner of the Moonshine told you Hallam threw the gun in the bushes?"

"I may have, but don't remember."

"Did you hear threats being made to Hallam by Officer Moreno?"

"No sir, I did not."

This line of questioning went on for some time, but there were no new revelations other then what was previously stated in Zinman's direct.

Hernandez then questioned Officer Artis about the .30-30 rifle. Artis explained that at some point, they ascertained that Yard Sr. gave Officer Moreno the stolen rifle, and they were going to secure a search warrant to look for more weapons at Yard's home. But after the incident, Artis said he did not follow up to the Yuma County substation, and he never submitted a statement.

Officer Artis was dismissed.

I was recalled to the stand, but Zinman was unable to elicit anything new that I hadn't already mentioned in my 15.7 and statements to I.A.D..

Then Zinman moved on to the "grabbing and shoving" of the Avenues murder suspect, Arnold Aguirre. Again, there were no new revelations.

On cross-examination, Hernandez didn't harm or help the defense.

The Board of Rights completed their case.

In Zinman's closing argument, he evoked Internal Affairs's motto: "We have a saying in the Advocate's office. When you have the facts on your side, argue the facts. When you have the law on your side, argue the law. And when you haven't got anything, you try to blow as much smoke as you can to obscure all facts."

How fitting the last sentence was, I thought to myself.

This whole affair was an immoral travesty of unthinkable injustice. That the Los Angeles Police Department would side with the likes of the Aryan Brotherhood's white supremacists over their own officers is a vulgar insult to all law enforcement.

Zinman went on and on, addressing the ten counts and how I was void of character and veracity. Then he exalted the character of the Moonshine Saloon witnesses.

Hernandez's closing argument was nothing more than an exercise in futility. His lack of preparation was glaringly evident throughout the Board of Rights, including in his closing statement.

On February 18, 1982, at approximately 1500 hours, the Chairman of the Board, Captain Bova, read their closing statement.

"The Board finds that the 'Accused' is guilty of:

Count 4, kicking Gerry Hallam in the body and striking him about the head and back with the butt of a rifle.

Count 6, making improper remarks to Gerry Hallam (tactical language).

Count 8, failing to promptly notify the department with a 15.7.

Count 9, (the Board combined counts 9 and 10 to a single count and reworded the charge) grabbing Arnold Aguirre by the throat and back of the neck and shoving him.

The Board therefore prescribes its penalty as follows: That Police Officer Alfonso Moreno be REMOVED from his position as police officer, effective December 31, 1981, with total loss of pay."

11
Barren Oak

THERE ARE TIMES when I think to myself that if Hallam had been successful in killing me, it would have been exponentially more merciful than what I have mentally endured all these years.

In addition to losing my job, I lost all the money I had put into the city pension fund. Finding work was impossible—I was viewed as an outcast by society and seen as a disgraced corrupt cop. The shame, anguish, and despair I've endured to this day is incalculable. The only work I could find was shithole security jobs in places like "dime-a-dance" halls in the seedy bowels of downtown Los Angeles.

In those years, 1979 to 1992, it was the height of the low-intensity wars in El Salvador, Guatemala, and Honduras. Masses of young girls from those war-torn countries were illegally streaming into the United States to find refuge and work in places like those degrading dance halls. My job was to keep them safe from the hordes of drunks and drugged-out customers, most of whom were also from those countries. And many of the other patrons were from the ranks of L.A.'s street gangs and our local dopers, drunks, and pimps.

I also found some part-time work at a Payless shoe store in downtown L.A. My job was to stand at the center of the store entrance giving the potential low-life thieves the thousand-yard stare to dissuade them from stealing the store empty. I worked ten-hour shifts with only a single half-hour break. That type of employment was as good as it was going to get for years.

My family and friends were unable to process my termination. Mom was always bragging about her son becoming a Los Angeles police officer. I was the first ever Marine and police officer in both the Adams and Moreno family trees.

There was always the lure of falling into alcohol and drugs to sedate my unspeakable pain. But I was fortunate enough to realize that would only sap my soul from fighting the corrupt City Hall and L.A.P.D. Instead, I worked out twice a day before and after work. Bill Wong, Poppin' Fresh (Danny Hart), Rick Beach, John Mahli, and Maria Elena stood at my six, and Mom was my Rock of Gibraltar.

When I could get away from the tangled schedule of working those demeaning jobs, Bill and I enjoyed running the hill trails around the Police Academy, then having a cold beer afterward. Being with Bill and Maria Elena was a time out of sorts from my new reality of ceaseless mental horror and fear for my family.

—

In another terrible twist of fate, in the early morning hours of October 29, 1983, Officer Dean Brinker called to tell me that Bill Wong and his partner, Art Soo Hoo, had been killed.

Bill and Art were working a flare-up gang war between Chinatown's Triad and Tong gangs. They were minutes from end of watch when they decided to give the hot spot one more pass. When their vehicle entered the intersection of Alpine and Broadway, their car was T-boned by a Buick Skylark speeding away from a drug deal gone bad. The suspect's vehicle was traveling between seventy and eighty miles per hour. The three suspects in the car—Teobaldo Villanueva (driver), Fausto Villareal (right-front passenger), and Primo Manriquez (seated in the rear)—were all illegal aliens from Mexico and members of the Sinaloa drug cartel in Mexico.

Manriquez (the rear passenger) only remained at the scene because of his injuries and was arrested. He was charged with being an accessory to murder and convicted, then released for time served.

The driver and right-front passenger fled back to Mexico. A short time after Bill and Art's murder, Villareal returned to the United States under an assumed name and enjoyed the fruits of this gracious nation before being arrested in May 2011 for an unrelated crime. He was fingerprinted and identified as one of the killers. He pleaded guilty to manslaughter and spent a short time in the joint.

The driver of the murder vehicle, Teobaldo Villanueva, has enjoyed a full life of freedom for the past thirty-five years. American authorities know his whereabouts, but he is under the protection of the Sinaloa Mexico drug cartel.

Bill's death has forever left a hole in my heart that will never heal. Through the years, I've called L.A.P.D. Robbery Homicide Division and spoken to various detectives to see if they are any closer in making an arrest. But during the last two decades, they have become less focused on Bill and Art's murder. Granted, some of them weren't born when Bill and Art were killed. But just the same, their killer is still out there, and our men and women in law enforcement need to be assured that if they are killed in the line of duty, they won't be forgotten like Bill and Art.

So, my brother and sister street coppers, take heed of the rats in the attic, for they do not have your six.

—

I continued to work in dives and began applying to fifteen police departments and six fire departments. I started with Long Beach and continued with Glendale, Pasadena, South Gate, Beverly Hills, El Segundo, Manhattan Beach, Hermosa Beach, Redondo Beach, Torrance, Santa Monica, Burbank, Downey, the Los Angeles County Sheriff's Department, and Culver City Police Department.

Applying to these P.D.s was nothing like what I experienced when I was erroneously disqualified nine separate times in five years when I first applied for the Los Angeles Police Department. However, this time I was up against a termination from the premier police department in the United States, so most of the P.D.s rejected me outright. A few of the departments were forthright with me and admitted that my police rating reports and seventy-plus commendations were incredibly unique in law enforcement. However, it was a question of liability if they hired me—if something went sideways, their department would pay for it in spades.

The six fire departments—Beverly Hills, Torrance, Redondo Beach, Downey, Los Angeles County, and the City—were extremely kind, but I was pushing thirty-nine years old and was a fired cop. The fire departments would often go through the trouble of getting me a cup of coffee while I was pleading for a job. I guess I was one pathetic sight.

Then, to my shock, I got a call back from Culver City Police Department. Their Chief of Police Ted Cook was a former Los Angeles police lieutenant. In 1968, while on the L.A.P.D., Officer Cook was one of the officers who went into harm's way when they pulled Officer Gary Murakami out of the line of fire after he took a shotgun blast to the face. Officer Murakami died of his wounds. It was only his second day out of the Academy. The suspect was killed at the scene. Officer Cook was a street cop's kind of cop.

Culver P.D. had an opening for a "lateral transfer" position. The position required that the applicant be either a current California police officer or had left law enforcement no more than two years prior. Before I took the oral exam, I spoke with Officer Mathews who was assigned to conduct the background phase of the applicants. I took all the documents relative to my termination, including my L.A.P.D. rating reports and commendations, to share with him.

I couldn't understand why Culver City, unlike all the other departments, was willing to spend all this time and effort looking into my case when there were nine other applicants for the position with no baggage. After hours and hours of questions, Officer Mathews scheduled me for an oral exam, physical agility test, physical, psychological test, background check, and a polygraph.

In the polygraph, I was asked about striking Crazy Gerry with the butt of the .30-30 rifle. The poly results confirmed my innocence. I also received the highest oral score of the nine applicants and successfully passed all the remaining tests.

On August 7, 1984, I was hired. But on August 20, 1984, I pulled the pin. That well-policed jurisdiction was much too civil for L.A.'s last street cop. But I will be forever grateful to Chief Cook and Officer Mathews.

Semper Fi.

⌒

The night after my trial, I was driving down Alameda Street. It's only about eight miles home from Parker Center, but it felt like a thousand miles of falling into a vortex of sheer darkness and doom. By now, of course, I had lost my Aston Martin, so I had to use Mom's 1972 white-and-red four-door Ford Victoria.

I stopped at a seedy liquor store and bought a quart of cheap East-side beer, the kind Dad drank. I couldn't bring myself to drive straight home and see that look on Mom's face. I knew no matter how hard I tried to hide it, she would see the unbearable pain in my soul. Just before I got to Mom's, it occurred to me to stop at Roosevelt Park and see if that old grand oak tree was still there by the rec room. That tree had given me so much comfort when I had sat up against its warm bark in other troubled times.

It was still there, but it appeared to be dying from some sort of fungus unlike the other much smaller trees around. It was barren of leaves, and its bark was hard, dry, and cold, like my heart. Just the same, I sat up against that old dying friend and opened my bottle of brew.

Nothing had really changed in this park. I saw the ubiquitous gangsters roaming about looking for their next victims. They were giving me the assessment stare. Was I an easy mark? I wasn't armed, so I gave them that Marine Corps, thousand-yard stare. It worked, and they left me alone.

I took my time sipping on my brew, but it was getting cold and dark. So, I left my old dying friend that cold night and went home where Mom was in the kitchen making dinner.

Epilogue

AFTER MY TERMINATION, I met with Officer Bunker at the Police Academy's Embers Room bar. I needed to pick up a couple items I had stored at the Academy. While we were in the bar, Captain Jess Rodriguez walked in with Lieutenant Kilgo from Robbery/Homicide Division. I was shocked with his temerity when he and Kilgo walked over to Dean and me! I'd never met Lieutenant Kilgo, but he was a legendary robbery/homicide detective and everyone knew who he was.

Lieutenant Kilgo spoke for Captain Rodriguez. "Jess [Captain Rodriguez] told me all about your termination and said you had an 'inadequate defense.' When you appeal your termination, emphasize that point!"

Rodriguez agreed. "Listen to him, listen to him, he knows what he's talking about."

They walked away, and Dean and I stood there in disbelief.

Days later, I obtained a copy of the Los Angeles Police Department's Board of Rights manual. I read the rules and procedures governing the conduct of a Board of Rights hearing. On page 3, section 140.75, there are nine guidelines a BOR is mandated to follow. Rule number 6 states, "If it appears that the case of either the accused or the department's is incomplete, through inability, inexperience, ignorance, or an inadequate investigation, it shall be the duty of the Board to question witnesses, subpoena additional witnesses, request additional investigation, or perform whatever function necessary to determine the true facts."

If my inadequate defense was so apparent to Captain Rodriguez,

Captains Bova and Harber were no doubt of the same mind. In addition to the corrupt I.A.D. investigation, and equally corrupt Board of Rights that resulted in my termination, I no longer had the legal right to bear arms and protect my mom, brothers, and sisters from the Aryan Brotherhood death threats.

Obviously, my logic in choosing the three captains for my Board was wholly ignorant. They were your generic thieves of dishonor and big city police corruption. Just the same, they were duty bound to stop the proceeding, per section 140.75, once it was apparent Hank Hernandez had not prepared a defense.

As for the Chairman of the Board of Rights, Captain Bova—who shot twenty-five-year-old Leonard Deadwyler to death, an African American who was feverishly driving his pregnant wife to the hospital—my calculus in picking him was unparalleled ignorance. Instead of being fired and prosecuted after that killing, the department had promoted Bova to Captain III, and he is now enjoying a retirement of $115,000 a year while Mr. Leonard Deadwyler lies in his grave.

The disclosures of the department's duplicity and corruption would surface on a continual basis for years to come. In early March 1982, some weeks after my termination, the department finally released the verdicts on Officers Dean Bunker and Mike Casey's personnel complaints. Both officers' complaints were completed months before my BOR, but they were not handled by I.A.D.. They were investigated and adjudicated at the officers' assigned division, Hollenbeck and Hollywood.

There was indeed a nefarious logic to why they withheld their findings until after my termination. Officer Bunker's two charges of misconduct—striking Ron Wood on the head with a pool cue without cause, and making false statements to another police agency (Yuma County Sheriff Department)—were adjudicated as unfounded by the department. The department found the ex-con (Hallam) and his white supremacists' testimonies "not credible" in Officer Bunker's charges of misconduct. Yet, the department found the same witnesses credible in my charges?

The department's duplicity did not stop there. Officer Bunker did not submit a 15.7 and was not charged with failing to notify the department of the off-duty altercation in Arizona. Lieutenant Art Melendrez, Officer Bunker's team lieutenant, wrote in his investigative administrative cover letter: "No formal report (15.7) was made by Officer Bunker since Officers Casey and Falls had already completed a 15.7 to their watch commander at Hollywood Division." However, I was found guilty for submitting a 15.7 "in an untimely manner" by the BOR.

Officer Mike Casey had faced four counts of misconduct: (1) having an improper relationship with his probationer, Officer Patty Falls; (2) not advising Officer Moreno that Officer Falls was not being held hostage by Crazy Gerry; (3) leaving the scene of a criminal investigation without informing the authorities; and (4) failing to respond to the Yuma County Sheriff's substation after being requested to do so. He was found guilty of the last three counts and received a twenty-two-day suspension.

Sometime after my termination, Sergeant Dave Gossman, who was still working at I.A.D., was unable to ethically tolerate the department's malfeasance in my termination. He formally submitted a sworn declaration in support of my Request for a Rehearing, per City Charter section 202, subsection 16. Dave was acutely aware that in doing this he would forever throw his career under the bus, but he did it just the same. In his declaration, he exposed Sergeant Zinman's proclamation, "Officer Moreno is going to be fired regardless of the evidence."

There was another stunning revelation in Sergeant Gossman's declaration. Ironically, Sergeant Gossman was Detective Skyys's robbery/homicide partner at Hollywood Division prior to Skyys's transferring to OCB CRASH. Under penalty of perjury (a felony), Sergeant Gossman stated that between May 22 and July 27, 1979, on several occasions while they were interrogating suspects and not getting anywhere, Skyys turned off the tape recorder and started "yelling and screaming at the suspect; then he would grab the suspects by the lapels or shirt sleeves and push or pull them while yelling at them."

Once the declaration was officially submitted to the department, Internal Affairs initiated a personnel complaint against Detective Skyys, I.A.D. report No. 84-1284. In one of many stunning hypocrisies and deceitful duplicities in the department's charge against Detective Skyys, the charge was titled "Improper Tactics" as opposed to

"Excessive Force" regarding grabbing and shoving suspects while interviewing them. However, in my case, I was charged with "Excessive Force."

On page 4 of Detective Skyys's I.A.D. investigation, it reads: "After a review of the case with Internal Affairs Division command, it was determined that to attempt to locate any suspects interviewed by Skyys would probably be nonproductive." Due to the fact that neither victims or witnesses to Skyys's alleged misconduct have been identified, and the passage of time since May to July 1979, this case was not presented to the Special Investigation Division of the Los Angeles District Attorney's Office. Detective Skyys was found innocent of all charges and promoted to the new head of the OCB CRASH detectives.

Sergeant Gossman was charged with "neglect of duty" for failing to report Detective Skyys's misconduct. He received a written "reprimand" and was never promoted above his position.

Sergeant Hank Hernandez was fast-tracked to lieutenant after my termination, and after retirement, he became the General Council for the Los Angeles Police Protective League.

Some months after my termination, I went before the Board of the Los Angeles Police Protective League and asked if they would appeal my firing to the Los Angeles County Superior Court. They agreed to champion my case and initiated the arduous legal process. The League appointed attorney Steve Pingel to prepare the brief. Steve interviewed countless witnesses, dissected the entire personnel complaint, including my police record, and he drove to Arizona and developed the critical "line-of-sight" issue. In effect, he did everything Hank Hernandez did not do.

Then came a hit that I have never recovered from. Both the Los Angeles Superior and Appellate Courts rejected my case in favor of the Los Angeles Police Department.

To this day, I have continued to file a "Request for Rehiring" (RFR), starting with Chief Daryl Gates on May 29, 1984. The brief included the "Fruit of the Poisonous Tree" argument regarding the statements made by Internal Affairs Sergeants Sewell, Lamb, and Zinman.

I emphasized the genesis of my troubles with the department when I reported Lieutenant Lynch underreporting the true number of gang-related crimes in Central Bureau to the Commander of the Bureau, Mark Kroeker. I included my unparalleled record of service and restraint, as well as the department's duplicity in finding Officer Bunker and Detective Skyys not guilty, and Captain Jess Rodriguez's revelation that I did not receive an adequate defense.

The brief also included several courageous declarations from Sergeants Ray Noetzel, Larry Mazur, Dave Gossman, Officers Dean Bunker and Mike Moulin, and Attorney Steve Pingel's comprehensive onsite investigation into the Colorado River altercation. I also included the Culver City Police Department's polygraph examination.

On October 11, 1984, Chief Gates replied in a letter. The last line of the curt letter reads:

"I find no reason to cause a further reinvestigation or conduct a rehearing into the original matter."

To date, I have petitioned every subsequent Los Angeles police chief with a copy of the RFR, including Willie Williams, Bayan Lewis, Bernard Parks, Martin Pomeroy, William Bratton, Michael Downing, and Charles Beck.

On February 8, 2010, and again on March 21, 2013, I petitioned Mayor Antonio Villaragosa for a Request for Rehearing. He did not respond.

On May 27, 2014, I personally delivered a hard copy of the RFR to Herb Wesson, President of the Los Angeles City Council, and e-mailed a copy to the fourteen other city councilpersons. Later that day, I addressed the entire City Council in chambers via the public comment's forum.

On May 28, 2014, I carried a hard copy of the RFR to Mayor Eric Garcetti's office. And once again on May 5, 2017, I delivered an updated RFR. I had this appeal videotaped.

Both the public address to the Los Angeles City Council and my hand-delivered copy of the RFR to Mayor Eric Garcetti can be viewed on YouTube in a video titled "L.A.'s Last Street Cop, parts 1 and 2."

To date, I have not received a single reply from the Los Angeles Police Department, the City Council, or the mayor's office. I am acutely aware that my unlawful termination from the Los Angeles Police Department did not occur under their watch. However, once the Chief of Police, the City Council, and the mayor became aware of this criminal behavior, they are both fiducially and morally bound to right this historic injustice.

On May 5, 2015, I took an additional polygraph examination by Mr. Joe Delia, one of America's premier polygraph examiners, at his office in Claremont, California. The results were identical to Culver City Police Department's—I am innocent of the Colorado River personnel complaint.

Appendix I: Gerry Hallam Interview

GERRY HALLAM, 11233 GREENWOOD WAY, ONTARIO, (714) 628-5072

Hallam was interviewed on August 12, 1981, at 1800 hours by
Sergeants Lamb and Sewell. The interview was not tape recorded
nor were any written statements taken at the time of the interview
due to Hallam's reluctance to discuss the matter. Written notes
were made of the interview on August 12, 1981, several hours after
the interview. The interview was conducted at Hallam's parents'
residence at 11233 Greenwood Way in Ontario, California.

Hallam admitted to being in Parker, Arizona, on July 12, 1981 [1]
and to being involved in the incident at the Moonshine Saloon. [2]
During the interview, Hallam referred to Moreno as Manchino. [3]
Hallam identified Moreno's photograph as the individual he was [4]
referring to as Manchino. Because of threats to Moreno's life, [5]
Hallam was not corrected as to the proper pronunciation of Moreno's [6]
name. Hallam made numerous threats to Moreno's life. He explained [7]
that he knew Moreno worked juvenile problems and that friends of [8]
his from "Emma"- (a Mexican prison gang) would locate him. When [9]
Hallam located Moreno, he was going to kill him. Hallam was [10]
upset over the fact that Moreno had hit him from behind when [11]
Hallam was not looking. The only justice Hallam wanted was to [12]
be placed in a room alone with Moreno. He indicated that he [13]
would kill Moreno if given the chance, even if it meant going [14]
to prison. [15]

Hallam and Wood were sitting at the bar (Moonshine Saloon) when
Fowler came up to the bar and sat by him. Hallam was unable to
identify Fowler's photograph but described her clothing as tight
pants, a blouse and high heels. Hallam thought that Fowler had
black hair but he was not sure. The woman was identified as
Fowler by investigators and referred to as Fowler. Fowler sat
down between Hallam and Wood. Fowler and Wood were involved in
a conversation but Hallam did not hear the conversation. Hallam
could not recall how he knew that Fowler was a police officer
but sometime during the conversation, he did learn that fact.
At some point, Wood stated to Fowler, "You have nice tits."
Fowler then pulled her blouse away from her body stating,
"You think so." When Fowler pulled her blouse away from her
body, both Hallam and Wood could see her breasts. Hallam thought
that since Fowler would expose herself. she was the type of woman
who would become involved in sexual conduct. Hallam felt confident
that he could have sexual relations with Fowler. Hallam became
involved in a conversation with Fowler. Hallam asked Fowler
whom she was with at the bar. Fowler pointed to either Moreno
or Casados. Hallam identified Moreno's photograph but was not
able to positively identify Casados' photograph. Hallam made
a comment to Fowler about her boyfriend. Hallam could not recall
the exact comment but did know that it was a derogatory remark

about his being a Mexican-American. Fowler responded, "He is not
a American, he is an Italian," to which Hallam responded, "A wap,
that is almost as bad as being a nigger." Fowler got up from
her stool and walked over to the other people in her group, who
were standing by the pool table. Approximately five or ten
minutes later, Hallam felt someone grab his right arm and begin
to pull him away from the bar. Hallam turned and observed that
Moreno was that individual. Moreno made some type of statement
about going outside. Hallam thought that he was about to be
hit and attempted to turn away from Moreno. Hallam was not able
to turn fast enough and Moreno hit him in the mouth area with a
closed fist. The impact of the blow split his lip open. Hallam
then grabbed Moreno around the head and was trying to hit Moreno,
when Moreno hit him in the groin area. Someone else grabbed Hallam
around the neck and started choking him. Hallam released Moreno
so that he could get free from the other individual. Hallam did
not see the other individual. While Hallam was struggling with
the other individual, Moreno grabbed him in a choke hold. Both
Hallam and Moreno fell to the ground. Moreno was on the ground,
facing upward, with Hallam on top of Moreno. Hallam was also facing
upward and Moreno was choking him. Hallam observed Wood attempting
to get him free from the choke hold when someone hit Wood on the
back of his head with a pool cue. Hallam reviewed the photographs
and identified Brinker's photograph, if Brinker was tall and balding,
as the individual who hit Wood with the pool cue. Wood fell
toward the bar as if stunned. As Moreno choked Hallam, Woody
attempted to pull Moreno off of Hallam. It appeared that Woody
was using all of his strength to pull Moreno's arm away from
Hallam's neck. At one point, Brinker yelled to Moreno to let go
of Hallam. Hallam recalls seeing skin underneath Woody's fingernails
from Moreno's forearm. When Woody was finally able to pull Moreno
off of Hallam, Hallam stood up and immediately exited the saloon.
Hallam went to his truck and got his shotgun. He had decided that
he was going to kill Moreno. As Hallam started toward the bar,
still being on the north side, Woody and another individual approached
him. They told him to put the gun away. Hallam saw Wood walking
up the road toward the main highway and started in his direction,
so that he could walk up the road with him. As he started across
the parking lot, he heard a noise by the trash bin. Hallam looked
in that direction and observed Fowler and another female. Hallam
walked over in their direction and both Fowler and the other female
got up and started to run. Hallam felt that it was fortunate that
they did run because he might have shot them. Hallam then walked
over to Wood and walked up the road with him. Hallam stated that
he hid the shotgun but would not state where he hid it. After a
short period of time, Hallam and Wood started walking back toward
the Moonshine Saloon. As they approached the saloon, Carla
(Troutman) came up to them and began talking to them. As they
were talking, Moreno and another individual came from behind a

73

vehicle which was parked next to the trash bin. Moreno was holding
a rifle and ordering Hallam and Wood to the ground. Moreno then
handcuffed both Hallam and Wood; prior to any local police units
arriving. Moreno then hit Hallam with the rifle butt four times.
He hit him in the back of the neck, behind the ear, to the top
of his head, and to the middle of his back. Moreno then kicked
him numerous times to the body and one time to the face. Hallam
was on the ground between the Moonshine Saloon and Carla's house
facing the motels. Wood was on Hallam's right side. Hallam
showed the investigators where he was missing a tooth) and explained
that he lost it when Moreno kicked him in the mouth. Hallam did
not see the other individual hit Wood, and he knew that the other
individual did not hit him. Hallam was next to the cement patio
area when Woody and the other individual stopped him. During the
time that Moreno was kicking and hitting Hallam with the rifle,
Carla was present and two kids were watching from the fence area.
After Hallam was handcuffed, Moreno approached, and in front of
Carla and a fireman working the rescue ambulance stated that if
given the chance, he would kill Hallam. Carla cold one of the
local agency officers and that officer kept Moreno away from
Hallam. During the entire time Moreno continued asking Hallam
where the shotgun was hidden. Hallam did not tell him where the
shotgun was hidden.

When Hallam was on the ground handcuffed, Moreno searched him.
This search took place after the Yuma officers had arrived.
During this search, Moreno removed Hallam's wallet. The wallet
contained Hallam's identification and six one hundred dollar
bills. (Hallam removed two one hundred dollar bills from his
pocket and stated, "Just like this because I always carry hundreds.")
Hallam described the wallet as a large brown snap type commonly
referred to as a trucker's wallet. Moreno then stated to Hallam,
"I have your wallet, your name, and address and know where you
live. Someday, I will kill you. I will shoot you and place a
gun underneath you." Later, at the Parker Jail facility, Moreno
again told Hallam he was "dead", that Moreno knew where Hallam
lived, and that he would "get him". Hallam was never given back
his wallet. (When asked if he was a member of the Aryan Brotherhood,
Hallam merely smiled.) Hallam stated although he does not normally
drink, while at the Moonshine he drank a Watermelon Slush.

The notes from which this statement was written were not read back
to Hallam due to the circumstances of the interview.

Appendix II:
Al Moreno Polygraph

JOE DELIA
CERTIFIED POLYGRAPH EXAMINER
415 W FOOTHILL BLVD, SUITE 125B
CLAREMONT, CALIFORNIA 91711

REPORT OF POLYGRAPH EXAMINER

SPECIFIC ISSUE EXAMINATION

SUBJECT: **AL MORENO**

TEST DATE: 5/09/15

TEST ISSUE: When Mr. Moreno took Hallam into custody, after the one compliance Tap to Jerry Hallam's shoulder with the butt of the rifle, did he/Moreno strike Hallam with his hands, feet or rifle.

Prior to the Polygraph Examination the above subject agreed to submit for a Polygraph Examination, where he signed my company waiver, see attached.

TEST RESULTS:
  NO DECEPTION INDICATED

Relevant Questions Asked;

> 5)   When you took Jerry Hallam into custody, other than the rifle compliance tap, did you strike him with your hands, feet or rifle?   Answer "NO"

> 7)   Did you lie to me today about when you took Hallam into custody that you did not strike him with any part of your body, other than the one compliance tap with the rifle? ANSWER "NO"

Evaluation of the collected charts on this examination showed a determination of "No Deception Indicated." It is my opinion, based on the results of his test, that the subject answered the above listed relevant questions truthfully.

POST TEST INTERVIEW: None.

The results of this test were discussed with the subject.

Joe Delia
Certified Polygraph Examiner

Date 5/09/15   Place CLAREMONT

1. I ALFONSO MORENO of my own free will, without promise of immunity, threats or coercion, agree to take a polygraph (lie detector test) to be given to me by an officer and/or employee of IDELIA _____ for the mutual benefit of myself and ALFONSO MORENO

I do hereby agree that the results of said test and such conclusion that may be drawn therefrom by IDELIA _____, its officers, agents and employees may be disclosed to ___ a.y. ___ its officers, agents and employees and to any other interested persons, both orally and in writing, for whatever uses they may determine.

I full well understand that the results of such a test and the conclusion drawn therefrom by IDELIA _____, its officers, agents and employees may prove unfavorable to me. I do, none the less, hold IDELIA _____, its officers, agents, and employees free and harmless from any claim I might otherwise have against them for any damages or liability to me resulting from the taking of the test and the disclosure of its results and the conclusions drawn therefrom.

I hereby remise, release, waive and forever discharge each of the above named corporations, firms, their respective officers, agents and employees from any and all action or cause of action, claim, demand or liability which I have now or may ever have resulting directly or indirectly from my taking said examination and the oral and written opinions rendered because of said examination. I understand that for mutual benefit both the interview and examination will be tape recorded.

IN WITNESS WHEREOF, I have hereunto set my hand and seal.

It is the law of the State of California that no Employer or prospective Employer may demand or require that you submit to a polygraph examination (lie detector test) as a condition of employment or continued employment. You cannot and shall not be denied employment based upon your refusal to submit to a polygraph exam.

I HAVE READ AND UNDERSTAND THE ABOVE and I confirm that MR. MORENO has requested that I submit to a polygraph examination (lie detector test). I hereby consent to the polygraph examination and understand and agree that I will not receive a copy of the report nor the charts and also agree that the report and charts are the property of the Police Department that I am testing for. For any information contact the above Police Dept. Background Investigator.

_____   × _____
Witnessed: Seal (Signature of person examined/time)

This exam was concluded at _____ on the above date. Having submitted myself freely to this exam, I hereby reaffirm my agreement as expressed above. I swear that during said exam there were no threats or harm done to me or any promises made to me during the entire time I have been here, either in connection with the examination or the signing of this form.

_____   × _____
Witnessed: Seal (Signature of person examined)

ZCT		5/9/2015	Page 1 of 1
ID	ER	Text Series Type: Zone	
1	Y	Is this the month of MAY?	
2	Y	Regarding THE INCIDENT YOU HAD WITH Jerry Hallam, do you intend to answer truthfully each question about that?	
3	Y	Are you completely convinced that I will not ask you a question on this test that has not already been reviewed?	
C9	N	Prior to 1980, did you ever lie to anyone ?	
₋R5	N	When you took Jerry Hallam into custody, other than the rifle complaince tap , did you strike him with your hands, feet or rife ?	
C6	N	Before your 30th birthday, did you ever lie to someone in authority ?	
⟋R7	N	Did you lie to me today about when you took Hallam into custody that you did not strike him with any part of your body, other than the one complaince tap with the rifle ?	
C4	N	Prior to 1980, did you ever lie to someone who trusted you ?	
8	N	Is there something else you are afraid I will ask you a question about, even though I have told you I would not?	

CVOS		5/9/2015	Page 1 of 1
ID	ER	Text Series Type: Rank	
1	Y	IS YOUR FIRST NAME AL ?	
2	N	DID YOU COME HER INTENDING TO LIE ABOUT ANYTHING?	
3	Y	WHAT DOES 6 TIMES 14 EQUAL? (84)	
4	N	DO YOU INTEND TO DO ANYTHING TODAY TO PRODUCE FALSE RESULTS?	
5	N	HAVE YOU USED ANY ILLEGAL DRUGS OR ALCOHOL IN THE PAST 24 HOURS?	

Index

Note: Page numbers in *italic* indicate figures.

Z